William Baldwin

A Myrrour for Magistrates

William Baldwin

A Myrrour for Magistrates

ISBN/EAN: 9783744684408

Printed in Europe, USA, Canada, Australia, Japan

Cover: Foto ©ninafisch / pixelio.de

More available books at **www.hansebooks.com**

A MYRROVR for Magistrates.

Wherein may be seene by examples passed in this realme, with howe greueous plagues, vyces are punished in great princes and magistrates, and how frayle and vnstable worldly prosperity is founde, where Fortune seemeth moste highly to fauour.

Newly corrected and augmented. Anno 1571.

Fœlix quem faciunt aliena pericula cautum.

Imprinted at London by Thomas Marshe dwellynge in Fleetstreete, neare vnto S. Dunstanes Churche.

Loue and Lyue.

TO AL THE NOBILITY,
and all other in office, God graunt wysdome and all thinges needefull for the preseruation of their Estates Amen.

PLATO amonge many of his notable sentences concerning the gouernmēt of a common weale hath this: Wel is that realme gouerned, in which the ambitious desyre not to beare offyce. Whereby you may perceiue (right honourable) what offyces are, where they bee duely executed: not gainfull spoyles for ye gredy to hunt for, but painfull toyls for the heedye to be charged with. You maye perceiue also by this sentence, there is nothing more necessary in a cōmon weal then that magistrates be diligent and trusty in their charges. And sure in what so euer realme suche prouision is made, that officers be forced to do their duties: there is it as harde a matter to get an officer, as it is in other places to repulse & shift of, those that with flattery, brybes, and other shifts, sue & preace for offices. For the ambitious (that is to saye prollers for power or gayne) seeke not for offices to helpe other, for which cause officers are ordayned: but with the vndoing of other, to enrich themselues. And therfore bar them once of this bayte, & force them to do their dueties, then will they geeue more to be ryd from their charges, than they did at ye first to come by thē: For they seeke onely their priuate profite. And therfore, wher

the

The Epistle.

the ambitious seeke no office: there no doubt, offices are duely ministred. And where offices are duely ministred, it cannot be chosen, but the people are good, whereof must nedes followe a good common weale. For if the magistrates be good, the people cannot be yll. Thus the goodnes or badnes of any Realme lyeth in the goodnes or badnes of the rulers. And therfore not without greate cause do the holy Apostles so earnestlye charge vs to pray for the magistrates: For in dede the wealth and quyet of euery common weale, the disorder also and miseries of þ same, come specially through them. I neede not go eyther to the Romaines or Grekes for the proofe hereof, neyther yet to þ Iewes, or other nations: whose common weales haue alwaye florished whyle their Magistrates were good, and decayed and ran to ruyne, when vicious men had the gouernment.

Our cowntrey stories (yf we reade and marke them) will show vs examples ynow, would God we had not sene mo than ynow. I purpose not to stand here vpon the particulers, because they be in parte set forth in the tragedies folowing. Yet by the way this I note (wishinge all other to do the lyke) namely, that as good gouernours haue neuer lacked their deserued prayses: so haue not the bad escaped infamy, besydes suche plagues as are horrible to heare of. For God (the ordeyner of offices) althoughe he suffer them for punishmēt of the people to be often occupied of such, as are rather spoylers and Iudasses, than toylers or Iustices (whom the scriptures call Hypocrites) yet suffreth he them not to scape vnpunished, because they dyshonour him. For it is Gods owne office, yea his chief office which they bear and abuse. For as Iustice is the chief vertue, so is þ ministracion thereof, the chiefest office: and therfore hath God establyshed it with the chiefest name, honouring and calling Kinges, and all officers vnder them by his own name: Gods. Ye be all Gods, as many as haue in your charge any ministratiō of iustice. What a fowle shame were it for any nowe to take vppon them the name and office of God, and in their doinges to shewe

them

The Epistle.

them selues deuils? God can not of Iustice, but plague suche shamelesse presumption and hypocrysy, and that with shameful death, diseases, or infamy. How he hath plagued euell rulers from tyme to tyme, in other nacions, you may see gathered in Bochas boke intituled The fall of Princes, trāslated into english by Lydgate a Monke of the Abbey of Bury in Suff. Howe he hath delt with some of our countrymē your auncestours, for sundry vyces not yet lefte, this booke named, A Mirrour for Magistrates, can shewe: which therfore I humbly offer vnto your honours, besechinge you to accepte it fauourablye. For here, as in a mirror or looking glasse, you shall se if any vice be found how the lyke hath bene punished in other heretofore, wherby admonished, I trust it wil be a good occasiō to moue mē to ye soner amendment. This is the chief end why thys booke is set forth, which god graūt it may attain The worke was begō & part of it printed in Quene Maries tyme but staid by such as thē were chiefe in office, neuertheles, through the meanes of ye right honorable Henry Lord Stafford, ye first part was lycensed, & imprinted ye first yeare of the raygne of this our moste noble & vertuous Queene, & dedicated to your honours with this preface. Since whiche tyme, although I wanted suche helpe as before, yet the sayde good Lorde Stafford hath not ceased to call vpon me, to publyshe so muche thereof as I hadde gotten at other mens hands, so that through his Lordships earnest meanes, I haue now also set foorth another parte, conteyning as much as I coulde obteyne at the handes of my frendes.   Whiche in the name of all the authors, I humbly dedicate vnto your honours, instantly wishing, that it may so lyke and delyte youre myndes, that your chearfull receiuing therof, may encourage worthy wits to enterprise and performe the rest. Whiche as soone as I maye procure, I entende through Gods leaue, and your fauourable allowaunce, to publish with all expedition. In the meane whyle my Lordes and Gods, (for so I may call you) I moste humbly beseche your honours fauourably to ac-

* iii.   cepte

The Epistle.

cepte this rude worke, and diligently to reade and consider it. And although you shall fynde in it, that some haue for their vertue bene enuied and brought vnto miserie: yet cease not you to be vertuous, but do your office to ý vttermost. Embrace vertue and suppresse the contrary, both in your selues and other, so shall God whose officers you are eyther, so mainteyne you, that no mallice shall preuaile, or if yt do, it shall be for your good, and to youre eternall glory both here and in heauen whiche I beseche God you may both seke and attain Amen.

Yours most humble
VV. B.

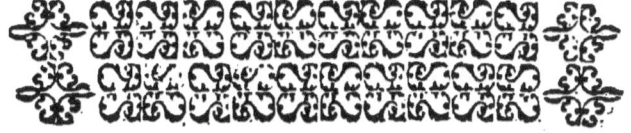

A TABLE
of the contentes of this booke.

1. The fall of sir Robert Tresilian & his felowes.   Folio. 1.
2. The infortunate end of the two Mortimers.   Fol. 4.
3. The murder of Thomas of Woodstocke Duke of Glocester.   Fol. 8.
4. The Lorde Mowbrey made Duke of Norfolke by K. Rycharde the. 2. and by him banished and miserably died in exile. Fol. 12.
5. King Richard the 2. miseraby murdred.   Fol. 16.
6. How Owen Glendour tooke on him to be prince of Wales, was chased to the mountaines, where he miserablye dyed for lacke of foode.   Fol. 19.
7. Henry Percy Earle of Northumberland for his traytrous attempt put to death.   Fol. 25.
8. Richarde Plantagenet Earle of Cambrydge put to death at Southampton.   Fol. 28.
9. Thomas Montague earle of Salisbury, chaunceably slayn at Orliaunce with a piece of ordinaūce.   Fol. 30.
10. King James the firste cruellye murdred by hys owne subiects.   Fol. 39.
11. Lord William De la pole Duke of Suffolke, worthely banished and beheaded.   Fol. 40.
12. Jacke Cade worthely punished for treasō.   Fol. 44.
13. The tragedy of Edmund Duke of Somerset, slaine in ye first battaile at S. Albanes.   Fol. 48.
14. Richard Plantagenet D. of Yorke, slaine through his ouer rashe boldenesse, and his sonne the earle of Rutlande for want of valyauncie.   Fol. 49.
15. The Lorde Clifforde for his abhominable cruelty came to a sodaine death.   Fol. 58.

16. The

The table.

16. The infamous end of the Lord Tiptoft Earle of Worcester. Fol. 60.
17. Richard Neuill Earle of Warwicke, & his brother John Lord Marquise Montacute slaine at Barnet. Fol 65.
18. The vertuous King, Henry the sixt cruelly murdred in the Tower of London. Fol. 68.
19. How George Plantagenet Duke of Clarence, brother to K. Edwarde the fowerth, was cruellye drowned in a vessell of malmesy. Fol. 72
20. A lamentaciō vpon the death of K. Edward the 4. Fol. 80
21. Sir Anthony Wooduille Lord Riuers, with his nephewe Lorde Richard Gray and others causles imprisoned and cruelly beheaded at Pomfret. Fol. 81.
22. The Lord Hastings betrayed by his counsailour Catesby, and murdred in the tower of London. Fol. 93.
23. Maister Sackeuils Induction. Fol. 103
    The Tragedy, of H. Duke of Buckingham. Fol. 113.
24. Collingbourne cruelly executed for making a foolish ryme Fol. 128.
25. Kynge Richard the third slaine at Bosworth. Fol. 144.
26 The fall of the blacke Smyth, and fatall ende of the Lord Awdeley. Fol. 151.
27. The complaint of Shores wyfe, one of the Concubynes of King Edward the fowerth. Fol. 161.
28. The vnworthy death of the worthy Duke Hūfrey of Gloceſter, protectour of England, contriued by false practises. Fol. 199.
29. The penance & exile of the Lady Elyanor Cobham Duches of Glocester, for witchcraft and sorcery.

FINIS.

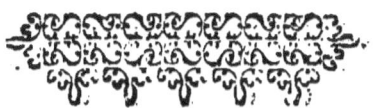

A BRIEFE MEMORIall of Sundrie vnfortunate Englishmen.

VVillyam Baldwin to the Reader.

When the Printer had purposed with himselfe to print Lidgates translation of Bochas, of the fall of Prynces, & had made pryuie thereto, many both honorable and worshipfull: hee was counsailed by dyuers of them to procure to haue the storye continued from wher as Bochas left, vnto this present tyme, chiefly of such as Fortune had dalyed with here in thys Jslande: which myght be as a Myrrour for mē of all estates & degres aswell Nobles as other to behold ye slippery deceytes of the wauering Lady, and the due rewarde of all kynde of vices. Whyche aduise lyked him so well, that hee requyred me to take paynes therein: but because it was a matter passinge my wyt and skill, and more thankelesse than gainfull to meddle in, I refused vtterly to vndertake it, except I might haue the helpe of such, as in wit were apt, in learninge allowed, and in iudgemente and estimation able to wield & furnish so waighty an enterprise, thinkinge so to shifte my handes. But he earneste & dilygent in his affayres, procured Athlas to set vn-

A.i.

Baldwine to

vnder his shoulder: for shortly after diuers learned
mē (whose many gifts nede few praises) consēted to
take vpon them part of the trauaile. And when cer:
taine of them to the nomber of seuen, were through
a general assent at an appointed time and place, ga:
thered together to deuise thereupon, I resorted vn:
to them, bearing with me the boke of Bochas, trā:
slated by Dan Lidgate, for the better obseruatiō of
his order: which although we liked wel, yet would
it not coueniētly serue, seyng that both Bochas and
Lidgate were deade, neither were there any aliue yͤ
medled with like argumente, to whome the vnfor:
tunate mighte make their mone. To make there:
fore a state mete for the matter, they al agreed that
I shoulde vsurpe Bochas rome, and the wretched
Princes complain vnto me: & toke vpō themselues,
euery man for his parte to be sundry personages, &
in their behalfes to bewaile vnto me their greuous
chaunces, heuy destenies, and wofull misfortunes.
This done, we opened such bookes of Cronicles as
we had there present, and Maister Ferrers, after he
had founde where bochas lefte, which was aboute
the ende of kinge Edwarde the thirdes raygne, to
beginne the matter, saide thus.
I meruaile what Bochas meanethe to forgette a:
mong his miserable Princes, such as were of oure
nacion, whose number is as greate as their aduē:
tures wonderfull: For to let passe all, both Britōs,
Danes, and Saxons, & to com to the last conquest,
what a sort are they, and som euen in his own time

or not

the Reader.

or not much before. As for example William Rufus the second king of Englãd after the Conquest, eyther by malice or misaduenture slaine in the new Forest, as he was in hunting there, by Walter Tirrell with the shotte of an Arrow. Robert Duke of Normandy eldest sonne to William Conqueror depriued of his inheritance of Englande, by the sayd Williã Rufus his secõd brother, and after by Henry his yongest brother hauing both his eyes put oute, miserablye imprisoned in Cardiffe Castel, whereas hee dyed. Lykewise the moste lamentable case of Williã, Richard, & Mary, children of the said Henry: drowned vpon the sea. And king Richard the first slaine with a quarrell in his cheife prosperity, Also king Iohn his brother (as som say) poisoned. Are not their Historyes rufull, & of rare example? But as it shold apeare, Bochas being an Italiã, minded most ye Romain & Italike story, or els perhaps he wãted the knowledge of ours. It were therefore a goodly and notable matter, to search and discourse oure whole story from the fyrst beginning of the inhabyting of the Isle. But seing the printers minde is to haue vs followe where Lidgate left, we will leaue that great labour to other that may entend it, and (as one being bold first to breake ye yse) I wil begin at the time of Richarde the second, a time as vnfortunate as the ruler therein. And forasmuch frende Baldwin, as it shalbe your charge to note and pen orderlye the whole processe: I will so far as my memorye and Iudgement serueth, somewhat further

A.ii.   you in

Baldwin to the Reader.

you in the truth of the story. And therfore omitting the ruffle made by Iacke Strawe and his meiney, with the murder of many notable men which therby happened, (for Iacke as ye knowe was but a pore prince) I will begin with a notable example, whiche within a while after ensued. And although ẏ perso͡ at who͡ I begin, was no king nor prince: yet sithens hee had a princely office, I wyll take vppon me the miserable person of syr Robert Tresilian chiefe Justice of England, and of other whiche suffered with him: therby to warne al of his aucthority & profession, to take heede of wronge Judgementes, misconstruinge of Lawes, or wresting the same to serue the Princes turnes, which rightfully brought them to a miserable end, which they may iustly lament in maner ensuinge.

The

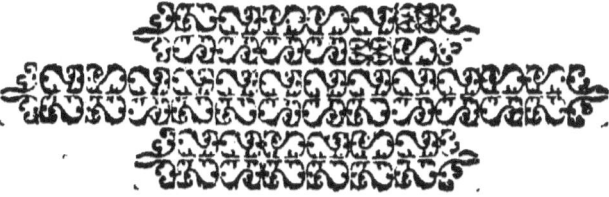

Robert Tresilian,

The fall of Robert Tresilian chiefe Iustice of England, and other his felowes, for mys-construing the lawes, and expouding them to serue the Prin-ces affections, Anno.
1388.

IN the rufull register of mischiefe and mischap,
Baldwin we besech the with our names to begin,
Whom vnfrendely Fortune did traine vnto a trap,
When we thought our state moste stable to haue bin:
So lightly lese they all, which all do wene to winne:
Learne by vs ye Laweyers and Iudges of the Land,
Upright and vncorrupt in dome alway to stande.

And printe ye this presydent to remaine for euer,
Enrolle and recorde it in Tables made of Brasse,
Engraue it in Marble that may be razed neuer,
Where Iudges of the Lawe may see, as in a Glasse,
What guerdon is for guyle, and what our wages was,
Who for our Princes pleasure corrupt with meede and awe
Wittingly and wretchedly did wrest the sence of Lawe.

A chaunge more new or straunge, when was there euer seene
Thē Iudges from the Bench, to come doune to the Barre
And counsaylours that were, most nigh to King and Quene
Exiled their countrey, from Court and counsaile farre,
But such is Fortunes play, which can both make and marre,
Exaltinge to most highe, that was before moste Lowe
And turning tayle agayne, the lofty doune to throwe.

And

Robert Tresilian,

And such as late afore, could stoutly speake and pleade
Both in court and countrye, carelesse of the tryall
Stand mute as Mummers without aduice or reade
All to seke of shifting, by trauerse or deniall
Which haue seene the daye, when for a golden Riall
By finesse and conning, could haue made black seme white
And moste extorted wronge, to haue appered righte.

Whilst thus on bench aboue, we had the highest place,
Our reasons were to strong, for any to confute,
But when at barre beneth, we came to pleade our case
Our wits were in the wane, our pleading very brute,
Hard it is for prisoners, with Iudges to dispute
When all men against one, and none for one shall speake
Who wenes himselfe moste wise, shall happely be to weake:

To you therefore that sit, these few wordes will I say,
That no man syts so sure, but he may haply stand,
Wherfore whilst you haue place, and beare the swinge & sway
By fauour without rygor, let pointes of Lawe be skand:
Pitty the poore prisoner that holdeth vp his hand,
Ne lade him not with lawe, who least of law hath knowen,
Remember ere ye dye, the case may be your owne.

Beholde me vnfortunate forman of this flocke,
Tresilian, sometime chiefe Iustice of this Lande,
A Gentleman by byrth, no staine was in my stocke,
Locketon, Holte, and Belknap, with other of my bande,
Which the Lawe and Iustice had wholy in our hande,
Under the seconde Richard a Prince of greate estate,
To whome and vs also, blinde Fortune gaue the mate.

In the common Lawes our skill was so profounde,
Our credite and aucthority suche and so estemed,
That what we concluded, was taken for a grounde,
Allowed was for Lawe, what so to vs best semed,
Lyfe, Death, Landes, Goods, and all by vs was demed,
Whereby with easy paine, greate gaine we did in set,
And euery thing was fisch, that came vnto our net.

At Sessions and at Sises, we bare the stroke and swaye,
In patentes and commission, of Quorum alway chiefe:
So that to whether syde, soeuer we did waye,
Were it by right or wrong, it past without repriefe,
The true man we let hang somewhiles to saue a thiefe,
Of Golde and of Siluer, our handes were neuer emptye
Offices, Fermes, and Fees, fell to vs in greate plentye.

But what thinge may suffise vnto the gredy man?
The more he hath in holde, the more he doth desire,
Happy and twise happy is hee, that wiselye can
Content himselfe with that, which reason doth requyre,
And moyleth for no more then for his needefull hyre:
But greedynes of minde doth seeldome kepe the syse,
To whome ynough and more doth neuer well suffise.

For like as dropsy pacients drincke and still be drye,
Whose vnstaunched thirst no lyquor can alaye,
And drincke they neuer so muche, yet thirst they by and by
So catchers and snatchers toyle both night and day,
Not needy but greedy, styll prolling for theyr praye,
O endelesse thirst of Golde, corrupter of all Lawes,
What mischiefe is on moulde whereof thou art not cause.

Thou

Robert Tresilian,

Thou madest vs forgette the faith of our profession,
When Sergeants we were sworn to serue the common Law,
Which was that in no point we shoulde make digression
From approued principles in sentence nor in sawe:
But we vnhappy wyghtes without all dreade and awe
Of the Iudge eternall, for worldes vaine promotion,
More to man then God did beare our hole deuotion.

The Lawes we did interprete and statutes of the Lande,
Not truly by the texte, but newly by a glose:
And wordes that were most plaine, whē they by vs were skand,
We tourned by construction to a welshmans hose,
Wherby many a one both life and land did lose:
Yet this we made our meane to mount aloft on mules,
And seruing times and turnes, peruerted Lawes and rules.

Thus climing and contending alway to the toppe,
From hye vnto higher, and than to be moste hye,
The honny dewe of Fortune so fast on vs did droppe,
That of King Richardes counsaile we came to be most nye:
Whose fauour to attaine we were full fine and slye
Alway to his profite, wh ere any thinge might sounde,
That way (all were it wrong) the Laws we did expound.

So working Lawe like waxe, the subiecte was not sure
Of life, land, nor goodes, but at the Princes will.
Which caused his kingdome the shorter time to dure,
For claiming power absolute both to saue and spill,
The Prince therby presumed his people for to pyll:
And set his lustes for Lawe, and will had reasons place,
No more but hange and drawe, there was no better grace.

Thus

and his Felowes.

Thus the King outleaping, the limits of his lawe
Not raigning but raginge, as youth did him entise,
Wise and worthy persons from Court did dayly drawe,
Sage counsaile set at naught, proud vauntours were in price,
And roysters bare the rule, which wasted all in vice,
Of ryot and excesse, grewe scarsitye and lacke,
Of lacking came taxinge, and so went welth to wracke.

The Barons of the Lande not bearinge this abuse,
Conspiringe with the Commons assembled by assent,
And seing neyther reason, nor treatye could induce,
The Kinge in any thing his rigour to relent,
Maugre his mighte they called a Parliament,
Franke and free for all men without checke to debate
As well for weale publike, as for the Princes state.

In this high assembly, great thynges were proponed
Touching the Princes state, his regaly and Crowne,
By reason that the King, which much was to be moned,
Without regarde at all of honour or renowne.
Myssedde by yll aduise, had tournd all vpsydowne.
For suerty of whose state, them thought it did behoue
His counsaylours corrupt, by reason to remoue.

Among whome, Robert Veer, called Duke of Irelande
With Mighell Delapole of Suffolke newe made earle,
Of Yorke also the Archbishop, dispatcht were out of hand,
With Brembre of London a full vncurteous churle
Some learned in the Lawe in exile they did hurle:
But I pore Tresilian because I was the chiefe,
Was damnded to the Galowes most vily as a thiefe.

B.i.   Lo the

Robert Tresilian,

Lo the fine of falshood, the stipend of corruption,
The fee of dowble fraude, the fruites it doth procure
Ye Iudges vpon earth, let our iuste punition,
Teach you to shake of bribes and kepe your handes pure.
Riches and promotion be vaine thinges and vnsure,
The fauour of a prince is an vntrusty staye,
But Iustice hath a fee, that shall remaine alwaye.

What glory can be greater before God or man,
Then by pathes of Iustice in iudgement to proceede:
So duely and so truely the Lawes alway to skan,
That right may take his place without rewarde or meede,
Set aparte all flattery and vaine worldly drede:
Set God before your eyes, the iuste Iudge supreme,
Remember well your reckening, at the day extreme.

Abandon all affray, be soothfast in your sawes,
Be constant and carelesse of mortall mens displeasure,
With eys shut & handes close, you should pronounce ÿ Lawes,
Estieme not worldly goods, thinke there is a treasure
More worth then Gold or stone a thousand times in valure,
Reposed for al suche as righteousnes ensue,
Wherof you can not fayle, the promise made is true.

If Iudges in our dayes, would ponder well in minde,
The fatall fall of vs, for wresting Lawe and right,
Such statutes as touch life should not be thus definde
By sences constrained, against true meaning quite,
As well they might affirme the blacke for to be white,
Wherefore we wish they would, our act and end compare,
And wayeng well the case, they will we trust beware.

FINIS, G. F. When

Roger Mortimer.

When maister Ferrers had finished this tragedye, whiche semed not unfit for the persons touched in the same. An other which in the meane time had staied upon sir Roger Mortimer, whose miserable ende (as it shoulde appeare,) was somwhat before ÿ others, saied as followeth. Although it be not greatly appertinent to our purpose, yet in my iudgement I think it would do wel to obserue the times of men, & as they be more auncient, so to place them: for I finde that before these, (of whome master Ferrers here hath spoken) there were two Mortimers, the one in Edwarde the iii. tyme, out of our date, an other slaine in Irelande in Richarde the secondes time, a yeare before the falle of these Justices: whose hystory sith it is notable & perãple fruitfull, it were not good to ouerpasse it
And therefore by your lycence and agremente,
I wyll take vpon me the personage of the
laste, who full of woundes mangled,
withe a pale countenaunce, and
grislye looke, may make his
mone to Baldwyn as
followeth.

B.ii.

Roger Mortimer.

*How the two Rogers, surnamed Morti-
mers, for their sundry vices*
ended their liues vnfor-
tunately the one. An.
1329. the other. 1387.

Among the riders of the rolling wheele,
That lost their holdes, Baldwin forget not me,
Whose fatal thred false Fortune nedes would reele,
Ere it were twisted by the sisters thre.
All folke be frayle, their blisses brittle be:
For proofe whereof although none other were,
Suffise may I, syr Roger Mortimer.

Not he that was in Edwardes dayes the thyrde,
Whom Fortune brought to boote and eft to bale,
With loue of whome, the King so much she sturde,
That none but he was heard in any tale:
And whiles she smooth, blew on this pleasant gale,
He was created Earle of March alas,
Whens enuy sprang which his destruction was

For welth breedth wrath, in such as welth do want,
And pride with folly in such as it possesse,
Among a thousand shall you fynde one skant,
That can in welth his lofty hart represse,
Which in this Earle due proofe did plaine expresse,
For where as he was somewhat haut before,
His high degree hath made him now much more.

Roger Mortimer.

For now alone he ruleth as him lust,
He recketh for reade, saue of King Edwards mother:
Which forced enuy foulder out the rust,
That in mens harts before did ly and smother.
The Peers, the people, as well the one as other,
Against him made so hanious a complaint,
That for a traytour he was taken and attaint.

Than all such faultes as were forgot afore,
They skower afresh, and somwhat to them ad:
For cruell enuy hath eloquence in store,
Whan fortune bids, to worse thinges meanely bad,
Fyue hainous crimes against him sone were had,
Fyrst that he caused the King to yeeld the Scot,
To make a peace, townes that were from him got:

And therewithall the Charter called Ragman,
That of the Scots he had bribed priuy gayne,
That through his meanes syr Edward of Carnaruan,
In Barkely Castell most traiterously was slaine:
That with his Princes mother he had layne,
And finally with polling at his pleasure,
Had robd the Kyng and commons of theyr treasure.

For these things lo which erst were out of minde,
He was condempned, and hanged at the last,
In whome dame Fortune fully shewed hyr kinde,
For whom she heaues she hurleth down as fast:
If men to come, would learne by other past,
This cosin of mine might cause them set aside,
High climing, bribing, murdering, lust, and pride.

B.iii.   But

Roger Mortimer.

The Fynall cause why I this processe tell,
Is that I may be knowen from this other,
My like in name, vnlike me though he fell,
Which was I thinke my graundsier or his brother:
To count my kin, dame Philip was my mother,
Deare doughter and heyre of douty Lionell,
The second sonne of a Kinge who did excell.

My father hight sir Edmund Mortimer,
True Earle of march, whence I was after Earle,
By iust discent these two my parents were,
Of which the one of Knighthood bare the ferll
Of womanhoode the other was the pearle:
Through theyr desert so called of euery wight,
Tyll death them tooke, and left me in their right.

For why the attaynder of my elder Roger,
(Whose shamefull death I toulde you but of late)
Was founde to be vniuste, and passed ouer,
Agaynst the lawe, by those that bare him hate:
For where by Lawe the lowest of free estate,
Should personally be hard ere iudgement passe,
They barred him this, where through distroyed he was.

Wherefore by doome of court in Parliament,
When we had proued our coosen ordered thus,
The King, the Lordes, and Commons of assent,
His lawles death vnlawfull did discus:
And both to bloode and good restored vs.
A president most worthy, shewed, and lefte
Lordes lines to saue that lawles might be refte

while

Roger Mortimer.

While Fortune thus did forder me a mayne
King Richards grace the second of that name,
(Whose dissolute lyfe did sone abridge his raine)
Made me his mate in earnest and in game:
The Lordes themselues so well allowed the same,
That through my titles duly comming downe,
I was made heyre apparaunt to the Crowne.

Who then but I was euery where esteemed?
Well was the man that might with me acquaynt,
Whome I allowed, as Lordes the people demed
To whatsoeuer folly had me bent,
To like it well the people did assent:
To me as prince attended greate and small,
I hoopt a day would come to pay for all.

But seldome ioy continueth trouble voyde,
In greatest charge cares greatest do ensue,
The most possest are euer most anoyed,
In largest seas sore tempestes lightly brue,
The freshest coulours soonest fade the hue,
In thickest place is made the depest wounde,
True proofe whereof my self to sone haue founde.

For whiles fayr Fortune luld me in her lap,
And gaue me giftes more than I did requyre,
The subtile quean behinde me set a trap,
Wherby to dash and lay all in the myre:
The Irishe men agaynst me did conspyre,
My landes of Ulster fro me to haue reft,
Which herytage my mother had me left.

B.iiii.   And

Roger Mortimer.

And whiles I there, to set all thinges in stay,
(Dimyt my toyles and troble thitherwarde)
Among mine owne, with my retinue lay,
The wylder men whom little I did regarde,
And had therefore the rechles mans rewarde:
When leaste I thought, set on me in such number,
That fro my corps my life they rent asunder.

Nought might auaple my courage nor my force,
Nor strength of men which were alas to fewe:
The cruell folke assaulted so my horse,
That all my helpes in peces they to hewe,
Our bloode distayned the grounde as drops of dewe,
Nought might preuaile to flye nor yet to yeelde,
For whome they take they murder in the fielde.

They knowe no law of Armes nor none will learne
They make not war (as other do) a play,
The Lord, the boy, the Gallowglas, the Kerne
Yeeld or not yeeld, whom so they take they slay,
They saue no prisoners, for raunsome nor for pay:
Theyr chyefest boote they count theyr bodyhs heade,
Theyr ende of war to se theyr enemy deade.

Amongest these men or rather sauage beastes,
I lost my life, by cruell murder slaine.
And therfore Baldwin note thou well my geastes,
And warne all Princes rashnes to refraine:
Byd them beware theyr enemyes when they faine
Nor yet presume vnequally to striue,
Had I thus done, I had bene man alyue.

But

Roger Mortimer, Folio. 7

But I dispised the naked Irish men,
And for they flew, I feared them the lesse:
I thought one man ynough to match with ten,
And through this carelesse vnaduisednes,
I was distroyed, and all my men I gesse,
At vnwares assaulted by our foen,
Which were in nomber fourty to vs one.

Se here the staye of fortunate estate,
The vaine assurance of this brittle life,
For I but yong, proclaimed prince of late,
Right fortunate in children and in wife,
Lost all at once by stroke of bloody knife:
Wherby assurde let men themselues assure,
That welth, and life, are doubtful to endure.
      FINIS. Ca.

After this Tragedye was ended mayster Ferrers saide, seing it is beste to place eche person in his order, Baldwin take you the Chronycles and marke them as they com: for there are many worthy to be noted, though not treated of. First the Lord Murrey a Scottishe man, who
                                           tooke

*T*honas Duke,

tooke his deaths wound through a stroke lent him by the Earle of Notynghā, whom he chalenged at the tylt. But to omit him, and also the fat Pryor of Tiptre, pressed to death with throng of people vpon Londō bridge at the Quenes entry, I wil come to the Duke of Glocester the kings vncle, a man myndynge the common welth, and yet at length miserably made awaye. In whose person yf yee will geeue eare, ye shall heare what I thinke mete to be saied.

Howe.

of Glocester.

How sir Thomas of Woodstocke Duke of Glocester, vncle to King Richard the second, was vnlawfully murdered. Anno. 1397.

Whose state stablisht is, in seming most sure,
And so far from daunger of Fortunes blastes,
As vy the compasse of mans coniecture,
No brasen piller may be fyrt more fast:
Yet wanting the stay of prudent forecast,
Whan froward Fortune list for to frowne,
May in a moment turne vpsyde downe.

In proofe whereof, O Baldwin, take payne,
To harken a while to Thomas of Woodstocke,
Addrest in presence his fate to complayne,
In the forlorne hope of English flocke:
Extract by discent from the royall stocke,
Sonne to Kinge Edward, third of that name,
And seconde to none in glory and fame.

This noble father to mainteyn my state,
With Buckingham Earldome did me indowe,
Both Nature and Fortune to me were grate,
Denying me nothing which they might allowe:
Their sundry graces in me did so flowe,
As bewty, strength, high fauour and fame,
Who may of God more wish then the same?

Brothers

Thomas Duke,

Brothers we were to the nomber of seuen,
I being the syxt, and yongest but one:
A more royall race was not vnder Heauen,
More stoute or more stately of stomacke and person,
Princes all perelesse in ech condition:
Namely syr Edward, called the blacke Prince,
When had England the lyke before or euer since?

But what of all this, any man to assure,
In state vncarefull of Fortuues variaunce:
Syth dayly and hourely we see it in vre,
That where most cause is of affiaunce,
Euen there is found most weake assurance,
Let none trust Fortune, but follow Reason:
For often we see in trust is treason.

This prouerbe in proofe ouer true I tried,
Finding high treason in place of high trust.
And most fault of faith where I most affyed:
Being by them that should haue been iust,
Trayterously entrapt, ere I coulde mistrust,
Ah wretched world what it is to trust thee,
Let them that will learne now harken to mee.

After king Edwarde the thirdes decease,
Succeded my Nephewe Richard to raigne,
Who for his glory and honours encrease,
With princely wages did me entertaine,
Agaynst the Frenchmen to be his Chiefteine:
So passing the seas with royall puissaunce,
With God and S. George I inuaded Fraunce.

Wasting

Wasting the countrey with sword and with fyre,
Ouerturning townes, high castels and towers,
Like Mars god of warre, enflamed with ire,
I forced the frenchmen tabandon their bowers:
Where euer we matcht I wan at all howers,
In such wise visiting both Citty and village,
That alway my souldiers were laden with pyllage.

With honour and triumph was my returne,
Was none more ioyous than yong King Richarde:
Who minding more highly my state to adourne,
With Glocester Dukedome did me rewarde:
And after in mariage I was prefarde,
To a daughter of Bohun an Earle honorable.
By whome I was of England high Constable.

Thus hoysted so high on fortunes wheele,
As one on a stage attending a playe,
Seeth not on which syde the scaffold doth reele,
Tyll timber and poales and all flie away:
So fared it by me, for day by daye,
As honour encreased I loked still hier,
Not seing the daunger of my fond desier.

For Fortunes floode thus running with full streame,
And I a Duke discended of great Kinges,
Constable of England, chiefe officer in the Realme,
Abused with esperaunce in these vaine thinges,
I went without feete, and flewe without winges:
Presuming so far vpon my high estate.
That dreade set apart, my prince I would mate,

Thomas Duke

For where as all Kings haue counsail of their choyse,
To whome they refer the rule of their Land,
With certain fam:liers in whome to reioyce,
For pleasure or profite, as the case shall stand,
I not bearing this, would needs take in hand,
Maugre his will, those persons to disgrace,
And such as I thought fyt to settle in their place.

But as an olde booke sayeth, who so will assaye
About the Cats necke to hang on any bell,
Had fyrst nede to cut the Cats clawes awaye
Least if the cat be curst, and not tamed well,
She haply with her nayles may clawe him to the fell:
So putting on the bell about the Cats necke,
By being to busie I caught a cruell checke.

Reade well the sentence of the Rat of renoune,
Which Pierce the plowman describes in his dreame,
And who so hath wit the sence to expoune,
Shall finde that to bridell the prince of a Reame,
Is euen (as who saieth) to striue with the streame:
Note this all subiects, and construe it well,
And busie not your brains about the Cats bell.

But in that ye be Lieges learne to obay,
Submitting your willes to your Princes Lawes,
It sitteth not a subiect to haue his own waye,
Remember this prouerbe of the Cats clawes:
For Princes like Lyons haue long and large pawes
That reache at Randon, and whome they once twitch,
They clawe to the boone before the skin itch.

But

But to my purpose, I being once bent,
Towardes the atchieuing of my attempt ate,
Fower bould Barons were of mine assent,
By oth and allyaunce fastly confederate:
First Henry of Derby an Earle of estate,
Richard of Arundell, and Thomas of warwicke.
With Mowbray the Marshall, a man most warlicke.

At Ratecote bridge assembled our bande,
The Commons in clusters came to vs that daye
To daunt Robert Veer, then Duke of Irelande,
By whome King Rycharde was ruled alway:
We put him to flight, and brake his aray,
Then maugree the King, his leaue or assent,
By Constables power we cald a Parliament.

Where not in Roabes, but with Bastardes bright,
We came for to parle of the Publike weale,
Confirming our quarrell with maine and with might,
With swordes and no words we tried our appeale,
In steede of Reason declaring our Zeale,
And whom so we knewe, with the King in good grace
We playnlye depriued, of power and of place.

Some with short processe were banisht the Land,
Some executed with cappytall paine,
Wherof who so list, the whole to vnderstand,
In the Parliament roll it appeareth plaine,
And furder how stoutly we did the King straine,
The rule of his Realme wholy to resigne,
To the order of those, whome we dyd assigne.

                                                        But

Thomas Duke,

But note the sequele of suche presumption,
After we had these miracles wroughte,
The Kinge inflamed with indignation,
That to such bondage he shoulde be brought,
Suppressing the ire of his inwarde thought:
Studied nought els but how that he might
Be highly reuenged of this high dispight.

Aggreued was also this latter offence,
With former matter his ire to renue:
For once at Windsore I brought to his presence,
The Mayor of London with all his retynue,
To aske a reckoning of the Realmes reuenue:
And the souldiours of Brest by me were made bolde
Their wages to claime when the town was solde.

These griefes remembred with all the remnaunt,
Hourded in his harte hate out of measure,
Yet openly in shewe made he no semblaunt,
By woord or by deede to beare dyspleasure:
But loue dayes dissembled do neuer endure,
And who so trusteth a foe reconcylde,
Is for the most part alwayes beguilde.

For as fyer ill quencht will vp at a starte,
And sores not well salued do breake out of newe,
So hatred hidden in an irefull harte,
Where it hath had long season to brewe,
Upon euery occasion doth easely renewe:
Not fayling at last, if it be not let,
To paye large vsury bisides the due det.

of Glocester.

Euen so it fared by this Frendshyp fayned,
Outwardly sounde, and inwardly rotten:
For whan the Kinges fauour in seming was gayned:
All olde dyspleasures forgeuen and forgotten,
Euen than at a sodeine the shaft was shotten,
Which pearced my hart voyde of mistrust.
Alas that a Prince should be so vniust.

For lying at Plashey my selfe to repose,
By reason of sicknesse which held me full sore:
The King espying me apart from those,
With whome I confedered in band before,
Thought it not meete, to tract the time more
But glad to take me at such auauntage,
Came to salute me with friendly visage.

Who hauing a band bound to his bent,
By coulour of kindenesse to visit his Eame,
Tooke tyme to accomplish his cruell entent:
And in a small vessell down by the streme,
Conueyed me to Calais out of the realme,
Where without processe or dome of my peares,
Not nature but murder abridged my yeares.

This act was odyous to God and to man,
Yet rygour to cloake in habit of reason,
By crafty compasse deuise they can,
Articles nine of right haynous treason:
But doome after death is sure out of season,
For who euer sawe so straunge a president,
As execution done before iudgement.

                        C.₄   Thus

Thomas Mowbray,

Thus hate harboured in depth of mindes
By sought occasion burst out of newe,
And crueltie abused the law of kinde,
Whan that the Nephue the vncle slewe,
Alas King Richard, sore maist thou rue:
Which by this fact preparedst the waye,
Of thy hard destenye to hasten the daye.

For bloud axeth bloud as guerdon dewe,
And vengeaunce for vengeaunce is iust rewarde:
O righteous god thy Judgementes are true,
For looke what measure we other awarde,
The same for vs agayne is prepard:
Take hede ye princes, by examples past,
Bloud will haue bloud, eyther fyrst or last.

FINIS. G. F.

WHe maister Ferrers had ended this fruitfulll tragedy, because no man was ready with any other, I, hauing perused the story which came next, saide: because you shal not say my masters but that I wyll somewhat do my parte, I will vnder your correction declare the tragedy of Thomas Mowbray, Duke of Northfolke, the chiefe woorker of the Duke of Glocesters destruction: who to admonish all counsaylours to beware of flattering princes or fallsely enuyinge or accusing their Peregalles, may lament his vices in maner following.   How

Duke of Northfolke. Fol. 12.

How the Lord Mowbray promoted by King Richarde the second, to the state of a Duke, was by him banished the Realme, the yeare of Chriſte. 1398. and after died miſerably in exile.

Though ſorrowe and ſhame abaſh me to reherſe,
My lothſome life and death of due deſerued,
Yet that the paynes thereof may other pearce,
To leaue the like, leaſt they be likewyſe ſerued,
Ah Baldwin marke, and ſee how that I ſwerued:
Diſſembling, Enuy, and Flattery, bane that be
Of all theyr hoſtes, haue ſhewed their power on me.

I blame not Fortune though ſhe did her parte,
And true it is ſhe can do litle harme,
She gyueth goodes, ſhe hampreth not the harte,
A minde well bent, is ſafe from euery charme:
Uice, onely vice, with her ſtout ſtrengthleſſe arme,
Doth cauſe the hart from good to yll encline,
Which I alas, do fynde to true by mine.

For where by byrth I came of noble race,
The Mowbreys heyre, a famouſe houſe and olde,
Fortune I thanke, gaue me ſo good a grace,
That of my prince I had what ſo I wolde:
Yet neyther was, toother greatly holde,
For I through flattery abuſed his wanton youth,
And his fond truſt augmented my vntruth.

C.ii.   He made

Thomas Mowbrey,

He made me fyrst the Earle of Notingham,
And Marshall of the realme, in which estate
The Pieres and people ioyntly to me came,
With sore complaint, against them that of late
Made officers, had brought the King in hate,
By making sale of Iustice, right, and Lawe,
And liuing naught: without all drede or awe.

I gaue them ayde these euyls to redresse,
And went to London with an army strong,
And caused the King, agaynst his will oppresse
By cruell death, all such as led him wrong:
The Lord chiefe Iustice suffered these among,
So did the Steward of his household head,
The Chauncellour scapt, for he aforehand fled.

These wicked men thus from the king remoued,
Who best vs pleased succeded in theyr place:
For which both King and Commons much vs loued,
But chiefely I with all stoode high in grace,
The king ensued my rede in euery case,
Whence selfe loue bred: for glory maketh proude,
And pride ay looketh alone to be allowde.

Wherefore to thend I might alone eniope
The Kinges good will, I made his lust my lawe:
And where of late I laboured to distroy,
Such flattering folke, as therto stoode in awe,
Now learned I among the rest to clawe:
For pride is such, if it be kindely caught,
As stroyeth good, and styrreth vp euery naught.

Duke of Northfolke,

Pride pricketh men to flatter for the pray,
To oppresse and poll for mayntenaunce of the same,
To malice such as match vnethes it may:
And to be briefe, pride doth the hart enflame,
To fyer what mischiefe any fraud may frame,
And euer at length the cuyls by it wrought
Confound the worker, and bring him vnto nought.

Beholde in me due proofe of euery part:
For pride fyrst forced me my Prince to flatter
So much, that what so euer pleased his harte
Were it neuer so euill, I thought a lawfull matter,
Which causd the Lordes a fresh agaynst him clatter:
Because he had his houldes beyond sea solde,
And seene his souldiers of theyr wages polde.

Though all these ils were doen by mine assent,
Yet such was lucke that ech man demed no:
For see the Duke of Glocester for me sent,
With other Lordes, whose hartes did bleed for wo,
To see the Realme so fast to ruin go.
In fault whereof, they saide the two Dukes were,
The one of Yorke, the other of Lancaster.

On whose remoue fro being about the King
We all agreed, and sware a solemne oth,
And whilst the rest prouided for this thing,
I flatterer I, to wyn the prayse of troth,
Wretch that I was brake fayth and promise both:
For I bewrayed the King, theyr whole intent,
For which vnwares they all were tane and shent.

       C.iii   Thus

Thomas Mowbray.

Thus was the warder of the common weale,
The Duke of Glocester gyltlesse made away,
With other mo, more wretch I so to deale,
Who through vntruth theyr trust did yll betray:
Yet by this meanes obtayned I nip pray,
Of King and Dukes I found for this such fauour,
As made me Duke of Northfolke for my labour.

But see how pride and enuy ioyntly run,
Because my Prince did more than me prefer,
Sir Henry Bolenbroke, the eldest sonne
Of Iohn of Gaunt, the Duke of Lancaster,
Proud I that would alone be blasing starre,
Enuyed this Duke, for nought saue that the shyne,
Of his desertes dyd glister more than myne:

To the end therfore his light should be the lesse,
I slily sought all shyftes to put it out:
But as the poyze that would the palme tree presse,
Doth cause the bowes spreade larger round about,
So spite and enuy causeth glory sproute.
And aye the more the top is ouertrode,
The deper doth the sound roote spreade abroade:

For when this Henry Duke of Hereforde sawe,
What spoyle the King made of the noble blood,
And that without all Iustice, cause, or lawe:
To suffer him so, he thought not sure nor good.
Wherfore to me twofaced in one hoode,
As touching this, he fully brake his minde,
As to his frende that should remedy fynde.

But

Duke of Northfolke.

But I, althoughe I knewe my Prince dyd yll,
So that my hart abhorred sore the same,
Yet myschiefe so through malice led my will,
To bring this Duke from honour vnto shame,
And toward my selfe, my soueraygne to enflame:
That I bewrayed his wordes vnto the King,
Not as a reade, but as a most haynous thyng.

Thus where my duty bounde me to haue tolde
My Prince his fault, and wild him to refrayne,
Through flattery loe, I dyd hys yll vpholde,
Which turnd at length both hym and me to payne:
Wo, wo to Kinges whose counsaylours do fayne,
Wo, wo to Realmes where such are put in trust,
As leaue the Lawe, to serue the Princes lust.

And wo to him that by his flattering rede,
Mayntepns a Prince in any kinde of vice:
Wo worth hym eke for enuy, pride, or mede,
That my reportes any honest enterprise,
Because I beast in all these poyntes was nice,
The plagues of all together on me lyght,
And due for ill, ill doers doth acquite.

For when the Duke was charged with my plaint,
He flat denyed that any part was true,
And claymde by armes to answere his attaynt,
And I by vse that warly featés well knewe,
To his desyre incontinently drewe:
Wherwith the King did seme right well content,
As one that past not much with whome it went.

C.iiii   At

At tyme and place appoynted we appeard,
At all poyntes armd to proue our quarels iust,
And whan our frendes on ech part had vs cheard,
And that the Haroldes bad vs do our lust,
With speare in rest we tooke a course to iust:
But ere our horses had run halfe theyr way,
A shout was made the King commaunded stay.

And for to auoyde the shedyng of our blood,
With shame and death which one must nedes haue had,
The Kyng through counsayle of the Lordes thought good
To banysh both, which iudgement strait was rad:
No meruayle than though both were wroth and sad
But chiefly I that was exild for aye
My enmy strauugd but for a ten yeares day.

The date expyrde, whan by this doulfull dome,
I should depart to lyue in bannisht band,
On payne of death to England not to come,
I went my way: the Kyng seasd in his hande
My nofsices, my honours, goods and land,
To pay the due as openly he tould,
Of mygty summes, which I had from him pold.

See Baldwin see, the salary of sinne,
Marke with what mede vyle vices are rewarded
Through pride and enuy I lose both kith and kinne,
And for my flattering playnt so well regarded,
Exile and slaunder are iustly me awarded:
My wyfe and heyre lacke landes and lawfull right,
And me theyr Lord made dame Dianaes Knyght.

It thesé

Duke of Northfolke,

If these mishaps at home be not ynoughe,
Adioyne to them my sorrowes in exile:
I went to Almayne fyrst, a land right roughe,
In which I found such churlish folke and vile,
As made me loeth my lyfe ech other while:
There lo, I learned what it is to be a gest
Abroade, and what to liue at home in rest.

For they esteeme no one man more than eche,
They vse as well the lackey as the Lorde,
And like theyr maners churlish in theyr spech,
Theyr lodging hard, theyr bourd to be abhord:
Their pleityd garmentes herewith well accord,
All iagde and frounst, with dyuers coulours deckt,
They swere, they curse, and drincke tyll they be fleckt.

They hate all such, as these theyr maners hate,
Which reason would, no wyseman should allowe,
With these I dwelt, lamenting myne estate,
Tyll at the length they had got knowledge, howe
I was exilde, because I did auow
A false complaynt agaynst my trusty freende:
For which they namd me traytour styll vnhende,

That what for shame and what for werines
I stale fro thence, and went to Uenise towne,
Where as I found more ease and frendlines,
But greater gryefe: for now the great renowne,
Of Bolenbroke whome I would haue put downe,
Was wart so greate in Brittayne and in Fraunce,
That Uenise through, ech man did him auaunce.

Thus

Thomas Mowbray.

Thus lo his glory grewe through greate dispite,
And I therby increased in defame:
Thus enuy euer doth her most acquite
With trouble, anguish, sorrowe, smart, and shame,
But sets the vertues of her foe inflame:
Lyke water waues, which clense the muddy stone,
And soyles themselues by beating thereupon.

Or eare I had soiournd there a peare,
Straunge tidinges came he was to England gone,
Had tane the Kyng, and that which touched him neare,
Enprisoned him with other of his fone,
And made him yeelde him vp his Crowne and throne:
When I these thinges for true by search had tryed,
Griefe griped me so, I pined away and dyed.

Note here the ende of pride, se Flatteries fyne,
Marke the reward of enuy and false complaynt,
And warne all people from them to decline,
Lest likely fault do finde the like attaynt.
Let this my life to them be a restraynt,
By others harmes who listeth take no hede:
Shall by his own learne other better rede.

FINIS. T. Ch.

This tragicall example was of all the companye well liked, howbeit a doubt was found therin, and that by meanes of the diuersitie of ye chronicles: for wher as Hall whose Chronicle in this worke, we chiefely followed, maketh Mowbray appellant & Bolinbroke defendant, Fabian reporteth the matter quite contrary, and that by record of the parliamēt rolle,

Duke of Northfolke.

Folio. 16

rolle, wherin it is playne that Bolinbroke was appellant and Mowbrey defendant. Wherfore what so euer shalbe saide here in the person of Mowbray, (who being a most noble prince had to much wrong to be so causeles defamed after his death) imagin ye same to be spoken againſt his accuser. Which matter sith it is more hard to decise, than nedeful to our purpose, whiche minde onely to disswade frō vices & exalt vertue, we refer to such as may com by ye recordes of ye acts of the parliamente, contented in the mean while with maister Halles iudgemēt, which maketh best for our forshewed purpose. This doubt thus let passe. I woulde (sayde maſter Ferrers) saye somwhat for king Richard, after whose depriuing, his brother & diuers other made a maske, myndinge by king Henries deſtruction to haue reſtored hym, whiche maskers matter so runneth in this, that I doubt which ought to go before, but seing no mā is redy to say ought in their behalfe, I will geue (who so liſteth) leaſure to thinke therupō, and in ye meane time to further youre enterprise, I will in king Rychards behalfe recount such part of his story, as I think most necessary. And therfore imagin Baldwin ye you see the corps of thys Prince all to be mangled, with blewe woundes, lyeng pale & wan all naked vpon the cold ſtones in Paules church, the people ſtandinge round about hym, and makynge his complainte in maner as foloweth.

How

K. Richard the ii.

Howe Kinge Richard the seconde was for his euell gouernaunce deposed from his seate, in the yeare 1399. and myserably murdered in pryson the yere folowyng.

Happy is the Prince, that hath in welth the grace
To followe vertue, keping vices vnder,
But wo to him whose will hath wisdomes place:
For who so renteth ryght and lawe asunder,
On him at length all the worlde shall wonder,
Hygh byrth, choyse fortune, force, nor princely mace,
Can warrant Kyng or Keyser fro the case,
Shame sueth sinne, as raynedrops do the thunder.
Let Princes therfore vertuous lyfe embrace,
That wylfull pleasures cause them not to blunder.

Behould my hap, see how the seely rout
On me do gase, and ech to other say:
See where he lyeth, but late that was so stout,
Loe howe the power, the pride, and rich aray,
Of myghtie rulers lightly fade away.
The King which erst kept all the Realme in doute,
The veriest rascall now dare checke and loute:
What moulde be Kinges made of, but carian clay?
Beholde his woundes how blew they be about,
Which while he liued, thought neuer to decay.

K. Richard the ii.

Me thinke I heare the people thus deuise
Wherfore Baldwin, syth thou wilt nowe declare
Howe Princes fell, to make the liuing wise,
My lawlesse life, in no point see thou spare,
But paynt it out, that rulers may beware
Good counsayle, Lawe, or vertue to dispise.
For Realmes haue rules, and rulers haue a lise,
Which if they breake, thus much to say I dare.
That eythers griefes the other shall agrise
Tyll one be lost, the other brought to care.

I was a King, who ruled all by lust
Forcyng but light, of Iustice, right, or Lawe,
Putting always flatterers false in trust,
Ensuing such, as could my vices clawe:
By faithfull counsaile passing not an hawe,
As pleasure pricte, so needes obay I must:
Hauing delite to fede and serue the gust,
Three meales a day could scarse content my mawe,
Me liked least to Torney or to Iust.
To Venus sporte my fansy did me drawe.

Which to maintaine, my people were sore polde
With Fines, Fiftenes, and loanes by way of prest,
Blanke Charters, Othes, and shyftes not knowen of olde,
For which the commons, did me sore detest.
I also sould the noble towne of Brest,
My falt wherein because mine vncle tolde,
(For Princes actes, may no wise be controld)
I found the meanes his bowels to vnbrest,
The worthy Peeres, which his cause did vphold,
With long exile, or cruell death opprest.

Non

K. Richard the ii.

None ayde I lackt, in any wicked deede,
For gaping Gulles whome I promoted had
Would furder all in hope of higher mede,
There can no King ymagin ought so bad,
But shall fynde some that will perforne it glad:
For sicknes seldome doth so swiftly brede,
As humours pll, do growe the griefe to feede,
Thus Kinges estates of all be worst bestad,
Abusde in welth, abandoned at nede,
And nearest harme when they be least adrad.

My lyfe and death the truth of this hath tryde:
For while I fought in Ireland with my foes,
Myne vncle Edmunde whome I left to guide
My realme at home, rebelliously arose,
Percyes to helpe, which plied my depose:
And cald fro Fraunce, Earle Bolenbroke whome I
Exiled had for ten yeares there to lye:
Who cruelly did put to death all those,
That in mine ayde durst looke but once awry,
Whose number was, but slender I suppose.

For comming backe this soden stur to staye,
The Earle of Worcester whome I trusted moste,
(Whiles I in Wales at Flint my Castle laye,
Both to refresh and multiply myne oste)
There in my hall, in sight of least and most,
His staffe did breake, which was my householde stay,
Bad ech make shyft, and rode him selfe away.
See Princes, see the strength whereof we bost,
Whome most we trust, at nede do vs betraye:
Through whose false fayth my land and life I lost.

K. Richarde the ii.

My Stuard false, thus being fled and gone,
My seruauntes slye shranke of on euery syde,
Then caught I was, and led vnto my foen,
Who for theyr Prince, no pallace did prouide,
But prison strong, where henry puft with pride,
causd me resigne, my Kingly state and throne,
And so forsaken and left as post alone,
These holowe frendes, by Henry soone espyed,
Became suspect and fayth was geuen to none,
Which caused them from faith agayne to slyde.

And strayt conspierd, theyr newe King to put downe,
And to that end a solemp oth they swore,
To render me my royall seate and crowne,
Wherof themselues, depriued me before,
But late medcynes can helpe no sothbynde sore:
When swelling floodes hath ouer flowen the towne
To late it is, to saue them that shall drowne,
Tyll sayles be spred, a shyp may kepe the shore,
No ankerholde can kepe the vessell downe,
With streme and stere perforce it will be bore.

For though the Peers set Henry in his state,
Yet could they not displace him thence agayne:
And where they easely, depriued me of late,
They could restore me, by no manner payne.
Thinges hardly mend, but may be mard amayne.
And whan a man is fallen in froward fate,
Still mischiefes light, one on anothers pate:
And meanes well ment all mishaps to restrayne
Waxe wretched mones, wherby his ioyes abate.
Due proofe whereof, in this appeared playne,

f o;

K. Richard the, ii.

For whan the King did knowe that for my cause,
His Lords in maske, would kill him on a night,
To dash all doutes he tooke no further pause:
But Pierce of Exton a cruell murdering knight,
To Pomfret Castell, sent hym armed bright,
Who causeleſſe kild me there againſt all lawes,
Thus lawles life to lawelces death ey drawes.
Wherfore bid Kinges be rulde and rule by right.
Who woorketh his will, and ſhunneth wiſdomes ſawes,
In ſnares of woo, ere he beware ſhall lyght.

FINIS. G. F.

When he had ended this so woefull a Trage-
gedy, and to all princes a right worthy in-
ſtructiō, we pauſed: hauing paſſed through
a miſerable time ful of piteous tragedys. And ſeing
ÿ reygne of Henry the fourth enſued, a man more
ware and proſperous in his doyngs, although not
untroubled with warres both of outforthe and in-
warde enemies, we began to ſerche what Peeres
were fallen therein, whereof the nomber was not
ſmall: & yet becauſe their examples were not much
to be noted for oure purpoſe, we paſſed ouer all the
Maſkers of whome kinge Richardes brother was
chiefe: whiche were all ſlaine and put to deathe for
theyr trayterous attempte. And ſyndinge Owen
Glendoure nexte, one of Fortunes owne whelpes,
and

Owen Glendour. **Fol. 19**

and the Percies his confederates, I thought them vnmeete to be ouerpassed, and therefore sayde thus to the sylent company: what my maisters is euery man at once in a browne study? hath no man affection to any of these stories? you minde so much some other belyke, that these do not moue you: and to say the truthe, there is no special cause why they should. How be it Owen Glendour, because hee was one of Fortunes owne darlinges, and affected to be Prince of Wales, althoughe to his owne mischiefe and destruction, rather then he should be forgotten, I will take vpon me by your fauour to saye somewhat in his persone: which Owen coming out of the wylde mountaines of Wales like the image of death (in all pointes (his hart onely excepted) as a ghost forpined with extreme famine, colde, & hunger, may lament his great missortune after this manner.

(∴)   D i

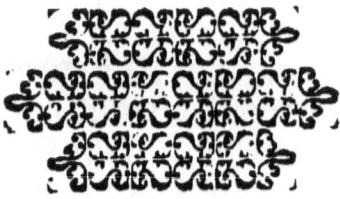

Owen Glendour.

Howe Owen Glendour seduced by false prophe-
cies, tooke vpon him to be Prince of VVales, and
was by Henry prince of Englande chased to
the mountaynes, vvhere he miserably died for
lacke of foode. Anno. 1401.

I Pray thee Baldwin sith thou doest entend,
To shew the fall of such as climbe to hye,
Remember me, whose miserable end
May teach a man his vicious life to flye.
Oh Fortune, Fortune, out on thee I crye.
My liuely corps thou hast made leane and slender,
For lacke of foode, whose name was Owen Glendour.

A Welshman borne, and of the Troyan blood,
But ill brought vp, whereby full well I fynde,
That neyther byrth nor linage make vs good,
Though it be true that Cat will after kynde
Fleshe gendreth fleshe, but not the soule or mynde:
They gender not, but fouly do degender,
When men to vice from vertue them surrender.

Eche thing by nature tendeth to the same
Whereof it came, and is disposed like:
Doune sincks the mold, vp mounts the fiery flame,
With horne the hart, with hoofe the horse doth strike,
The Wolfe doth spoile, the suttle Foxe doth pike,
And to conclude, no fish, flesh, foule or plant
Of their true dame, the propertie doth want.

But

But as for men, sith seuerally they haue
A mynde whose maners are by learning made,
Good bringing vp alonly doth them saue
In honest actes, which with their parentes fade,
So that true gentry standeth in the trede
Of vertuous life, not in the fleshly line:
For bloud is brute, but Gentry is deuine.

Experience doth cause me thus to say,
And that the rather for my countrey men,
Which vaunt and boast themselues aboue the daye,
If they may strayne their stocke fro worthy men:
Which let be true, are they the better than?
Nay far the worse, if so they be not good,
For why they staine the bewty of their bood.

How would we mocke the burden bearing mule,
If he would brag he were an horses sunne,
To presse his pride (might nothing els him rule)
His boastes to proue no more but bid him rum:
The horse for swiftnes hath his glory wonne.
The mule could neuer the more aspyer,
Though he should proue that Pegas was his ster.

Ech man may crake of that which was his owne,
Our parentes vertues, are theirs and no whit ours:
Who therfore wyll of noble byrth be knowen,
Ought shyne in vertue like his auncessours,
Gentry consisteth not in landes and towers:
He is a churle though all the worlde were his,
Yea Arthurs heyre if that he liue amisse.

D ij   For

Owen Glendour.

For vertuous life a Gentleman doth make
Of her possessour all be he poore as Iob,
Yea though no name of elders he can take:
For proofe take Merlin fathered by an Hob.
But who so sets his mynde to spoyle and rob,
Although he come by due discent from Brute,
He is a chorle, vngentle, vile, and brute.

Well, thus did I for want of better wyt,
Because my parents naughtely brought me vp:
For Gentlemen (they sayde) was nought so fyt
As to attast by bould attemptes the cup,
Of conquests wyne, whereof I thought to sup:
And therefore bent my selfe to rob and ryue,
And whome I coulde of landes and goods depryue.

For Henry the fourth dyd then vsurpe the Crowne,
Despoyled the Kyng, with Mortimer the heyre:
For which his subiects sought to put him downe,
And I whyle Fortune offered me so fayre,
Dyd what I might his honour to appayre:
And tooke on me to be the Prince of Wales,
Entitle thereto by prophecies and tales.

For whiche, suche Idle as wayte vpon the spoyle,
From euery part of Wales vnto me drew:
For loytering youth vntaught in any toyle
Are redy aye all mischiefe to ensue.
Through helpe of these so greate my glory grewe,
That I defyed my King through lofty harte,
And made sharpe warre on all that tooke his parte.

See

Owen Glendour,

See lucke, I tooke Lord Raynold Gray of Rythen,
And him enforst my daughter to espouse,
And so vnraunsomed I held him still and sytheu;
In Wigmore land through battayle rigorous,
I caught the right heyre of the crowned house:
The Earle of March sir Edmond Mortimer,
And in a dungeon kept him prisonner.

Than all the marches longing vnto Wales,
By Syuerne west I did inuade and burne:
Destroyed the townes in mountaines and in vales,
And rich in spoyles had homeward safe returne:
Was none so bould durst once agaynst me spurne,
Thus prosperously doth Fortune forwarde call,
Those whome she mindes to geue the sorest fall.

Whan fame had brought these tidinges to the King,
(Although the Scots than vexed him right sore)
A mighty army agaynst me he did bring:
Whereof the French king being warned afore,
Who mortall hate agaynst king Henry bore,
To greue our fo he quickly to me sent,
Twelue thousand Frenchmen armed to war and bent.

A part of them led by the Earle of marche
Lord James of Burbon, a valiant tried knight,
With held by wyndes to Wales ward forth to march,
Tooke land at Plymmouth priuely on a night:
And whan he had done all that he durst or might,
After that a meyney of his men were slaine
He stole to ship and sailed home againe.

Owen Glendour.

Twelue thousand moe in Milford did ariue,
And came to me then lieng at Denbigh
With armed Welshmen thousandes double fyue,
With whome we went to Worcester well nigh,
And there encampt vs on a mount on high,
To abide the King who shortly after came
And pitched his field, on a hill hard by the same.

There eyght daies long our hoastes lay face to face,
And neyther durst others power assaile:
But they so stopt the Passages the space,
That vitailes could not come to our auaple,
Where through constrained our hartes began to fayle:
So that the frenchmen shranke away by night,
And I with mine to the mountaines tooke our flight:

The King pursued greatly to his cost,
From hilles to woods, from woods to valleis plaine:
And by the way his men and stuffe he lost.
And whan he saw he gayned nought but paine,
He blewe retreate and gat him home againe:
Then with my power I boldly came abrode,
Taken in my countrey for a very God.

Immediatly after fell a Joly Iarre
Betwene the King, and Percies worthy bluds,
Which grew at last vnto a deadly warre:
For like as drops engender mighty fluds,
And licle seedes sprut forth great leaues and buds,
Euen so small striues, if they be suffered run,
Brede wrath and war, and death or they be don.

Owen Glendour.

The King would haue the raunsome of such Scots,
As these the Percies tane had in the field:
But se how strougly lucre knits her knots,
The King will haue, the Percies will not pield,
Desire of goods some craues, but graunteth seeld:
Oh cursed goods desire of you hath wrought
All wickednes, that hath or can be thought,

The Percies deemed it meeter for the King,
To haue redemed theyr cosin Mortimer,
Who in his quarrell all his power did bring,
To fight with me, that tooke him prisoner,
Than of theyr pray to rob his souldier:
And therfore willed him see some meane were found,
To quite forth him whom I kept vily bound.

Because the King misliked their request.
They came them selues and did accord with mee,
Complayning how the kingdome was opprest
By Henries rule, wherefore we did agree
To put him downe, and part the realme in three:
The North part theirs, Wales wholy to be mine;
The rest, to rest to therle of Marches line.

And for to set vs hereon more agog,
A Prophet came (a vengeance take them all)
Affirming Henry to be Gogmagog,
Whome Merline doth a Mouldwarp euer call,
Accurst of God that must be brought in thrall
By a Wolfe, a Dragon, and a Lion strong,
Which should deuide, his kingdome them among.

D.iiii.   This

Owen Glendour.

This crafty dreamer made vs three such beastes,
To thinke we were the foresaide beastes in dede.
And for that cause our badges and our creastes,
We searched out which scarsely well agreed:
Howbeit the Haroldes redy at such a neede,
Drewe doune such issues from olde auncesters,
As proued these ensignes to be surely oures.

Ye crafty Welshmen, wherfore do ye mocke,
The Noble men thus with your fayned rymes?
Ye Noble men why fly ye not the flocke,
Of such as haue seduced so many times?
False Prophesies are plauges for diuers crimes,
Which God doth let the deuilish sort deuise,
To trouble such as are not godly wise.

And that appeared by vs three beastes in dede.
Through false perswasion highly borne in hand,
That in our feate we coulde not chuse but spede,
To kill the King and to enioy his land:
For which exployt we bound our selues in band,
To stand contented ech man with his parte,
So fully folly assured our foolysh hart.

But such they say as fishe before the net,
Shall seldom surfet of the pray they take,
Of thinges to come the haps be so vnset,
That none but fooles may warrant of them make:
The full assured, successe doth oft forsake.
For Fortune findeth none so fyt to flout,
As suresby sots which cast no kinde of doubt.

How

Owen Glendour.

How sayest thou Henry Hotspur, do I lye:
For thou right manly gauest the King a feelde,
And there wast slaine because thou wouldst not flye?
Syr Thomas Percy thine vncle forst to peeld,
Did cast his head a wonder sene but seeld,
From Shrewsbury towne to the top of London bridge.
Lo thus fonde hope, did both theyr lyues abridge.

Whan King Henry this victory had wonne,
Destroyed the Percyes, put theyr power to flyght,
He did appoynt prince Henry his eldest sonne:
With all his power to mete me if he myght:
But I discomfyt, through my partners fight,
Had not the hart to mete him face to face,
But fled away and he pursued the chase.

Now Baldwin marke, for I calde prince of Wales,
And made beleue I should be he in dede,
Was made to flye among the hilles and dales,
Where all my men forsooke me at my nede.
Who trusteth loyterers seeld hath lucky speede:
And whan the capitains courage doth him fayle,
His souldiers hartes a litle thing may quayle.

And so Prince Henry chased me, that lo
I found no place wherein I might abyde:
For as the dogges pursue the sely Doe,
The brache behinde, the boundes on euery side,
So traste they me among the mountaynes wide:
Whereby I founde, I was the hartlesse hare,
And not the beast Colprophete did declare.

And

Owen Glendour.

And at the last: like as the litle roch,
Must eyther be eat, or leap vpon the shore
When as the hungary pickerell doth approch,
And there fynde death which it escapt before:
So double death assaulted me so sore
That eyther I must vnto my enuy peeld,
Or starue for hungar in the barrayn feeld.

Here shame and payne awhile were at a strife
Payn bad me yeeld, shame bad me rather fall:
The one bad spare, the other bad spend my life,
But shame (shame haueit) ouercame at last.
Than hunger gnew, that doth the stone wall brast,
And made me eate both grauell, durt and mud,
And last of all, my dung, my flesh, and blud.

This was mine ende to horrible to beare,
Yet good ynough for a life that was so yll,
Wherby O Baldwin warne all men to beare
Their youth such loue, to bring them vp in skill.
Byd princes flye Colmophets lying hyll:
And not presume to clime aboue theyr states,
For they be faultes that foyle men, not theyr fates.

            FINIS.   When

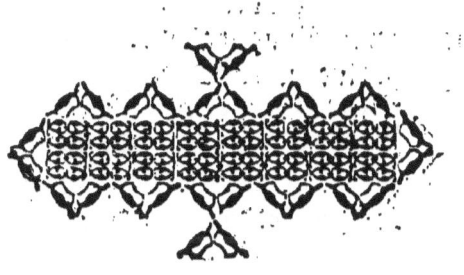

When starued Owen had ended his hungry exhortation, it was well inough liked, how beit one found a doubt worth the mouing, and that concerning this title, Earle of March: for as it appereth, ther wer 3. men of 3. diuers natiōs together in one time entituled by that honour: First syr Edmund Mortimer, whom Owen kept in pryson, an Englishman: the second the Lorde George of Dunbar a valiaunt Scot, banished out of his countrey, and well estemed of Henry the fowerth: the third Lorde James of Bourbon a Frenchman, sent by the french king to helpe Owen Glendour. These three men had this tytle all at once, whiche caused him to aske how it was true that euery one of these coulde be Earle of Marche: whereto was aunswered, that euerey country hath Marches belonging vnto them, & those so large, that they were Earldomes and the Lords therof intitulyd therby: so y lord Edmūd Mortimer was Earle of March in England, Lord James of Burbon of y marches of Fraunce, and Lord George of Dunbar Earle of the Marches in Scotland. For otherwise neyther could haue interest in others title. This doubt thus dissolued, maister Ferrers said: if no man haue affection to the Percies, let vs passe the times both of Henry the fourth and the fyft, and come to Henrye the sixt in whose time Fortune (as she doth in y mynority of princes) bare a great stroke among the nobles. And yet in Henry the fourths time are examples which I would wishe Baldwin that you should not

Henry Percy.

not forget, as the conspiracye made by the Byshop of Yorke, and the Lorde Mowbray, sonne of him whom you late treated of: pricked forwarde by the Earle of Northumberland, father to sir Henry Hotspur, who fled himselfe, but his parteners were apprehended & put to death, with Bainton and Blinkinsops, which could not se theyr duty to their king, but tooke part with Percy that banished Rebell. As he was proceding, he was desired to stay by one which had pondered the storie of the Percies, who briefely saide. To thende Baldwin that you maye know what to say of the Percies whose story is not all out of memorye (and it is an notable story) I wyll take vpon me the person of the Lorde Henry Percy Erle of Northumberlãd, father of syr Henry Hotspur, in whose behalfe this may be saide as followeth
(∴)   How

Earle of Northūberland. Fol. 25
Howe Henry Percy Earle of Northumberland, was for his couetous and trayterous attempt put to death at Yorke. Anno. 1407.

Morall Seneck true fynde I thy saying,
That neyther kin, riches, strength, or fauour
Are free from Fortune, but are ay decaying:
No worldly welth is ought saue doubtfull labour,
Mans lyfe in earth is like vnto a tabour,
Whiche nowe to myrth doth mildly men prouoke
And strayght to war, with a more sturdye stroke.

All this full true I Percy finde by proofe,
Which whilom was Earle of Northumberland:
And therfore Baldwin for my Piers behoofe,
To note mens falles sith thou hast tane in hand,
I would thou should my state well vnderstand:
For fewe Kinges were more than I redouted,
Whome double Fortune lifted vp and louted.

As for my kinne their noblenesse is knowen,
My valiaunt acts were folly for to prayse,
Wher through the Scots so oft wer ouerthrowe,
That who but I was doubted in my dayes:
And that king Richard found at all assayes,
For neuer Scots rebelled in his raigne,
But through my force were eyther caught or slayne.

A bj.

Henry Percy.

A brother I had was Earle of Worcester,
Alwayes in office and fauour with the King,
And by my wyfe dame Elinor Mortimer,
A sonne I had which so the Scots did sting,
That being yong, and but a very spring,
Henry Hotspur they gaue him vnto name,
And though I saye it, he did deserue the same.

We three triumphed in king Richardes tyme,
Tyll Fortune ought both hym and vs a spite:
But chiefly me, whome clerely from any cryme,
My king did banyshe from his fauour quite,
Proclayming me a trayterous knight:
Where through false slaunder forced me to be
That which before I did moste deadly flee.

Let men beware how they true folke defame,
Or threaten on them the blame of vices nought,
For infamy bredeth wrath, wreke followeth shame:
Eke open slaunder often times hath brought
That to effect, that erst was neuer thought
To be misdemed, men suffer in a sort.
But none can beare the griefe of misreport.

Because my kyng did shame me wrongfully,
I hated him and in dede became his foe:
And whyle he did at war in Ireland lye,
I did conspire to turne his weale to woe:
And through the duke of Yorke and other moe,
All royall power from him we quickly tooke
And gaue the same to Henry Bolenbroke.

                                           Ney the

Earle of Northuberland. Fol. 26

Neyther did we this onely for this cause,
But to say truth, force draue vs to the same:
For he despising God and all his lawes,
Slew whome he would, made sinne a very game,
And seing neither age nor coūsaile could him tame.
We thought it well done for the kyngdomes sake,
To leaue his rule that did all rule forsake.

But when syr Henry had attaynd his place,
He straighte became in all pointes worse than he,
Destroied the piers, & slew king Richardes grace,
Against his othe made to the Lordes and me:
And sekyng quarels howe to disagre,
He shamelesly required me and my sonne
To yeld him Scots which we in field had wonne.

My Nephue also Edmund Mortimer
The very heyr apparant to the crowne,
Whom Owen Glendour held as pryisoner,
Vilely bound in dungeon depe cast downe,
He would not raunsome but did felly frown,
Against my brother and me which for him spake,
And hym proclaymed traytour for our sake.

This foule despite did cause vs to conspire
To put hym downe as we did Richard erst,
And that we might this matter set on fire
From Owens iaple, our coosin we remeerst,
And vnto Glendour all our griefes reherst,
Who made a bond with Mortimer and me,
To priue the King and part the realme in three.

But

Henry Percy.

But when kyng Henry heard of this deuise,
Toward Owen Glendour he sped hym very quicke,
Mynding by force to stop hur enterprise:
And as the deuill would, than fell I sicke,
Howbeit my brother and sonne more politike
Than prosperous, with an hoast from Scotland brought,
Encountred him at Shewesbury where they fought.

The one was tane and kild, the other slayne,
And shortly after was Owen put to flight:
By meanes whereof I forced was to fayne,
That I knewe nothing of the former fyght.
Fraude oft auayles more than doth sturdy myght:
For by my fayning I brought him in beliefe,
I knewe not that wherin my part was chiefe.

And while the king thus tooke me for his frende,
I sought all meanes my former wrong to wreake,
Which that I might bring to the soner end,
To the byshop of Yorke I did the matter breake,
And to therle Marshall likewyse did I speake.
Whose father was through Henries cause exiled,
The bishops brother with trayterous death defiled.

These strapt assented to do what they could,
So did the Lord Hastinges and Lorde Fauconbridge
Which altogether promised they would,
Set all their power the kynges dayes to abridge.
But se the spite, before the byrdes were flydge
The kyng had woord and seasoned on the nest
Whereby alas my frendes were all opprest.

Earle of Northumberland

The bloody tyrant brought them all to ende
Excepted me, which into Scotland scapt,
To George of Dunbar therle of March, my frend,
Who in my cause all that he could ey scrapt:
And when I had for greater succour gapt,
Both at the Frenchmen and the Flemings hand,
And could get none I tooke such as I fand.

And with the help of George my very frend.
I did inuade Northumberland full bold,
Wheras the folke drew to me styll on end,
Bent to death my party to vphold:
Through help of these, full many a fort and hold,
The which the King right manfully had mand,
I easely wonne, and seised in my hand.

Not so content (for vengeance draue me on)
I entred Yorkshyre there to wast and spoile,
But ere I had far in the countrey gone
The shirpffe therof, Rafe Rokesby did assoyle
My trobled hoast of much part of our toyle
For he assaulting freshly tooke through power,
He and Lord Bardolph both at Bramham more.

And thence conueyed vs to the town of York,
Untill he knew what was the Kings entent:
There loe Lord Bardolph kinder than the Storke,
Did lose his head, which was to London sent,
With whome for frendship mine in like case went,
Thys was my hap my fortune or my faute,
This life I led and thus I came to naught.

      E.i.   Where

Richard Plantagenet.

Wherefore good Baldwin will the Piers take hede,
Of slaunder, mallice, and conspiracy,
Of couetise, whence all the rest procede:
For couetise ioynt with contumacy,
Doth cause all mischiefe in mens hartes to brede,
And therfore this to Esperance my woord.
Who causeth bloodshed shall not escape the swoord.

FINIS.

By that this was ended, I had founde out the story of Richarde Earle of Cambridge: & because it contained matter in it, thoughe not very notable, yet for the better vnderstanding of the rest, I thought it mete to touch it, and therfore said as followeth: you haue said well of ye Percies & fauourably: For in dede as it should appeare, the chiefe cause of their conspiracy against king Henry, was for Edmund Mortimer their cousins sake whome the kinge very maliciouslye proclaymed to haue yelded him selfe to Owen coulourably, whan as in dede he was taken forcibly against his wyll & very cruelly ordered in prison. And seinge we are in hand with Mortimers matter, I will take vppon me the person of Richard Plantagenet earle of Cambridge, who for his sake likewise dyed. And therefore

Earle of Cambridge.

fore I let passe Edmund Holland Earle of Kent, whome Henry the fourth made admirall to skoure the Seas, because ẏ Britons were abrode: which Earle (as many thinges happen in war) was slain with an arrow at ẏ assault of Briack: shortly after whose death this king dyed, & his son Henrye ẏ fyft of that name, succeded in his place. In the beginning of this Henry the fyfts raigne dyed this Richard, & with him Henrye the Lorde Scrope and other in whose behalfe this may be saide.

Richard Plantagenet,

How Richard Plantagenet Earle of Cambridge entending the Kings Destruction, was put to death at Southamton. Anno. Dom. 1415.

Aste maketh waste, hath commonly ben sayde,
And secrete mischiefe sceld hath lucky spede:
A murdering minde with proper poyze is wayd,
All this is true, I finde it in my crede.
And therfore Balwin warne all states take hede,
How they conspire any other to betrappe,
Least mischiefe ment light in the miners lappe.

For I Lord Richard heyre Plantagenet,
Was Earle of Cambridge and right fortunate,
If I had had the grace my wit to set,
To haue content me with mine own estate:
But O false honours, breders of debate,
The loue of you oure lewd hartes doth allure,
To lese our selues by seking you vnsure.

Because my brother Edmund Mortimer,
Whose eldest sister was my wedded wife,
I meane that Edmunde that was prisoner
In Wales so long through Owens busie strife,
Because I say that after Edmundes life,
His rightes and titles must by law be mine,
For he ne had, nor could encrease his line.

Because

Earle of Cambridge.

Because the right of realme and crowne was ours,
I serched meanes to help him thereunto.
And where the Henries held it by their powrs,
I sought a shyft their tenures to vndo,
Which being force, sith force or sleight must do,
I voyde of might, because their powr was strong,
Set pryuy sleight against their open wrong.

But sith the death of most part of my kin
Dyd dash my hope, through out the fathers dayes
I let it slip, and thought it best begin,
Whanas the sonne should dred least such assaies:
For force through spede, sleight spedeth through delayes,
And seeld doth treason time so fitly fynde
As whan all dangers most be out of minde.

Wherefore while Henry of that name the fifte,
Prepard his army to go conquer Fraunce,
Lord Scroope and I thought to attempt a drifte,
To put him downe my brother to auaunce:
But were it Gods will, my lucke, or his good chaunce,
The King wist wholy whereabout we went
The night before to shipward he him bent.

Then were we straight as traytours apprehended,
Our purpose spied, the cause therof was hid,
And therfore loe a falfe cause we pretended,
Where throught my brother was fro daunger rid:
We said for hier of French Kings coyne, we did
Behight to kill the King: and thus with shame
We staind our selues, to saue our frende fro blame.

           E iii   Whan

Thomas Montague,

When we had thus confest so foule a treason,
That we deserued, we suffered by the law.
See Baldwin see, and note as it is reason
How wicked dedes to woful endes do draw,
All force doth fayle no craft is worth a strawe,
To attayne thinges lost and therfore let them go,
For myght ruleth right, and will though truth say no.

FINIS.

When stout Richarde had stoutely sayde his minde, belyke saide one, this Richard was but a litle man, or els litle fauoured of writers, for our chronicles speake very litle of him. But seing we be com now to king Henries voyage into Fraunce, we cannot lacke valiaunt men to speke of for among so many as were led & sent by the kinge out of this Realme thyther, it can not be chosen but some, and that a greate somme, were slain among them: wherfore to speke of them all, I thincke not nedefull. And therfore to let passe Edward Duke of Yorke, and the Earle of Suffolke, slain both at the battaile of Agincourt, as were also many other. Let vs end the tyme of Henry the fift, and come to his sonne Henrye the sixte: whose nonage brought Fraunce and Normandy out of bondage, and was cause that so fewe of our noble men died aged. Of whome to let passe the nomber, I will take vppon me:

Earle of Salisbury. Folio. 30.

mee the person of Thomas Montague Earle of Salisbury, whose name was not so good at home (and yet he was called ẏ good Earle) as it was dreadfull abroade: who exclamyng vpon the mutability of Fortune may iustly saye in manner as followeth.

E.iiii. How

Thomas Montague,

How Thomas Montague Earle of Salisburye in the middest of his glory, was chaunceably slaine at Orleaunce with a piece of Ordinaunce the .3. of Nouēber. Anno. 1428.

What fooles be we to trust vnto our strength,
Our wit, our courage, or our noble fame,
Which time it selfe must nedes deuour at length,
Though froward Fortune could not foyle the same.
But seing this Goddesse giueth all the game,
Which still to chaunge doth set her only lust,
Why toyle we so for thinges so hard to trust?

A goodly thing it is suerly good report,
Which noble hartes, do seke by course of kinde:
But seen the date so doutfull and so short,
The way so rough wherby we do it finde,
I cannot chose but prayse the princely mynde
That preaseth for it, though we fynde oppresst,
By foule defame those that deserue it best.

Concerning whom marke Balwyn what I say,
I meane the vertuous hindred of their brute,
Among which nomber recken well I may,
My valiaunt father Ihon Lord Montacute,
Who lost his life I iudge through iust pursute:
I say the cause and not the casuall speede,
Is to be wayed in euery kinde of dede,

             This

Earle of Salisburie,

This rule obserued, how many shall we fynde
For vertues sake with infamy opprest:
How many again through help of Fortune blinde,
For ill attemptes atchieued, with honour blest:
Successe is worst oftimes whan cause is best:
Therfore say I: God send them sory haps
That iudge the causes by their afterclaps.

The end in dede is iudge of euery thing,
Which is the cause or latter point of time:
The fyrst true verdict at the first may bring,
The last is slow, or slipper as the slime,
Oft chaunging names of innocence and crime.
Duke Thomas death was Iustice two yearrs long,
And euer sence, sore tyranny and wrong.

Wherfore I pray thee Baldwyn way the cause,
And praise my father as he doth deserue:
Because Earle Henry, King against all lawes,
Endeuoured King Richard for to starue,
In iayle, wherby the regall crowne might swarue
Out of the line to which it than was due,
(Wherby God knowes what euell might ensue)

My Lord Iohn Holland Duke of Excetter,
Which was dere cosin to this wretched King,
Dyd moue my father, and the Earle of Glocester,
With other Lordes to ponder well the thing:
Who seing the myschiefe that began to spring,
Did all consent this Henry to depose,
And to restore King Richard to the rose.

And

Thomas Montague,

And while they did deuise a prety trayue,
Wherby to bring their purpose better about,
Which was in maske this Henry to haue slaine,
The Duke of Aumerle blew their counsaile out:
Yet was their purpose good, there is no dout.
What cause can be more worthy for a Knyght,
Than saue his king, and help true heyrs to right?

For this with them my father was distroyed,
And buried in the dunghill of defame.
Thus euill chaunce their glory dyd auoyde,
Wheras theyr cause doth claime eternall fame.
Whan dedes therfore vnluckely do frame,
Men ought not iudge the aucthours to be nought,
For right through might is often ouerraught.

And God doth suffer that it should be so,
But why, my wit is feble to decise,
Except it be to heape vp wrath and wo
On wicked heades that iniuries deuise.
The cause why mischiefs many times arise,
And light on them that would mens wronges redresse,
As for the rancour that they beare I gesse.

God hates rigour though it furder right,
For sinne is sinne, how euer it be vsed:
And therfore suffereth shame and death to lyght,
To punish vyce, though it be well abused.
Who furdereth right is not therby excused,
If through the same be do sum other wrong:
To euery vice due guerdon doth belong.

Whan

Earle of Salisbury.

What preach I now I am a man of warre,
And that my body I dare say doth professe,
Of cured woundes beset with many a skarre,
My broken Iaw vnheald can say no lesse.
O Fortune, Fortune cause of all distresse,
My father had great cause thy fraude to curse
But much more I, abused ten times worse

Thou neuer flattredst him in all thy life,
But me thou dandledst like thy darling deare:
Thy gyftes I found in euery corner rife,
Where euer I went I met thy smyling cheare:
Which was not for a day or for a yeare,
But through the raigne of three right worthy kinges,
I founde thee forward in all kinde of thinges.

The while King Henry conquered in Fraunce
I sued the warres and still found victory,
In all assaultes so happy was my chaunce,
Holdes yeld or won did make my enemies sory:
Dame Prudence eke augmented so my glory,
That in all treaties euer I was one,
Whan weyghty matters were agreed vpon.

But whan this King this mighty conquerour,
Through death vnripe was both his realmes bereft,
His sely infant did receyue his power,
Pore litle babe full yong in cradell left,
Where crowne and Scepter hurt him with the heft.
Whose worthy vncles had the gouernaunce,
The one at home the other abroade in Fraunce.

And

Thomas Montague,

And I which was in peace and war well skilled,
With both these rulers greatly was estemed:
Bare rule at home as often as they willed,
And fought in Fraunce whan they it nedefull demed,
And euery where so good my seruice semed,
That English men to me great loue did beare,
Our foes the French, my force fulfilled with feare.

I alwayes thought it fitly for a Prince,
And such as haue the regiment of Realmes,
His subiects hartes with mildenes to conuince,
With iustice mixt, auoyding all extreames.
For like as Phebus with his cherefull beames,
Doth freshly force the fragrant flowers to florish,
So rulers myldenes subiects loue doth norish.

This found I true: for through my mylde behauiour,
Their harts I had with me to liue and dye,
And in their speche bewrayer of their fauour,
They cald me still good Earle of Salisburie,
The Lordes confest the commons did not lye.
For vertuous life, free hart, and lowly minde,
With high and low shall alwayes fauour finde.

Which vertues chiefe becom a man of war,
Whereof in Fraunce I founde experience:
For in assautes due myldenes passeth far
All rigour, force and sturdy violence:
For men will stoutly sticke to their defence,
When cruell captaines couet after spoyle,
And so enforst, oft geue their foes the foyle.

Earle of Salisbury.

But when they knowe they shalbe frendly vsed,
They hazard not their heades but rather yelde:
For this my offers neuer were refused
Of any towne, or suerly very sceld.
But force and furies fyt befor the fielde
And there in dede I vsed so the same,
My foes would fly yf they but heard my name.

For whan Lord Steward and Earle Vantadore,
Had cruelly besieged Crauant towne,
Which he had wonne, and kept long time before,
Which lieth in Awxer on the River Youne,
To rayse the siege the regent sent me downe:
Where as I vsed all rigour that I might,
I killed all that were not saued by flight.

When therle of Bedford then in Fraunce Lord regent
Knewe in what sort I had remoued the siege,
In Brye and Champayne he made me vicegerent,
And Lieutenaunt for him and for my Liege:
Which caused me to go to Brye, and there besiege,
Mountaguillon with twenty weekes assaut,
Which at the last was yelded me for naught.

And for the Duke of Bretaynes brother Arthur,
Both Earle of Richmond and of Yuery,
Against his oth from vs had made departure,
To Charles the Dolphin our chiefe enemy,
I with the Regent went to Normandy,
To take his town of Yuery which of spight,
Did to vs dayly all the harme they might.

They

Thomas Montague,

They at the first compounded by a day
To yeeld, if rescues did not come before,
And while in hope to fight, we at it lay,
The Dolphin gathered men two thousand score,
With Earles Lordes and Captaines ioly store:
Of which the Duke of Alanson was guyde,
And sent them down to se yf we would bide.

But they left vs and down to Vernoyle went,
And made their vaunt they had our army slayne,
And through that lye, that town from vs they hent,
Which shortly after turned to their payne:
For there both armies met vpon the plaine:
And we eyght thousand whom they flew, not slew before,
Did kill of them, ten thousand men and more.

When we had taken Vernoyle thus agayne,
To driue the Dolphin vtterly out of Fraunce,
The Regent sent me to Aniow and to Mayne,
Where I besieged the warlike town of Mawns
There Lord of Toysers Baldwins valiaunce
Did well appeare, which would not yeeld the town,
Tyll al the towers and walles were battered down,

But here now Baldwin take it in good part,
Though that I brought this Baldwin there to yeeld
The Lyon fearce for all his noble hart,
Being ouer matched, is forst to flye the field.
If Mars him selfe there had ben with his shield
And in my stormes had stoutly me withstoode,
He should haue yeeld, or els haue shed my blood.

Earle of Salisburie.

This worthy Knight both hardy, stout, and wise,
Wrought well his feat: as time and place require,
When Fortune failes, it is the best aduice
To strike the sayle least all ly in the myre.
This haue I said to thend thou take no ire,
For though no cause be found, so nature frames,
Men haue a zeale to such as beare theyr names.

But to returne, in Mayn wan I at length,
Such townes and forts as might eyther help or hurt,
I manned Payon and Suzans town of strength,
Fort Barnard, Thanceaur, and S. Cales the curt,
With Lile sues Bolton, standing in the durt:
Eke Gwerland, Suze, Loupeland and Mountsure,
With Malycorne, these wan I and kept full sure.

Besides all this I tooke nere forty holdes,
But those I razed euen with the ground.
And for these dedes, as sely shepe in foldes,
Do shrinke for feare at euery little sound,
So fled my foes before my face full round:
Was none so hardy that durst abide the fight,
So Mars and Fortune furdered me their knight.

I tell no ly so gastfull grew my name,
That it alone discomfited an hoast:
The Scots and frenchmen well confesse the same,
Els will the towne which they lyke cowards lost.
For whan they sieged Beauron with greate boast,
Being fourty thousand Britaynes, French, and Scots,
Fyue hundred men did vanquish them like sots.

Thomas Montague.

For while the Frenchmen freshly assaulted still,
Our Englishmen came boldly forth at night,
Crying sainct George, Salisbury, kill, kill, kill,
And offered freshly with their foes to fight,
And they as frenchly tooke themselues to flight,
Supposing suerly that I had bene there,
Se how my name did put them all in feare.

Thus was the Dolphins power discomfited,
Fower thousand slaine, their campe tane as it stoode,
Wherby our town and souldiers profited,
For there were vitayles plentifull and good:
This while was I in England by the rood,
To appease a strife that was right foule befall,
Betwene Duke Humfrey and the Cardinall.

The Duke of Exceter shortly after died,
Which of the King at home had gouernaunce,
Whose roume the Earle of Warwicke then supplied,
And I tooke his and sped me into Fraunce.
And hauing a zeale to conquere Orlpaunce,
With much a do I gat the Regents ayd,
And marched thyther, and siege about it layde.

But in the way I tooke the town of Payne,
Where murdered were for stoutnes many a man:
But Baugencey I tooke with litle payne,
For which to shew them fauour I began:
This caused the townes of Mewne and Jargeman,
That stoode on Loyer: to profer me the keyes,
Ere I came nere them, welny by two dayes.

See

Earle of Salisbury.

See here how Fortune forward can allure,
What baytes she layeth to bring men to their end
Who hauing hap lyke this, but hopeth sure,
To bring to bale what euer he entendes?
But soone is sower the swete that Fortune sends:
Whan hope and hap, whan health and welth is hiest,
Than wo and wracke, disease, and nede be nihest.

For while I, suing this so good successe,
Layde siege to Orlyaunce on the riuer side,
The Bastard (Cuckolde Cawnies son I gesse,
Who thought the Dukes, who had the town in gide,
Came fiersly forth, when he his time espied;
To rayse the siege but was bet backe againe,
And hard pursued both to his losse and payne.

For there we wan the bulwarke on the bridge,
With a mighty tower standing fast thereby.
Ah cursed tower that didst my dayes abridge,
Would God thou hadst ben furder, eyther I:
For in this tower a chamber standes on hye,
From which a man may biew through all the town
By certaine windowes yron grated downe.

Where on a day, now Baldwyn note mine ende,
I stoode in bewing where the town was weake,
And as I busily talked with my frend,
Shot fro the towne, which all the grate did breake
A pellet came and droue a mighty fleake
Against my face, and tare away my cheeke,
For payne wherof I dyed within a weeke.

F.i.

See

James the first.

See Baldwin see the vncertayne of glory,
How sodayne mischiefe dasheth all to dust.
And warne all princes by my broken story,
The happiest fortune chiefly to mistrust,
Was neuer man that alway had his lust:
Than such be fooles, in fancy more then mad,
Which hope to haue that neuer any had.

FINIS.

Hys straunge aduenture of the good Earle draue vs all into a dumpe, inwardly lamētyng his wofull desteny, out of whiche we were awaked after this sort.

To what end (saide one) muse we so muche on the matter. This Earle is neyther the fyrst nor the last whom Fortune hath foundred in ye heigth of their prosperity. For all through the raigne of this vnfortunate king Henry, we shall synde many whiche haue bene likewise serued, whose chaunces sith they be martiall & therfore honorable, maye the better be omitted. And therfore we will let go the Lordes Molynes and Poyninges, slayne both at the siege of Orleaunce shortle after the death of this Earle. Also the valiaunt Earle of Arundell destroyed with a bowlet at ye assaut of Gerbory, whose storyes neuer the lesse are worth the hearing. And to quyckē vp your

Kinge of Scots.

vp your spites, I wil take vpon me a tragicall person in dede, I meane kyng Iamy slayne by his seruauntes in his priuy chamber: who although he be a Scot, yet seing he was brought vp in Englande, wher‍e hee learned the language, his example also so notable, it were not mete it shold be forgotten.
And therefore marke Baldwyn what I thinke he may say.

James the firste

How King Iames the firſt for breaking his othes and bonds, was by Gods ſufferannce miſerably murdered of hys owne ſubiectes. An:1437.

If for examples sake thou write thy booke,
I charge the Baldwyn thou forget me not:
Whom Fortune alwayes frowardly forſooke,
Such was my lucke, my merit or my lot.
I am that Iames King Roberts ſon the Scot,
That was in England priſonner all his youth,
Through myne uncle Walters trayterous untruth.

For whan my father through diſeaſe and age,
Unwieldy was to gouern well his land,
Becauſe his brother walter ſemed ſage,
He put the rule thereof in to his hand.
Than had my father, you ſhall underſtand,
Of lawfull barnes, me and one onely other,
Nempt Dauy Rothſay, who was mine elder brother.

This Dauy was prince of Scotland and ſo take,
Tyll his aduoutry cauſed men complayn:
Which that he might by moniſhment forſake,
My father prayed myne uncle take the paine.
To threaten him hys vyces to refrayne.
But he falſe traytour butcherly murdering wretche,
To get the crowne began to fetch a fetch.

Kiuge of Scots,

And fynding now a proffer to his pray,
Deuised meanes my brother to deuoure,
And for that cause conuayed him day by day
From place to place, from castle vnto tower,
To Faulkland fort, where like a tormentour
He starued him, and put to death a wife
Whom through a rede he suckt to saue his life.

O wretched death, fye cruell tyranny,
A Prince in prison lost for fault of foode?
Was neuer enmy wrought such vilany.
A trusted brother distroy his brothers bloud
Wo worth so frendly, fye on double hood.
Ah wretched father se thy son is lost,
Sterued by thy brother whom thou trustedst most.

Of whom when some began to finde the fraude,
And yet the traytour made himselfe so clere,
That he should seme to haue deserued laude,
So wofull did he for his prince appere,
My doutfull father louing me full dere,
To auoyde all daunger that might after chaunce,
Sen me away but nine yeares ould to Fraunce.

But windes and wether were so contrary,
That we were driuen to the English coast,
Which realme with Scotland at that tyme did vary
So that they tooke me prisoner not as hoaste:
For which my fyther fearing I were lost,
Conceiued shortly such an inward thought,
As to the graue immediately hym brought.

Thus

James the first,

Than had myne vncle all the regiment
At home, and I in England prisonner lay,
For to him selfe he thought it detriment,
For my release any raunsom for to pay,
For as he thought he had possest his pray:
And therfore wisht I might in durance dure
Tyll I had dyed, so should his raygne be sure.

But good King Henry seing I was a chyld,
And heir by right vnto a realme and crowne,
Dyd bring me vp not (like my brother) wilde,
But vertuously in feates of high renowne:
In liberall artes, in instrumentall sowne:
By meane whereof when I was after King,
I dyd my realme to ciuill order bring.

For ere I had ben prisonner eyghtene yere,
In which short space two noble Princes dyed,
Whereof the fyrst in prudence had no pere,
The other in war most valyaunt throughly tryed,
Whose roume his sonne babe Henry eke supplied:
The peers of England which did gouerne all,
Dyd of their goodnes help me out of thrall.

They maried me to a cosin of their King,
The Duke of Somersets daughter riche and fayre.
Releast my raunsom saue a triflyng thyng:
And after I had done homage to the heyr,
And sworne my frendshyp neuer should appayre,
They brought me kyngly furnisht to my land,
Which I receyued at mine vncles hand.

Whereof

Whereof my Lordes and commons were full glad,
So was myne uncle chiefly as he sayed,
Who in his mouth no other matter had,
Saue punish such as had my brother trayed.
The faut wherof apparantly he layed,
To good Duke Murdo, his elder brothers son,
Whose father dyed long ere this was don.

My cursed uncle slyer than the snake,
Whice would by craft vnto the crowne aspyer,
Because he sawe this Murdo was a stake,
That stayed vp the top of his desyre,
(For his elder brother was duke Murdoes syer)
He thought it best to haue him made away,
So was he suer (I gone) to haue his pray.

And by his craftes the traytour brought to passe
That I destroyed Duke Murdo and his kyn,
Pore innocentes, my louing frends alas.
O Kings and princes what plight stand we in,
A trusted traytour shall you quickly winne
To put to death your kin and frendes most iust:
Take hede therfore, take hede whose rede ye trust.

And at the last to bring me hole in hate,
With God and man at home and eke abrode,
He counsayld me for surance of my state:
To help the Frenchmen, then nigh ouertrode
By Englishmen: and more to lay on lode,
Wyth power and force all England to inuade,
Agaynst the oth and homage that I made.

F.iiii.   And

James the firste.

And though at first my couscience did grudge,
To breake the boundes of frendship knitt by oth,
Yet after profe (see mischiefe) I dyd iudge,
It madnesse for a King to kepe his troth.
And semblably with all the worlde it goth.
Syns oft assayed are thought to be no sinne,
So soyleth synne the soule it sinketh in.

But as diseases common cause of death,
Bring daunger most, when least they pricke and smart,
Which is a signe they haue expulst the breath
Of lyuely heate which doth defend the hart:
Euen so such sins as felt are on no part
Haue conquerd grace, and by their wicked vze,
So kild the soule that it can haue no cure.

And grace agate, vice still succedeth vice,
And all to haste the vengeaunce for the furst.
I arede therfore all people to be wise,
And stop the bracke whan it begins to burst.
Attaste no poyson (vice is venim wurst,
It mates the minde) beware eke of to much,
All kyll through muchnes, some with onely touche.

When I had learnd to set my oth at nought,
And through much vse the sence of sinne exiled,
Agaynst King Henry what I could I wroght,
My fayth my oth vniustly foule defiled.
And while sly Fortune at my doinges smyled,
The wrath of God which I had well deserued,
Fell on my necke, for thus loe was I serued.

                                                    Ere I

Ere I had raygned fully fiftene yeare,
While time I lay at Pertho at my place,
With the Quene my wife and children me to cheare,
My murdringe vncle with the double face,
That longed for my kingdome and my mace,
To slay me there suborned Robert Grame,
With whome his nephue Robert Stuart came.

And whan their time fit for their purpose found,
Into my priuy chamber they astart,
Where with their swords they gaue me many a wound,
And slue all such as stucke vnto my parte:
There loe my wife did shew her louing hart,
Who to defend me felled one or twaine,
And was sore wounded ere I could be slaine.

Se Baldwin Baldwin, the vnhappy endes,
Of such as passe not for their lawfull oth:
Of those that causles leaue theyr faithe or frendes,
And murder kinsfolke through their foes vntroth,
Warne warne all Princes, all like sinnes to loth,
And chiefly such as in my realme be borne,
For God hates highly all that are forsworne.

FINIS.

When this was said, let king Iamy go sayd
mayster Ferrers: and retourne wee to oure
owne story, and see what broyles were a-
mong the nobilyty in the kinges minoritye. How
the

William De la pole.

the Cardinal Beauford maligneth ye estate of good Duke Humfrey the kinges vncle and protectour of the realme, & by what driftes he fyrst banissheth hys wyfe from him. And lastely how the good Duke is murderouslye made a waye through conspiracye of Quene Maygaret and other: both whose tragedies I entend at leysure to declare, for they be notable. Do so I pray you (said an other) But take hede ye demurre not vpon them. And I to be occupied in ye meane tyme, will shewe what I haue noted in the Duke of Suffolkes doinges, one of the chiefe of Duke Humfreys destroyers, who by the prouidence of God came shortly after in such hatred of the people, that the king him selfe could not saue him from a straunge and notable death, for being banisht the realme for the terme of fyue yeares, to appease the contynuall rumors and inwarde grudges that not onely the Commons but most parte of the nobility of England bare towardes him for the death of the Duke of Glocester and sayling towardes Fraunce, was met with a ship of Deuonshyre, and beheaded forthwith the fyrste day of may Anno. 1450, and the dead corps throwen vp at Douer vpon the sandes, whiche may lament hys deathe after thys manner.

Duke of Southfolke.

How Lord William Delapole Duke of Suffolke was worthely banyshed, for abusinge his Kinge and causing the destruction of the good Duke Humfrey. An. 1450.

Heauy is the hap wherto all men be bound,
I meane the death, which no estate may flye:
But to be banisht, beheded, and than drownd,
In sinke of shame from top of honors hye,
Was neuer man so serud I thinke but I,
Wherfore Baldwyn amongest the rest by ryght,
I clayme of the my wofull case to wryte.

My only lyfe in all poyntes may suffise,
To shew how base all baytes of Fortune be,
Which thawe lyke yse, through heate of enuies eyes:
Or vicious dedes which much possessed me.
Good hap with vice, long tyme cannot agree,
Which bring best fortunes to the basest fall,
And happyest hap to enuy to be thrall.

Called I was Wyllyam De la Pole,
Of Suffolke Duke in Quene Margarets dayes,
That found the meane Duke Humfreys bloud to coole,
Whose worthy actes deserue eternall prayse,
Wherby I note that Fortune cannot rayse
Any one aloft, without some others wracke:
Fluds drown no fieldes before they fynde a bracke.

But

William De la pole.

But as the waters which do breake the walles
Do lose their course they had within the shore,
And dayly rotting stinke within their stalles
For faut of mouing which they found before:
Euen so the state that ouer high is bore
Doth lose the life of peoples loue it had,
And rots it selfe vntyll it fall to bad.

For while I was but Earle, ech man was glad,
To say and do the best by me they myght:
And Fortune euer synce I was a lad,
Dyd smyle vpon me with a chearfull syght,
For whan my Kyng had doubed me a knight
And sent me forth to serue at war in Fraunce,
My lucky spede myne honour did enhaunce.

Where, to ompt the many feates I wrought
Under others guyde, I do remember one,
Which with my souldiers valyantly was fought,
None other Captayne saue my selfe alone,
I meane not now the apprinze of Pucell Ione
In which attempt my trauayle was not small,
Though the Duke of Burgoyne had the prayse of all.

But the siege of Awmarle is the feat I prayse:
A strong built towne, with castles, walles, and baultes,
With men and Weapon armd at all assayes:
To which I gaue nygh fyue tymes fyue assaultes,
Tyll at the last they yelded it for naughtes.
Yet Lord Ramburs like a valyaunt Knyght,
Defended it as long as euer he might.

But

Duke of Southfolke.

But what preuayled it these townes to winne,
Which shortly after must be lost agayne:
Wherby I see there is more glory in
The keping thinges than is in their attayne:
To get and kepe not, is but losse of payne.
Therfore ought men prouide to saue theyr winninges
In all attemptes, els lose they theyr beginninges.

Because we could not kepe the townes we won,
For they were more than we might easely wyeld
One yere vndid what we in ten had don:
For enuy at home and treason abrode, did yelde
King Charles his realme of Fraunce, madeh a rrain field:
For bloudy warres had wasted all encrease,
Which causde the Pope help pouerty sue for peace.

So that in Tourayn at the town of Toures
Duke Charles and other for their prince appered,
So did Lord Rosse and I than Earle, for oures:
And whan we shewed wherin ech other dered,
We sought out meanes all quarrels to haue clered,
Wherin the Lordes of Germany, of Spayne,
Of Hungary, and Denmarke, tooke exceding payne.

But sith we could no finall peace induce,
For neyther would the others couenantes here,
For eyghtene monthes we did conclude a truce:
And while as frendes we lay together there,
Because my warrant did me therein beare,
To make a perfyt peace and through accord,
I sought a mariage for my souerayne Lord.

And

William De la pole.

And for the French Kinges daughters were to small,
I fancied most dame Margaret his niece,
A louely Lady bewtiful and tall,
Fayre spoken, pleasant a very princely piece,
In wit and learning matchlesse hence to Grece,
Duke Rayners doughter of Aniow, King by stile
Of Naples, Ierusalem and of Scicil yle.

But ere I could the graunt of her attayne:
All that our King had of her fathers landes,
As Mauntes the cytye, the county whole of Mayne,
And most of Aniow duchy in our handes,
I did release him by assured bandes.
And as for dowry with her none I sought,
I thought no peace could be to derely bought.

But whan this mariage throwly was agreed
Although my King were glad of such a make.
His vncle Humfrey abhorred it in dede,
Because therby his precontract he brake,
Made with the heyr of the Earle of Arminacke,
A noble maide wtth store of goodes endowed,
Which more than this with lesse the Duke allowed.

But loue and bewty in the Kyng so wrought,
That neyther profit or promise he regarded,
But set his vncles counsaple styll at noughts
And for my paynes I highly was awarded.
Thus vertue staruees, but lustfoode must be larded,
For I made Marquyse went to Fraunce agayne,
And brought this bride vnto my soueraygne.

Duke of Southfolke.

At whome because Duke Humfrey ay repined,
Calling their mariage aduoutry (as it was)
The Quene did moue me, erst therto enclined,
To helpe to bring him to his Requiem masse,
Which sith it could for no crime cum to passe:
Hys life and doinges were so right and clere,
Through priuy murder we brought him to his bere.

Thus righteousnes brought Humfrey to rebuke,
Because he should no wickednesse allow,
But for my doynges I was made a Duke.
So Fortune can both bend and smoth her browe
On whome she list, not passing why or how.
O Lord how high, how sone she did me rayse,
How fast she fyld me both with prayes and prayse.

The Lordes and commous both of like assent,
Besought my soueraygne kneling on their knees,
To record my doynges in the parliament,
As dedes deseruing euerlasting fees.
In which attempt they did no labour lesse,
For they set not my prayse so fast in flame,
As he was redy to reward the same.

But note the end, my dedes so worthy demed
Of Kyng, of Lordes, and Commons altogether,
Were shortly after treasons false estemed,
And all men curst Quene Margets comming hither,
For Charles the french king in his feates not lyther,
Whan we had rendered Rayner Mauntes and Mayne,
Found meane to wyn all Normandy agayne,

Thys

Willyam De la pole.

This made the people curſe the mariage,
Eſteming it the cauſe of euery loſſe:
Wherfore at me with open mouth they rage,
Affirming me to haue brought the realme to moſſe:
Whan King and Queene ſawe thinges thus go a croſſe,
To quiet all a parliament they called,
And cauſed me in priſon to be thralled.

And ſhortly after brought me forth a brode,
Which made the Commons more than double woode:
And ſome with weapons would haue laid on lode,
If their graund captain Blewberd in his moode,
Had not in time with wiſdome ben withſtode:
But though that he and more were executed,
The people ſtill their worſt againſt me bruted.

And ſo applied the parliament with bylles,
Of haynous wronges and open trayterous crimes,
That King and Quene were forſt againſt their willes,
Fro place to place to adiourne it diuers times.
For Princes power is like the ſandy ſlimes,
Which muſt perforce geue place vnto the waue,
Or ſue the windy ſourges whan they raue.

Their life was not more dere to them than I,
Which made them ſearch all ſhyftes to ſaue me ſtyll,
But ay my foes ſuch faultes did on me trye,
That to preſerue me from a worſer pyll,
The King was fayne full ſore againſt his will:
For fyue yeares ſpace to ſend me in exile,
In hope to haue reſtorde me in a while.

           But

Duke of Southfolke.

But marke how vengeaunce wayteth vpon vice,
To shun this storme, in sayling towardes Fraunce,
A Pyrates Barke, that was of litle price,
Encountred me vpon the seas by chaunce,
Whose captain there, tooke me as in a traunce,
Let passe my shyppes, with all their frayt and loade,
And led me backe agayne to Douer roade.

Where vnto me recounting all my faultes,
As murdring of Duke Humfry in his bed,
And how I had brought all the realme to naughts,
Causing the King vnlawfully to wed,
There was no grace, but I must lose my head.
Wherfore he made me to shryue me in his bote,
And on the brinke my necke in two he smote.

This was myne end: which was by reason due
To me, and such as others deaths procure,
Therfore be bould to write, for it is true,
That who so doth such practise put in vre,
Of due reward at last shalbe most sure,
For God is iust, whose stroke delayed long,
Doth light at last with payn more sharpe and strong.

FINIS. VV. B.

When this was said: euery man reioysd to heare of a wicked person so righteously punished: for though Fortune in many points be iniurious to Princes, yet in this and such like she is most righteouse: and only deserueth the name of
G. i. a Goddesse,

Jacke Cade.

a goddesse, whan she prouideth meanes to punish & destroy tyrantes. And when we had a while considered the driftes of the kinge and quene to haue saued this Duke: & yet they could not: It is worth ye labour(said one)to way the workes & iudgements of God: whiche seynge they are knowen most euidently by comparing contraries, I will touche the story of Jacke Cade in order next followinge. Whome kyng Henrye with all his puissaunce was no more able for a while to destroy (yet was he hys rebellious enemy) than he was to preserue ye Duke of Suffolke his derest frende: by which two examples doth appeare howe notablye God disposeth all thinges, and that no force stretcheth farther, than it pleaseth him to suffer. For this Cade beinge an Irishcman but of meane parentage, of no ability,& lesse power, accompanied with a fewe naked Kentishemen, caused ye king with his army at al points appointed, to leaue the field, and suffer him to do whatsoeuer he lusted for a tyme, but in the ende hee was slaine at Hothfielde in Suffer, and caried thence to London in a cart,and there quartered. In whose behalfe, seing he is one of Fortunes whelpes, I will troble you a while to heare the processe of his enterprise, whiche he maye declare in manner followinge. How

Iacke Cade.

How Iacke Cade naming hymselfe Mortimer, traterously rebelling agaynst his King in Iune. Anno. 1450. was for his treasons & cruell doyngs worthely punished.

Shall I call it Fortune or my froward folly,
That lifted me vp and layed me downe belowe?
Or was it courage that made me so ioly,
Which of the starres and bodies grement growe?
What euer it were this one poynt suer I knowe,
Which shalbe mete for euery man to marke:
Our lust and willes our euils cheifly warke.

It may be well that planets do encline,
And our complexions moue our myndds to yll,
But such is reason, that they bring to fine
No worke vnayded of our lust and will:
For Heauen and Earth are subiect both to skill.
The skyll of God ruleth all it is so strong,
Man may by skill gyde thinges that to him long.

Though lust be sturdy and will enclined to nought,
This forst by mixture that by heauens course,
Yet through the skill God hath in reason wrought
And geuen man, no lust nor wil to course,
But may be stayed or swaged of the sourse,
So that it shall in nothing force the mynde:
To worke our wo, or leaue the proper kynde.

But

Jacke Cade.

But though this skill be giuen to euery man
To rule the will, and kepe the minde aloft,
For lacke of grace full fewe vse it can,
These worldly pleasures tickle vs so oft:
Skyll is not weake, but will strong, flesh is soft
And yeldes it selfe to pleasure that it loueth,
And hales the mynde to that it most reproueth.

Now if this hap wherby we yelde our mynde
To lust and will, be Fortune as we name her,
Than is she iustly called false and blinde,
And no reproch can be to much to blame her:
Yet is the shame our owne when so we shame her,
For suer this hap if it be rightly known,
Commeth of our selues, and so the blame our own.

For who so liueth in the schole of skill,
And medleth not with any worlds assayes,
Forsaketh pompes and honors, that do spill
The myndes recourse to Graces quiet stayres,
His state no Fortune by no meane appayres:
For Fortune is the folly and plague of those
Which to the world their wretched wylles dispose.

Among which fooles (marke Baldwyn) I am one,
That would not stay my selfe in myne estate.
I thought to rule but to obay to none,
And therfore fell I with my King at bate.
And to the end I myght him better mate,
John Mortimer I caused my selfe be called,
Whose kingly bloud the Henries nye had thralled.

Jacke Cade.

Thys shyft I vsed the people to perswade
To leaue theyr Prince, on my syde more to sticke,
Where as in dede my fathers name was Cade,
Whose noble stock was neuer worth a sticke.
But touchyng wyt I was both rype and quicke,
Had strength of lims, large stature, comely face,
Which made men wene my lynage were not base.

And seyng stoutnes stuck by men in Kent,
Whose valyant hartes refuse none enterpryse,
With false perswasions strapte to them I went,
And sayd they suffered to great iniuries:
By meane whereof I caused them to rise,
And battayle wise to come to Black heath playne,
And thence their griefs vnto the King complayne.

Who being deafe (as men say) on that eare
For we desyred release of subsedies,
Refused roughly our requestes to heare,
And came agaynst vs as his enemies:
But we to tary him sought out subtilties,
Remoued our campe, and backe to Senocke went,
After whome the Staffords with their power was sent.

Se here how Fortune setting vs a flote,
Brought to our nets a porcion of our pray.
For why the Staffords with their army hote,
Assayled vs at Senocke where we laye:
From whence alyue they parted not away,
Whiche whan the Kings retinue vnderstoode,
They all affirmed my quarrell to be good.

G.iii.   Whiche

Jacke Cade.

Which caused the King, and Quene whome all did hate,
To rayse their campe, and sodainly depart:
And that they might the peoples grudge abate,
To impzison some full soze agaynst their hart.
Lozde Saye was one, whome I made after smart,
For after the Staffozds and their hoast was slayne,
To Blackheath fyeld I marched back agayne.

And where the King would nothing heare befoze,
Now was he glad to send to knowe my mynde:
And I therby enflamed much the moze,
Refused his grauntes so folly made me blynde.
For this he flew and left Lozd Scales behynde,
To help the towne and strengthen London tower,
Towards which I marched fozward with my power.

And found there all thinges at myne owne desire.
I entred London, did there what I list.
The treasurer, Lozd Saye, Ioyd conspire
To haue condemned: wherof when I mist,
(For he by lawe my malice did resist)
By foçce I tooke hym in Guyldhall fro the heape,
And headed him befoze the crosse in Cheape.

Hys son in law Iames Cromer shriue of Kent
I caught at Myle end, whereas then he lay:
Beheaded him and on a poale I sent,
Hys head to London where his fathers laye.
With these two heades I made a prety play,
For pyght on poales I bare them through the strete,
And for my spozt made ech kisse other swete.

Than

Jacke Cade.

Than brake I prisons let forth whome I wold,
And vsed the City as it had ben myne:
Tooke from the marchaunts, mony ware and Gold,
From some by force, from other some by fyne.
This at the length did cause them to repyne,
So that Lord Scales consenting with the Mayre,
Forbad vs to their City to repayre.

For all this while mine hoast in Southwarke lay,
Who whan they knew our passage was denyed,
Came boldly to the bridge and made a fraye,
For in we would, the townes men vs defyed:
But whan with strokes we had the matter tryed,
We wan the bridge and set much parte on fyer,
This done to Southwark backe we did retyer.

The morow after came the Chauncellour,
With generall pardon for my men, halfe gone,
Which heard and read, the rest within an houre,
Shranke all away ech man to shifte for one.
And whan I saw they left me post alone,
I dyd dysguyse me like a knyght of the post,
And into Sussex rode away in poste.

And there I lurked tyll that cursed coyne,
That restlesse begle sought and found me out,
For straight the King by promyse did enioyne,
A thousand marke to who so euer mought
Apprend my corse, which made them seeke about:
Among the which one Alexander Iden,
Found out the hole where in the foxe was hidden.

G iiii   But

Jacke Cade.

But ere he tooke me I put hym to his trumps,
For yeeld I would not while my handes would holde,
But hope of money made him stur his stumps,
And to assault me valyauntly and bolde.
Two hores and more our combat was not colde,
Tyll at the last he lent me such a stroke,
That downe I fell and neuer after spoke.

Than was my carkasse caryed like a hog,
To Southwarke borow where it lay a night,
The next day drawen to Newgate like a dog,
All men reioysing at the rufull sight:
Than were on poales my perboyld quarters pight,
And set aloft for vermin to deuour,
Mete graue for rebels that resist the power.

Full litle know we wretches what we do,
When we presume our princes to resist.
We war with God, agaynst his glory to,
That placeth in his office whome he list:
Therfore was neuer traytour yet but mist
The marke he shot, and came to shamefull ende,
Nor neuer shall tyll God be forst to bend.

God hath ordayned the power, all princes be
His lieutenantes or debities in realmes,
Agaynst their foes therfore fighteth he,
And as his ennies driues them to extreames,
Their wise deuises proue but doltish dreames.
No subiect ought for any kynde of cause,
To force the Prince, but yeld him to the lawes.

            Wherfore

Wherfore Baldwin warne men folow reason,
Subdue their willes, and be not Fortunes slaues,
A shamefull ende doth euer followe treason,
There is no trust in rebelles, rascall knaues,
In Fortune lesse, which worketh as the waues:
From whose assautes who listeth to stand fre,
Must followe skyll, and so contented be.

FINIS.

By sainct Mary (said one) if Jacke were as wel learned, as you haue made his oration, what so euer he was by birth, I warrant him a gentilman by his learning. How notably á philosopher lyke hath hee described Fortune and the causes of worldly cumbraunce? howe lyke a deuyne hath he determined the states both of officers and rebelles. For in dede officers be gods deputies, and it is gods office which they beare: and it is he which ordayneth therto such as himselfe listeth, good whan he fauoureth the people, and euill when he wil punish them. And therfore whosoeuer rebelleth againste any ruler eyther good or bad, rebelleth agaynste God and shalbe suer of a shamefull ende: For God cannot but mainteyne his deputy. Yet this I note by the way concerning rebels and rebellions. Although the deuill raise them, yet God alwayes vseth them to his glorye, as a parte of his iustice. For whan kings & chiefe rulers, suffer their vnder officers to misuse their subiects, and wil not heare nor remedy their peoples wrongs whan they
complayne

Eadmund Duke

complayne, than suffereth God the rebell to rage, and to execute that parte of his Justice, whiche the parciall prince would not,

For the Lorde Saye a very corrupt officer, and one whome notwithstanding the king alwayes mainteyned, was destroyed by this Jacke, as was also the Byshop of Salisburye (a prowde and couetous prelate) by other of the rebelles. And therfore what soeuer prince desireth to lyue quietly without rebellion must do his subiects right in all thinges, & punishe suche officers as greue or oppresse theym: thus shall they be suer from all rebellion. And for ye clerer opening hereof it were well done to set foorth this Lord Sayes tragedy. What nede that (sayd another) seing the lyke example is sene in the Duke of Suffolke, whose doinges are declared sufficiently already. Nay let vs go forward for we haue a greate many behinde that may not be omitted, and the tyme as you se passeth away. As for this Lorde Saye whome Cade so cruelly killed and spitefullye vsed after his death (I dare saye) shalbe knowen therby what he was to all that reade or heare this story. For God woulde neuer haue suffered hym to haue ben so vsed, except he had first deserued it. Therfore let hym go and with him the Bishop, and all other slayne in that rebellyon which was raysed as it may be thought through some drift of ye Duke of Yorke, who shortly after began to endeuour him selfe by all meanes to attayne the crowne, and therfore gathered an army in Wales and marched towardes

of Somerset.

wardes Londō: but ẏ kyng with his power taried
& met him at sainte Albons, where whyle the kyng
and he were about a treaty, Richarde Neuile Earle
of Warwicke, cheefe of the faction of the house of
Yorke, set vpon the kinges army, gate the victorye
and slue Eadmund Beauford Duke of Somerset.
Where also the same day were slaine in the quarrell
of king Henry the syxt, Henry Percy the seconde of
of that surname, Earle of Northumberland, Hū=
frey Earle of Stafford son and heyre to Humfrey
Stafford Duke of Buckingham, John Lord Clif=
ford, Babthorp the kinges Attorney and his son
and heyre, besydes many mo of the nobility.
But because the Duke of Somerset
was the chiefe of that parte, pas=
sing ouer the rest, let vs onely
heare hym speake for all.

Eadmund Duke

*The tragedy of Eadmūd Duke of Somerset,
slaine in the firste battaile at Sainte Albanes, the 23. day of May, in the 32.
yeare of Henrye the sixte.
Anno; 1454.*

Some I suppose are borne vnfortunate,
Els good endeuours could not ill succede,
What shall I call it? yll fortune or fate;
That som mens attempts haue neuer good spede,
Their trauaile thankles, all bootles their hede:
Where other vnlike in working or skill,
Outwrestle the world, and wyeld it at will.

Of the first nomber I count my selfe one,
To all mishap I wene predestinate,
Beleue me Baldwin there be few or none,
To whome Fortune was euer more ingrate.
Make thou therfore my life a Caueat,
That who so with force wyll worke agaynst kynde,
Sayleth (as who sayth) agaynst the streame and wynde.

For I of Somerset which Duke Eadmund hight,
Extract by discent from Lancaster lyne,
Were it by folly, or Fortunes despyte,
Or by yll aspect of some croked sygne,
Of mine attempts could neuer se good fine:
What so I began did seldome well end:
God from such Fortune all good men defend.

                                                      Where

Where I thought to saue, most part I did spill,
For good hap with me was alway at warre,
The linage of Yorke whome I bare so yll,
By my spite became bright as the morning starre,
Thus somewhiles men make when fayn they would marre.
The more ye lop tres, the greater they growe,
The more ye stop streames, the higher they flowe.

Maugre my spite, his glory grewe the more,
And myne, as the mone in the wane, waxt lesse:
For hauing the place which he had before,
Gouernour of Fraunce, nedes I must confesse,
That lost was Normandy without redresse,
Yet wrought I alwaies that wit might contriue,
But what doth it boote with the streame to striue.

Borne was I neyther to war ne to peace,
For Mars was maligne to all my whole trade:
My byrth I beleue was in Ioues decrease,
When Cancer in his course being retrograde,
Declined from Sol to Saturnus shade,
Where aspects were good, opposities did marre,
So grew myne vnhap both in peace and warre.

A straunge natiuity in calculation,
As all my lyues course, did after well declare,
Whereof in a briefe to make relation,
That other by me may learne to beware,
Ouerlight credence was cause of my care,
And want of foresight in geuing assent,
To condemne Humfrey that Duke innocent.

Humfrey

Eadmund Duke

Humfrey I meane that was the protectour,
Duke of Glocester of the royall bloud,
So long as he was Englands dyrectour,
King Henries title to the crowne was good.
This Prince as a piller most stedfastly stood:
Or like a prop set vnder a vyne,
In state to vpholde all Lancasters lyne.

O heedles trust, vnware of harme to come.
O malice headlong swyft to serue fond will,
Dyd euer madnes man so much benome,
Of prudent forecast, reason, wit, and skill,
As me blinde Bayard consenting to spill
The bloud of my cosin, my refuge and stay,
To my destruction making open way?

So long as the Duke, bare the stroke and sway,
So long no Rebels quarrels durst begin,
But when the poste, was pulled once away,
Which stoode to vpholde the King and his kin,
Yorke and his banders proudly preased in,
To chalenge the crowne by title of right,
Beginning whit lawe, and ending with might.

Abroade went bruites in countrey and towne,
That Yorke of England was the heyre true,
And how Henry had vsurped the crowne
Agaynst all right, which all the realme myght rue:
The people than embrasing titles newe,
Yrkesome of present and longing for chaunge,
Assented sone because they loue to raunge.

True

of Somerset.

True is the text which we in scripture reade,
Ve terræ illi cuius rex est puer.
Wo to that land whereof a childe is heade,
Whether childe or childish, the case is one sure,
Where Kinges be yong, we dayly see in vre,
The people awlesse, by weakenes of their head,
Leade their liues lawlesse, hauing none to dread.

And no lesse true is this text agayne,
Beata terra cuius rex est nobilis.
Blest is the land where a stout King doth rayne,
Where in good peace ech man possesseth his,
Where yll men feare to fault or do amis,
Where a stout Prince is prest, with sword in hand,
At home and abroade his enemies to withstand.

In case King Henry had bene such a one,
Hardy and stoute as his fathers afore,
Long mought he haue sate in the royall throne,
Without any feare of common vprore.
But dayly his weakenesse shewed more and more,
Which boldnes gaue, to the aduersary band,
To spoyle him at last both of lyfe and land.

His humble hart was nothing vnknowen,
To the gallants of Yorke and their retinue,
A ground lying lowe is soone ouerflowen,
And shored houses cannot long contynue,
Joyntes cannot knit wheras is no synowe.
And so a prince, not dred as well as loued
Is from his place, by practise sone remoued.

Well

Eadmund Duke

Well mought I see had I not wanted brayne,
The worke begon to vndermyne the state,
When the chiefe link was loosed fro the chayne,
And that some durst vppon bloud royal grate,
How tickle a hold had I of myne estate:
When the chiefe post lay flat vppon the flore,
Mought not I thinke my staffe then next the dore?

So mought I also dame Margaret the Quene,
By meane of whome this mischiefe first began,
Dyd she trow ye, her selfe not ouerwene
Death to procure to that most worthy man?
Which she and hers afterward mought well ban,
On whome did hang, as I before haue sayde,
Her husbandes life, his honour and his ayde.

For whilst he liued which was our stable stay,
Yorke and his pympes were kept as vnder yoke,
But when the piller remoued was away,
Then burst out flame, that late before was smoke,
The traytour couert than cast of his cloake,
And from his den came forth in open light,
With tytles blinde which he set forth for right.

But this to bring about him first behoued,
The King and his kin asunder for to set:
Who being perforce or practise remoued,
Then had they auoyded the principall let,
Which kept the sought pray so long from the net:
The next poynt after, was themselues to place
In rule aboue the rest, next vnto his grace.

Therfore

of Somerset.

I was the fyrst whome they put out of place,
No cause pretending but the common weale,
The crowne of England was the very case,
Why to the Commons they burned so in zeale.
My faultes were c'oakes their practise to conceale,
In counsayle hearing consider the entent,
For in pretence of truth, treason oft is ment,

So their pretence was onely to remoue,
Counsayle corrupt from place about the Kyng,
But O ye Princes, you it doth behoue,
This case to construe as no fayned thing,
That neuer traytour did subdue his King,
But for his plat, ere he could furder wade,
Agaynst his frendes the quarrell first he made.

And if by hap he could so bring about,
Them to subdue at his own wish and will,
Then would he waxe so arrogant and stout,
That no reason his outrage might fulfyll.
But to procede vpon his purpose still
Tyll King and Counsayle brought were in one case:
Such is their folly, to rebelles to geue place.

So for the fish casting forth a net,
The next poynt was in driuing out the plat,
Commons to cause iu rage to fume and fret,
And to rebell, I cannot tell for what,
Requiring redresse of this and of that:
Who if they spede, the stander at recept,
Grasp wyll the pray for which he doth awayt.

H.i.   Then

Eadmund Duke

Then by surmise of some thing pretended,
Such to displace as they may well suspect,
Lyke to withstand their mischief entended,
And in their roumes their banders to elect,
The aduerse party proudly to reiect.
And then with reportes the simple to abuse,
And when these helpes fayle, open force to vse.

So this Dukes traynes were couert and not seke,
Which ment no lesse, that he most pretended.
Lyke to a Serpent couert vnder grene,
To the weale publike seemed wholy bended:
Zelous he was and would haue all thing mended,
But by that mendment nothing els he ment,
But to be King, to that marke was his bent.

For had he bene playne, as he ment in dede,
Henry to depose from the royall place,
His hast had bene waste, and much worse his spede,
The King then standing in his peoples grace.
This Duke therfore set forth a goodly face,
As one that ment no quarrell for the crowne,
Such as bare rule, he onely would put downe.

But all for nought, so long as I bare stroke,
Serued these dryftes, and proued all but vayne,
The best helpe then, was people to prouoke,
To make commocion and vprores a mayne:
Which to appease, the Kyng himselfe was fayne,
From blacke heathe in Kent, to send me to the Tower.
Such was the force of rebels in that hower.

The

of Somerset.

The tempest yet therewyth was not ceased,
For Yorke was bent his purpose to pursue,
Who seyng how sone I was released,
And yll successe of sufferaunce to insue:
Then lyke Judas, vnto hys Lord vntrue,
Estemyng tyme lost any lenger to deferre,
By Warwickes ayde proclaymed open warre.

At S. Albanes towne both our hoastes dyd mete,
Which to try a fielde was no equall place,
Forst we were to fight in euery lane and strete,
No feare of foes could make me shun the place:
There I and Warwicke fronted face to face,
At an Inne dore, the Castell was the sygne,
Where with a sword was cut my fatall lyne.

Oft was I warned to come in Castel none,
Hauing no mistrust of any common sygne,
I dyd imagine a Castell buylt with stone,
For of no Inne I could the same deupne:
In Prophets skill my wyt was neuer fyne,
A foole is he that such vayne dreames doth bred,
And more foole of both that will by them be led.

My life I lost in that vnlucky place,
With many Lordes that leaned to my parte:
The Earle Percy had no better grace,
Clyfford for all his courage could not shun the darte,
Buckingham heyr was at this mortall marte,
Babthorp the Attorney for all his skyll in lawe,
In this poynt of pleadyng apppered very rawe.

H ii. So

Eadmund Duke

So poore King Henry disarmed of his bandes,
Hys frendes slayne wanting all assistence,
Was made a pray vnto his enemies handes,
Priued of power and princely reuerence,
And as a pupyll voyde of all experyence,
Innocent playne, and symply witted,
Was as a Lambe vnto the wolfe committed.

A Parlyament than was called with speede,
A Parlyament, nay a playne conspiracy,
When agaynst ryght it was decreede,
That after the death of the syxt Henry
Yorke should succede vnto the regally,
And in his lyfe the charge and protection,
Of King and realme at the Dukes dyrection.

And thus was Yorke declared protectour,
Protectour sayd I, nay Prodytor playne.
A rancke rebell the princes dyrectour,
A vassall to leade his Lord and souerayne,
What honest hart would not conceyue disdayne
To see the foote surmount aboue the head,
A monster is in spite of nature bred.

Some happyly heare will moue a farther doubt,
And as for Yorkes parte allege an elder right,
O braynlesse hedes that so run in and out.
Whan length of tyme a state hath firmely pyght:
And good accord hath put all stryfe to flyght,
Were it not better such tytles still to slepe,
Than all a realme about the tryall wepe?

From

of Somerset.

From the female, came Yorke and all his leede,
And we of Lancaster from the heir male,
Of whome three Kinges in order dyd succede,
By iust discent: this is no fayned tale.
Who would haue thought that any storme or gale
Our shyp could shake, hauing such anker hold:
None I thinke sure, vnlesse that God so would.

After this hurle the King was fayne to flee,
Northward in post for succour and relefe.
O blessed God how straunge it was to see,
A rightfull prince pursued as a thiefe:
To the O England, what can be more repriefe:
Then to pursue thy prince with armed hand,
What greater shame, may be to any land:

Traytours dyd tryumph, true men lay in the dust,
Reuing and robbing roisted euery where,
Will stoode for skill, and law obeyed lust,
Might trode downe right, of King there was no feare.
The tytle was tryed onely by shyeld and speare.
All which vnhaps that they were not forsene,
Suffolke was in fault who ruled King and Quene.

Some here perhaps, do looke I should accuse
My selfe of some sleight, or subtiltie vniust
Wherin I should my princes eares abuse
Agaynst the Duke, to bring him in mistrust
Some parte whereof, though nedes confesse I must,
My fault onely cosisted in consent
Leaning to my foes, whereof I do repent.

                                    P.iii.

Eadmund Duke

Yf I at fyrst whan brandes began to smoke,
The sparkes to quench by any way had sought,
Neuer had England felt this mortall stroke,
Which now to late lamenting helpeth nought.
Two poyntes of wyt to dearely haue I bought,
The fyrst that better is tymely to forsee,
Then after ouer late a counsaplour to be.

The second is, not easely to assent
To aduise geuen agaynst thy faythfull freude,
But of the speaker pouder the intent,
The meanyng full, the poynt, and finall ende.
A Saynt in showe in proofe is found a Feende,
The subtile man the simple to abuse,
Much pleasaunt speach and eloquence doth vse.

And so was I abusde and other mo
By Suffolkes sleyghts, who sought to please the Quene,
Forecasting not the misery and wo
Which thereof came, and soone was after sene:
With glosing tong he made vs fooles to wene
That Humfrey dyd to Englands crowne aspyre,
Which to preuent, his death they dyd conspyre.

What should I more of myne vnhaps declare,
Whereof my death at last hath made an end:
Not I alone was voyde of all this care,
Some besydes me there were that dyd offend.
None I accuse, nor yet my selfe defend,
Faultes I know I had, as none lyues without,
My chiefe fault was folly I put the out of dout.

                                    Folly

of Somerset.

Folly was the chiefe, the noughty tyme was next,
Which made my fortune subiect to the chiefe:
If England then with strife had not bene vext,
Glory might haue growen whereas ensued griefe,
Yet one thing is, my comfort and reliefe,
Constant I was in my Princes quarell,
To dye or lyue and spared for no parell.

What though Fortune enuyous was my foe,
A noble hart ought not the soner yelde,
Nor shrinke abacke for any weale or woe,
But for his prince lye bleeyng in the fyeld:
If pryuy spight at any tyme me helde,
The price is payde: and greuous is my guerdon,
As for the rest God (I trust) will pardon.

FINIS. G. F.

After this tragedye ended, one saide seinge this Duke hath so vehementlye exclamed agaynste the Duke of Yorkes practises, it were well done to heare what hee can saye for hym selfe. For after the fyrst battell at S. Albanes hee was made protectoure, whiche so muche greeued Quene Margaret & her complices, that priuy grutches & open dissēbling neuer ceased tyll the Duke & his allyes were fayn to fly both field and realme, he into Ireland & they to Calaies. Whence they came again with an army, whereof Richard Neuil earle of Salisbury was leder, and marched toward Couentry where the kinge was, and had gathered an

H iiii.   army

Richard Plantagenet

army to subdue them, and encoūtred thē at Northhampton on the 10 day of July in the yeare of grace 1460. fought with them, lost the fielde, & was taken himselfe, & many of his frendes slayne, as Hūfrey Stafford Duke of Buckingham, John Talbot the second of that name earle of Shrewesbury, John Uicount Beaumont, Thomas Lorde Egremont, Syr William Lucy and dyuers other. But ouerpassing all these & many mo because they were honourably slain in ye field, let vs come to hym who was the chief cause therof, that is to saye, Richarde Plantagenet Duke of Yorke slayn in the battell at Wakefield on Christmas euen, and Eadmūd earle of Rutland his yong son, who was there murdered by the Lord Clifforde as he would haue fled into ye towne to haue saued himselfe.

Therfore imagine that you se a tall mans body full
of freshe woundes, but lackynge a heade,
holding by the hand a goodly childe, whose
breaste was so wounded that his harte
might be sene, his louely face and eyes
diffygured with dropping teares,
his heare through horror standing vpright, his mercye
crauing handes all to be māgled, and all
his body embrued with his own blond.
Out of the wesand pipe of whiche
headles bodye came a shriekinge voice sayinge as
followeth.   How

Duke of Yorke.

How Richarde Plantagenet Duke of Yorke was slain through his ouer rash boldnes, and hys son the Earle of Rutland for his lacke of valyaunce.
Anno Do. 1460.

TRust Fortune (quod he) in whome was neuer trust,
O folly of men that haue no better grace,
All rest, renowne, and dedes ly in the dust,
Of all the sort that sue her slipper trace.
What meanest thou Baldwyn for to hyde thy face?
Thou nedest not feare although I mysse my head:
Nor yet to mourne, for this my son is dead.

The cause why thus I leade him in my hand,
His skyn with blood and teares so sore be staynd,
Is that thou mayest the better vnderstand,
How hardly Fortune hath for vs ordaynd:
In whome her loue and hate be hole contaynd.
For I am Richard Prince Plantagenet,
The Duke of Yorke in royall race beget.

For Richard Earle of Cambridge, eldest sonne
Of Edmund Langley, thyrd son of King Edward,
Engendred me whereof the course dyd runne
Of Mortimers to be the issue garde:
For when her brother Edmund dyed awarde,
She was sole heyre by due discent of lyne,
Wherby her rightes and tytles all were myne

But

Richard Plantagenet

But marke me now I pray thee Baldwin marke,
And see how force oft ouerbereth right:
Way how vsurpers tyrannously warke,
To kepe by murder that they get by myght,
And note what troubles daungers do alyght
On such as seke to repossesse their owne,
And how through rygour right is ouerthrowne.

The Duke of Hereford, Henry Bolenbroke,
Of whom Duke Mowbray tould the now of late,
Whan voyde of cause he had Kyng Richard tooke:
He murdered him, vsurped his estate,
Without all right or tytle, sauing hate
Of others rule, or loue to rule alone:
These two excepted tytle had he none.

The realme and Crowne was Edmund Mortimers,
Whose father Roger, was King Richards heyre:
Which caused Henry and the Lancasters
To seeke all shiftes our housholdes to appayre,
For suer he was to sit besyde the chayre
Were we of power to clayme our lawfull right,
Wherfore to crop vs he did all he myght.

Hys cursed son ensued hys cruell path,
And kept my giltlesse cosin strayt in duraunce:
For whome my father hard entreted hath,
But lyuing hopelesse of his lyues assuraunce,
He thought it best by politike procuraunce,
To pryue the Kyng and so restore his frende:
Which brought him selfe to an infamous ende.

Duke of Yorke.

For whan King Henry of that name the fyft,
Had tane my father in this conspiracy,
He from sir Edmund all the blame to shyfte,
Was fayne to say the French Kings ally,
Had hyred him thys trayterous act to try
For which condemned shortly he was slayne,
In helping right this was my fathers gayne.

Thus whan the linage of the Mortimers,
Was made away by his vsurping lyne,
Some hangd, some slayne, some pyned prisoners:
Because the crowne by right of law was myne,
They gan as fast agaynst me to repine:
In feare alwayes least I should stur them to stryfe,
For gylty hartes haue neuer quyet lyfe.

Yet at the last in Henries dayes the sixt,
I was restored to my fathers landes,
Made Duke of Yorke: where through my mynde I fyxt
To get the Crowne and kingdome in my handes,
For ayde wherein I knyt assured bandes
With Neuils stocke, whose daughter was my make
Who for no wo would euer me forsake.

O Lorde what hap had I through mariage,
Fower goodly hopes in youtth my wife she bore.
Right valiaunt men and prudent for their age,
Such bretherne she had and nephues still in store
As none had erst, nor any shall haue more:
The Earle of Salisbury, and his son of Warwicke,
Were matchlesse men from Barbary to Barwicke.

Through

Richard Plantagenet

Through helpe of whome and Fortunes louely looke.
I vndertooke to claime my lawfull right,
And to abash such as agaynst me tooke,
I raysed power at all pointes prest to fight:
Of whome the chiefe that chiefly bare me spight,
Was Somerset the Duke, whome to annoy
I alway sought, through spite, spite to destroy.

And maugre him, so choyse lo was my chaunce,
Yea though the Quene that all rulde tooke his part,
I twise bare rule in Normandy and Fraunce,
And last lyeutenant in Ireland, where my hart
Found remedy for euery kinde of smart.
For through the loue my doynges there dyd brede,
I had their help at all tymes in my nede.

This spitefull Duke, his seely King and Quene,
With armed hoastes I thrise met in the field,
The first vnfought through treaty made betwene,
The second ioynde wherin the Kyng dyd yelde,
The Duke was slayne, the Quene enforst to shyeld
Her selfe by flyght. The third the Quene dyd fyght,
Where I was slayne being ouer matcht by might.

Before this last were other battayles three,
The first the Earle of Salisbury led alone,
And fought on Blorehcath, and got victory:
In the next was I and my kinsfolke euery one,
But seing our souldiers stale vnto our foen,
We warely brake our company on a night,
Disolued our hoaste, and tooke our selues to flight.

Duke of Yorke.

This Boy and I in Ireland dyd vs saue,
Myne eldest son with Warwicke and his father
To Calais got, whence by the reade I gaue
They came agayne to London, and dyd gather
An other hoast whereof I spake no rather:
And met our foes, slew many a Lord and Knight,
And tooke the King and draue the Quene to flight.

Thys done I came to England all in haste,
To make clayme vnto the Realme and Crowne:
And in the house while parliament did last,
I in the Kings seate boldly sate me downe,
And claymed it where at the Lords did frowne,
But what for that, I dyd so well procede,
That all at last confest it myne in dede.

But syth the Kyng had rayned now so long,
They would he should contynue tyll he dyed,
And to the end that than none dyd me wrong,
Protectour and heyre apparant they my cryed.
But sith the Quene and others this denyed,
I sped me towarde the North where than she lay,
In mynde by force to cause her to obay.

Whereof she warnd prepared a mighty power,
And ere that myne were altogether redy,
Came swyft to Sandale and besieged my bower:
Where like a beast I was so rash and heady,
That out I would, there could be no remedy,
With scant fyue thousand souldiers, to assayle
Fower tymes so many, encampt to most auayle.

And

Richard Plantagenet

And so was slayne at fyrst: and while my chylde
Scarse twelue yeare olde, sought secretly to parle,
That cruell Clifford, Lord, nay Lorell wylde,
While the infant wept, and prayed him rue his smart,
Knowing what he was, wyth dagger cloue his hart,
Thys done he came to the campe where I lay dead.
Despoylde my corps and cut away my head.

And whan he had put a paper crowne thereon,
As a gawzing stocke he sent it to the Quene.
And she for spyte commaunded it anon
To be had to Yorke: where that it mought be sene,
They placed it where other traytours bene.
This myschiefe Fortune dyd me after death,
Such was my lyfe, and such my losse of breath.

Wherfore see Baldwyn that thou set it forth,
To the ende the fraude of Fortune may be knowen,
That eke all princes well may way the worth
Of thynges, for which the seedes of war be sowen:
No state so sure but soone is ouerthrowen.
No worldly good can counterpeyze the prise,
Of halfe the paynes that may thereof arise.

Far better it were to lose a piece of right,
Than lymmes and lyfe in sousing for the same,
It is not force of frendshyp nor of myght,
But God that causeth thinges to fro or frame,
Not wit but lucke doth wield the winners game.
Wherfore if we our follyes would refrayn,
Tyme would redresse all wronges we boyd of payn.

Duke of Yorke.

Wherfore warne Princes not to wade in war
For any cause except the realmes defence:
Their troublous tytles are vnworthy far
The blud, the lyfe, the spoyle of innocence.
Of frendes of foes beholde my foule expence,
And neuer the neare: best therfore tary time,
So right shall raygne, and quyet calme ech cryme.

FINIS.

With that mayster Ferrers shooke me by the sleue, saying: why howe now man do you forget youre selfe? belyke you mynde oure matters very much So I do in dede (said I) for I dreame of them. And whan I had rehearsed my dreame, we had long talke concerninge the nature of Dreames, which to stint and to bring vs to oure matter agayne, thus sayd one of them: I am glad it was your chaunce to dreame of Duke Rychard, for it had bene pity to haue ouerpassed hym.
And as concerninge this Lorde Clifford whiche so cruelly killed his son, I purpose to geue you notes: Who (as hee well deserued) came shortely after to a sodayne death, and yet to good for so cruell a tyrant. For on Palmesonday nexte followinge, being the Nine and twenty daye of Marche, in the yeare of Christ a thousand four hundreth threscore & one, thys Lord Clyfford wyth Héry Percy, the 3. Earle of Northuberland, ẏ Erle of Westmerland, the

Lord Clyfford.

the Lorde Dacres, the Lorde Welles & other were slaine at Towton in Yorkeshyre. Wherfore as you thought you saw and heard ye headles Duke speake thorow his necke, so now suppose you se this Lord Clifforde all armed saue his head, w his breast, plate all gore bloud runing frō his throate wherein an headlesse arrowe sticketh, through which woūd he saith thus.

How the Lorde Clifford for his straunge and abho-
mynable crueltye, came to as straunge and so-
dayne a death. Anno. 1461.

Wen confession areth open pennaunce,
And wisdome would a man his shame to hyde:
Yet sith forgeuenes commeth through repentaunce,
I thinke it best that men their crymes ascryed,
For nought so secret but at length is spyed:
For couer fyer and it will neuer lynne
Tyll it breake forth, in lyke case shame and synne.

As for myselfe my faultes be out so playne,
And published so abroade in euery place,
That though I would I cannot hyde a grayne.
All care is booteless in a curelesse case,
To learne by others griefe some haue the grace,
And therfore Baldwin write my wretched fall,
The bryefe whereof I briefly vtter shall,

I am

Lord Clyfford.

I am the same that slue Duke Richards chylde,
The louely babe that begged lyfe with teares:
Wherby my honour fouly I defylde.
Pore sely Lambes the Lyon neuer teares:
The feble mouse may ly among the beares:
But wrath of man his rancour to requite,
Forgets all reason, ruth, and vertue quite.

I meane by rancour the parentall wreke
Surnamd a vertue (as the vicious say).
But litle knowe the wicked what they speake,
In boldening vs our enemies kyn to slay,
To punish sinne is good, it is no nay.
They wreke not sinne, but merit wreke for sinne,
That wreke the fathers faultes vpon his kinne.

Because my father Lord Iohn Clyfford dyed
Slayne at S. Albanes, in his princes ayde,
Agaynst the Duke my hart for malice fryed,
So that I could from wreke no way by stayed.
But to auenge my fathers death, assayd
All meanes I might the Duke of Yorke tannoy:
And all his kin and frendes to kill and stroy.

This made me with my bloody dagger wound
Hys giltlesse sonne that neuer agaynst me stode:
Hys fathers body lying dead on ground
To pearce with speare, eke with my cruell sworde
To parte his necke and with his head to boord,
Inuested with a paper royall crowne,
From place to place to beare it vp and downe.

                                                               I b.   But

Lord Clyfford.

But cruelty can neuer scape the scourge
Of shame, of horror, or of sodayn death.
Repentaunce selfe that other synnes may pourge,
Doth fly from this, so sore the soule it slayeth,
Despayre dissolues the tyrants bitter breth:
For sodayn vengeaunce sodainly alights
On cruell deedes, to quite their cruell spights.

This finde I true, for as I lay in wait
To fight with Duke Richards eldest son,
I was destroyed not far from Dintingdale
For as I would my gorget haue vndone
To euent the heate that had me nigh vndone,
An headles arrow strake me through the throte
Where through my soule forsoke his filthy cote:

Was this a chaunce? no sure Gods iust award,
Wherein due iustice playnely doth appeare:
An headles arrow payed me my rewarde,
For heading Richard lying on his bere,
And as I would his childe in no wise beare,
So sodayne death bereft my tong the power,
To aske for pardon at my dying hower.

Wherfore good Baldwin warne the bloudy sort,
To leaue their wrath, their rigour to refrayne:
Tell cruell iudges horror is the port
To which they saile through shame and sodayn payne:
Hell haleth tyranntes downe to death amayne.
Was neuer yet nor shalbe cruel deede,
Left vnrewarded with as cruell meede.

FINIS.

What

Tiptoft Earle of Worcester. Folio. 60.

When this tragedy was ended, O Lord said an other, how horrible a thinge is deuision in a realme, to howe manye mischefes is it the mother, what vice is not therby kindled, what vertue left vnquenched?

For what was the cause of the Duke of Yorkes death, and of the cruelty of this Clifforde, saue the variaunce betwene kynge Henrye and the house of Yorke: which at length besides millions of the comons, brought to destruction all the noblitye. For Edward the Dukes eldest sonne immediatly after his father was slaine, through help of the Neuilles, gaue the king a battaile, wherat besides this Clyfford and xxxvi. thousand other souldiers were slayn their captaines, therles of Northūberland & Westmerland, with the Lords Dacres and Welles: the winning of whiche fielde brought Edwarde to the Crowne, and the losse draue kinge Henrye and his wife into Scotland. But as few raignes beginne without bloud, so kinge Edwarde to kepe order, caused Thomas Courtney erle of Deuonshyre, and John Veer Earle of Oreforde, and Aubrey Veer eldest son to the said earle, wyth diuers other hys enemies, to bee attainted and putte to death. And shortly after he did execution vpō the Duke of Somerset and the Lords Hungerford and Rosse, whō hee tooke prisonners at Exham fielde. For thither they came with kinge Henrye oute of Scotlande, with an army of Scottes, and fought a battayle, whyche was lost and moste parte of them slaine.

I ii.   And

Tiptoft Earle of Worcester.

And because these are all noble men I wyll leaue them to Baldwins discretion.
But seynge the Earle of Worcester was the chiefe instrument, whom king Edward vsed as well in these mens matters, as in lyke bloudy affayres, because he should not be forgottē, ye shal heare what I haue noted concerning his tragedy.

The infamous end of the Lorde Tiptoft Earle of VVorcester, for cruelly executinge his Princes butcherly cōmaūdementes.
Anno. 1470.

He gloryous man is not so loth to lurke,
As the infamous glad to lye vnknowen:
Which maketh me Baldwin disalow thy wurke,
Where princes faultes so openly be blowen.
I speake not this alonely for myne owne
Which were my princes (yf that they were any)
But for my Piers, in nomber very many.

Or myght report vprightly vse her tong,
It would lesse greue vs to augment the matter.
But suer I am thou shalt be forst among,
To frayne the truth the liuing for to flatter:
And other whiles in poyntes vnknowen to smatter.
For tyme neuer was, nor neuer I thinke shalbe
That truth vnshent should speake in all thinges free.

Thys

This doth appeare (I dare say) by my story,
Which dyuers wryters dyuersly declare
But story wryters ought for neyther glory,
Feare, nor fauour, truth of things to spare.
But still it fares as alway it did fare,
Affections, feare, or doubtes that dayly brue:
Do cause that stories neuer can be true.

Unfruitfulll Fabian followed the face
Of tyme and dedes, but let the causes slip:
Which Hall hath added but with double grace,
For feare I thinke lest trouble might him trip:
For this or that (saith he) he felt the whip.
Thus story wryters leaue the causes out,
Or so rehearse them as they were in dout.

But seing causes are the chiefest thinges
That should be noted of the story wryters,
That men may learne what ends all causes bringes,
They be vnworthy the name of Chroniclers,
That leaue them cleane out of their registers,
Or doubtfully report them: for the fruite
Of reading stories standeth in the suite.

And therfore Baldwyn eyther speake vpright
Of our affayres, or touch them not at all:
As for my selfe I way all thinges so light,
That nought I passe how men report my fall.
The truth wherof yet playnely shewe I shall,
That thou maist wryte and other therby rede,
What thinges I did wherof they should take hede.

A iii.   Thou

Tiptoft Earle of Worcester.

Thou hast heard of Tiptofts Earles of Worcester,
I am that Lord that liued in Edwardes dayes
The fourth, and was his frend and counsailour,
And butcher to as common rumor sayes.
But peoples voice is neither shame nor prayse:
For whom they would aliue deuour to day,
To morow dead they will worship what they may.

But though the peoples verdite go by chaunce,
Yet was their cause to call me as they did
For I enforst by meane of gouernance,
Dyd execute what euer my King did bid,
From blame herein my selfe I cannot ridd :
But fye vpon the wretched state that must
Defame it selfe to serue the princes lust.

The chiefest crime wherewith men do me charge,
Is death of the Earle of Desmunds noble sonnes.
Of which the Kings charge doth me clere discharge,
By strayt commaundement and iniunctions:
Theffect wherof so rigorously runnes,
That eyther I must procure to se them dead,
Or for contempt as a traytour lose my head.

What would mine enemies do in such a case
Obay the King or proper death procure?
They may well say their fancy for a face,
But lyfe is swete and loue hard to recure.
They woulde haue done as I dyd I am sure:
For seldom will a welthy man at ease,
For others cause his prince in ought displease.

How

How much lesse I which was lieutenant than
In the Irish Isle, preferred by the King:
But who for loue or dread of any man
Consents to accomplishe any wicked thing,
Although chiefe fault therof from other spring,
Shall not escape Gods vengeance for his dede,
Who scuseth none that dare do ill for drede.

This in my King and me may well appeare,
Which for our faultes did not escape the scourge:
For whan we thought our state most sure and clere,
The wynd of Warwicke blew vp such a sourge
As from the realme and crowne the King did poure,
And me both from mine office, frendes and wyfe,
From good report, from honest death and lyfe.

For the Earle of warwicke through a cancarde grudge
Which to King Edward causelesse he did beare,
Out of his realme by force did make him trudge.
And set King Henry again vpon his chaire.
And then all such as Edwardes louers were
As traitours tane, were greuously opprest,
But chiefly I because I loued him best.

And for my goods and liuinges were not small,
The gapers for them bare the world in hand
For ten yeares space, that I was cause of all
The executions done within the land.
For this did suche as did not vnderstand
Myne enimies drift, thinke all reports were true:
And so to hate me worse than any Iewe.

Tiptoft Earle of Worcester.

For seldom shall a ruler lose his life,
Before false rumors openly be spred:
Wherby this prouerbe is as true as rife,
That rulers rumors hunt about a head,
Frowne Fortune once all good report is fled:
For present shew doth make the mayny blinde,
And such as see dare not disclose their minde.

Through this was I King Edwards butcher named,
And bare the shame of all his cruell dedes:
I cleare me not, I worthely was blamed,
Though force was such I must obay him nedes.
With hiest rulers seldom well it spedes,
For they be euer nerest to the nyp,
And fault who shall, for all fele they the whip.

For whan I was by parliament attainted,
Kinge Edwards euils all were counted mine.
No truth auayled so lies were fast and painted,
Which made the people at my life repine,
Crying Crucifige kill that butchers lyne:
That whan I should haue gone to Blockham feast,
I could not passe so sore they on me preast.

And had not bene the officers so strong
I thinke they woulde haue eaten me aliue,
Howbeit hardly haled from the throng,
I was in the flete fast throwded by the shriue.
Thus one dayes life their malice did me giue:
Which whan they knewe, for spite the next day after,
They kept them calme so suffered I the slaughter.

Tiptoft Earle of VVorcester.

Now tel me Baldwin what fault doest thou fynde
In me, that iustly should such death deserue?
None sure except despye of honour blynde,
Which made me seke in offices to serue:
What mynde so good that honours make not swerue?
So mayst thou see it onely was my state
That caused my death and brought me so in hate.

Warne therfore all men wisely to beware,
What offices they enterpryse to beare:
The hiest alway most maligned are,
Of peoples grudge, and princes hate in feare.
For princes faultes his faultors all men teare,
Which to auoyde, let none such office take,
Saue he that can for right his prince forsake.

FINIS.

His Earles tragedy was not so soone fynished, but one of the company had prouided for another, of a notable person Lord Tiptofts chief enemy: concerning whom he said: Lord God what trust is there in worldly chaunces? what stay in any prosperity? for se the Earle of Warwick which caused the Earle of Worcester to be apprehended, attainted and put to death, triumphing with his olde imprisonned and new vnprisonned Prince kinge Henry, was by and by after and his brother with him, slaine at Barnet field by king Edwarde, whom he had before time damaged diuers waies.

As

Richard Neuill.

As first by his frendes at Banbury fielde, where to reuēge the death of hys cosin Henry Neuill sir John Coniers and Jhon Clappam his seruaunts slew v. thousand Welshmen, and beheaded their captains; the earle of Pembroke, and sir Richard Harbert his brother after they were yelded prisoners, of whome sir Richarde Harbert was y͑ fallest gentlemā both of his person & hands that euer I read or heard of. At which tyme also, Robin of Riddsdale, a rebell of therle of Warwicks raising, tooke the earle Riuers king Edwards wifes father, and his son John, at his manour of Graftō, & caried thē to Northhampton, & there with out cause or proces beheaded thē. Which spites to requite, kinge Edward caused the Lorde Stafford of Southwike, one of Warwicks chiefe frends, to be taken at Brent march, and headed at Bridgewater.

This caused the earle shortly to rayse his power, to encounter the king which came againste him with an army, beside Warwicke at Wolney, where hee wan the field, tooke the king prisoner, and kept him a while in Yorkshire in Middleham castell: whence (as some say) he released him again, but other think he corrupted his kepers & so escaped. Then through the Lords the matter was taken vp betwene them & they brought to talke together, but because they could not agre, y͑ earle arayped a new army, wherof he made Captaine the Lorde Welles sonne, which broyle king Edward minding to appease by pollicy foaly distained his honour committing periury: for

hee

Earle of Warwicke.

he sent for the Lorde Welles and his brother Syr Thomas Dymocke, vnder safe conduite promising them vpon his faithe to kepe them harmelesse: But after, becaufe the Lord Welles sonne wold not dissolue his army, beheaded them both & wẽt with his power into Lincolnshire and there fought with sir Robert Welles, and flew ten thousande of his souldiers (yet ran they away so fast, that casting of their clothes for the more spede, caused it to be called Lose coate field) and tooke sir Robert and other, & put them to death in the same place.

This misfortune forced the Earle of Warwicke to faile into Fraunce where he was entertained of the king a while and at last with suche poore helpe as he procured there of Duke Rainer and other, he came into England againe, and encreased suche a power in king Henries name, that as the Lorde Typtofte saide in his tragedy, king Edward vnable to abide him, was fayn to fly ouer the washes in Lincolneshire to get a ship to faile out of his kingdom to his brother in lawe the Duke of Burgoine: So was king Henry restored again to the kingdom. Al these despites and troubles the Earle wrought againste king Edward. But Hẽry was so infortunate that ere halfe a yeare was expyred, king Edward came backe again, & enprisoned him and gaue the Earle a fielde, wherein he slew both him and his brother.

I haue recounted thus much before hãd for the better opening of the story, which if it should haue ben spoken in his tragedie woulde rather haue made a

volume

Richard Neuill.

volume than a Pamphlete. For I entende onely to saye in the tragedye, what I haue noted in the Earle of Warwickes person wishinge that these other noble men, whom I haue by the way touched, should not be forgotten.

And therfore ymagin that you see this Earle lyinge
with his brother in Poules church in his coate
armure, with such a face and costinance
as he bereth in portraiture ouer the
dore in Poules at the goynge
down to Jhesus Chap-
pell from the south end of the quier
stayres, and say-
inge as fol-
loweth.

How

Earle of Warwicke. Folio. 65

How sir Richard Neuill Earle of VVarwicke, and his brother Iohn Lord Marquise Montacute, through theyr to muche boldnesse were slaine at Barnet. the 14. of Aprill. Anno. 1471.

Among the beauy heape of happy Knightes
Whome Fortune stald vpon her staylesse stage,
Oft hoyst on hye, oft pight in wretches plights,
Beholde me Baldwin, A per se of my age,
Lord Richard Neuill, Earle by mariage
Of Warwicke Duchy, of Sarum by discent,
Which erst my father through his maryage hent.

Wouldst thou beholde false Fortune in her kynde
Note well my selfe so shalt thou se her naked:
Full fayre before, but to to foule behynde,
Most drowsie styll whan most she semes awaked:
My fame and shame her shift full oft hath shaked,
By enterchaunge alow and vp aloft,
The Lysard lyke that chaungeth hew full oft.

For while the Duke of Yorke in life remaynde
Myne vncle deare, I was his happy hand:
In all attempts my purpose I attaynde,
Though King and Quene and most Lords of the land
With all their power dyd often me withstand:
For God gaue Fortune, and my good behauiour
Dyd fromt heir prince steale me the peoples fauour.

Richard Neuill.

So that through me in fieldes right manly fought:
By force myne vncle tooke Kyng Henry twise:
As for my cosin Edward I so wrought,
When both our sters were slayn through rash aduice.
That he atchiefde his fathers enterpryse:
For into Scotland King and Quene we chased,
By meane whereof the Kingdome he enbraced.

Which after he had enioyed in quiet peace,
(For shortly after was King Henry take,
And put in prison) his power to encrease,
I went to Fraunce and match hym with a make
The French Kinges doughter, whome he dyd forsake:
For while with payne I brought this sute to passe,
He to a widowe rashely wedded was.

This made the French King shrewdly to mistrust,
That all my treaties had but yll pretence,
And whan I sawe my King so bent to lust,
That with his faith he past not to dispence,
Which is a prin̄ es honours chief defence:
I could not rest till I had found a meane,
To mend his misse, or els to marre him cleane,

Wherefore I me allyed with his brother George,
Encensing him his brother to maligne
Through many a tale I did against him forge:
So that through power that we from Calais bring
And found at home, we frayed so the King,
That he did fly to Freseland ward amayne,
Wherby King Henry had the crown agayne.

Than

Earle of Warwicke.

Than put we the cherle of Worcester to death,
King Edwards frende a man so foule defamed:
And in the while came Edward into breth.
For with the Duke of Burgoine so he framed,
That with the power that he to him had named,
Unloked for he came to England streight,
And got to Yorke and tooke the town by sleight.

And after through the sufferaunce of my brother,
Which lyke a beast occasion foully lost,
He came to London safe with many other,
And tooke the towne to good King Henries cost:
Who was through him from post to piller tost,
Till therle of Oxeford, I and other more,
Assembled power his fredome to restore.

Wherof King Edward warned came with spede,
And camped with his hoast in Barnet towne,
Where we right fearce encountred him in dede
On Easter day right early on the downe:
There many a man was slaine and striken downe
On eyther side and neyther part did gayne
Till that I and my brother both were slayne.

For we to hart our ouermatched men,
Forsooke our stedes, and in the thickest throng
Ran preacing forth on foote, and fought so then
That downe we draue them were they neuer so strong.
But ere this lucke had lasted very long
With nomber and force we were so fouly cloyed,
And rescue fayled, that quite we were destroyed,

Now

Richard Neuill.

Now tell me Baldwyn hast thou hard or read
Of any man that dyd as I haue done?
That in his tyme so many armies led,
And victory at euery voyage won?
Hast thou euer hard of subiect vnder sonne,
That plaast and baast his soueraynes so oft,
By enterchaunge, now low, and than alaft?

Perchaunce thou thinkst my doynges were not such
As I and other do affyrme they were.
And in thy mynde I see thou musest much
What meanes Ihsde, that should we so prefer:
Wherin because I will thou shalt not erre,
The truth of all I will at large recyte,
The short is this: I was no hypocrite.

I neuer dyd nor sayd saue what I ment,
The common weale was still my chiefest care,
To priuate gayne or glory was I neuer bent,
I neuer past vpon delicious fare.
Of nedefull foode my bourd was neuer bare,
No creditour did curse me day by day,
I vsed playnnesse, euer pitch and pay.

I heard pore souldiers and pore workemen whine
Because their dutyes were not truely payde.
Agayne I saw how people did repine
At those through whome their payments were delayde:
And proofe dyd oft assure (as scripture sayde)
That God doth wreke the wretched peoples greues,
I saw the polles cut of fro polling theues.

Thys

Earle of Warwicke.

This made me alway iustly for to deale.
Which whan the people plainely vnderstoode,
Because they saw me minde the common weale
They still endeuoured how to do me good,
Ready to spend their substaunce, life and bloud,
In any cause wherto I did them moue:
For suer they were it was for their behoue.

And so it was. For whan the realme decayed
By such as good King Henry sore abused,
To mend the state I gaue his enemies ayd:
But whan King Edward sinfull pranks still vsed,
And would not mend, I likewise him refused:
And holpe vp Henry, better of the twayne,
And in his quarrell (iust I thinke) was slaine.

And therfore Baldwin teach by proofe of me,
That such as couet peoples loue to get,
Must se their works and words in all agree:
Lyue liberally and kepe them out of det,
On common weale let all their care be set:
For vpright dealing, dets paid, pore sustayned,
Is meane wherby all harts are throwly gayned.

FINIS.

As sone as the Earle had ended this admonition, sure (said one) I thinke the Earle of Warwick although he were a glorious mā hath said no more of him selfe than what is true. For if he had not had notable good vertues, or vertuous qualities, & vsed laudable means in his trade

of lyfe

K. Henry the sixte.

of lyfe, the people woulde neuer haue loued him as they did: But God be with him, and send his soule rest for sure his body neuer had any. And although he died yet ciuill warres ceased not. For immediatlye after his death came Quene Margaret with a power out of Fraunce, bringing with her her yong sonne Prince Edward: & with suche frendes as she fond here, gaue king Edward a battel at Thewkesbury wher both she and her sonne were taken prisoners, with Eadmund Duke of Somerset her chief captaine: whose sonne Lord John, and the Earle of Deuonshyre were slaine in fight, and the Duke himselfe with diuers other immediately beheaded. Whose infortunes are worthye to bee remembred, chiefly prince Edwards whom ye king, for speaking truth, cruelly stroke with his gauntlet, and his brethren cruelly murdered. But seinge the tyme so far spent, I will passe them ouer, and with them Fawconbridge that iolye rouer, beheaded at Southapton: whose commocion made in Kent, was cause of sely Henries destruction. And seyng king Henrye himselfe was cause of the destruction of many noble princes, being of al other most vnfortunate himself, I will declare what I haue noted in his vnluckye lyfe: who wounded in prison with a dagger, maye lament his wretchednesse in maner folowing.

How

K. Henry the sixt. Folio. 68

How King Henry the sixte a vertuous prince, was after many other miseries, cruelly murdered in the Tower of London the 22. of May. Anno. 1 4 7 1.

If euer wofull wight had cause to rue his state,
Or by his rufull plight to moue men moane his fate.
My piteous plaint may please my mishap to reherse,
Wherof ý leaſt moſt lightly hard, ý hardeſt hart may pearce.

What hart so hard can heare of innocent opreſt,
By fraud in worldly goods, but melteth in the breſt?
When giltleſſe men be ſpoild, impriſonned for their owne,
Who waileth not their wretched caſe to who ý caſe is knowe.

The Lyon licks the sores of sely wounded shepe,
The dead mans corſe may cauſe the Crocodile to wepe,
The waues that waſte the rocks refreſh the rotten redes,
Such ruth the wrak of innocence in cruell creatures bredes.

What hart is then so hard but will for pity bleed,
To heare, so cruell lucke so cleare a lyfe ſuccede:
To see a sely soule with wo and sorrow souſſe,
A King depriude, in priſon pent, to death with daggers douſt.

Would God the day of birth had brought me to my bere,
Then had I n'uer felt the chaunge of Fortunes chere,
Would God the graue had gript me in her greedy woumbe,
What crown in cradel made me King to ople of holy thoumbe.

K. ii. Would

K. Henry the sixt.

Would God the rufull tombe had bene my royall trone,
So should no Kingly charge haue made me make my mone:
O that my soule had flowen to heauen with the ioy,
Whan one sort cryed, God saue the King another, *Vive le Roi.*

So had I not bene washt in waues of worldly wo,
My minde to quiet bent, had not bene tossed so:
My frendes had ben aliue my subiects not opprest,
But death or cruell desteny, denyed me this rest.

Alas what should recount the cause of wretches cares,
The starres do rule them vp, Astroitomy declares:
Our humours saith the leach, the double true do vies
Both will of God, or ill of man, the doubtfull cause assignes.

Such doltish heades as dreame that all things driue by haps,
Count lacke of former care for cause of after claps,
Attributing to man a power fro God bereft,
Abusing vs and robbing him through their most wicked theft.

But God doth guyde the world, and euery hap by skill,
Our wit and willing power are payzed by his will:
What wit most wisely wardes, and will most deadly syhes,
Though al our powr wold presse it doun, vndoth dash our warest
                                                     (wurkes.

Than destenie, our sinne, Gods will or els his wreake,
Do worke our wretched woes, for humours be to weake:
Except we vse them so, as they prouoke to sinne,
For though our lust by humours fed all vicious dedes begin,

K. Henry the sixte.

So sinne and they be one, both working like effect,
And cause the wrath of God to wreake the soule infect.
Thus wrath and wreake deuine, mans sinnes & humours ill
Concurre in one, though in a sort, ech doth a course fulfill.

If likewise such as say the welkin Fortune warks,
Take Fortune for our fate and sterres therof the marks,
Then desteny with fate and Gods will all be one:
But if they meane it otherwise, skath causers skies be none.

Thus of our heauy haps chiefe causes be but twaine,
Wheron the rest depend, and vnder put remaine.
The chiefe the will deuine, calde desteny and fate,   (hate.
The other sinne through humors holp, which God doth highly

The fyrst appointeth paine for good mens exercise,
The second doth deserue due punishement for vice:
This witnesseth the wrath, and that the loue of God,
The good for loue, the bad for sinne, God beateth with his rod.

Although my sundry sinns do place me with the worst,
My haps yet cause me hope to be among the fyrst:
The eye that searcheth all and seeth euery thought,
Is iudge how sore I hated sinne, and after vertue sought.

The solace of my soule my chiefest pleasure was,
Of worldly pompe, of fame, or game, I did not passe:
My kingdomes nor my crown I prised not a crume
In heauen were my riches heapt, to which I sought to com.

K.iii.   Yet

K. Henry the sixte.

Yet were my sorrows such as neuer man had like,
So diuers stormes at once, so often did me strike:
But why, God knows, not I, except it were for this
To shew by paterne of a prince, how brittle honour is.

Our kingdomes are but cares, our state deuoide of stay,
Our riches redy snares, to hasten our decay:
Our pleasures priuy pricks our vices to prouoke, (smoke.
Our pope a pumpe, our fame a flame, our powr a smouldring

I speake not but by proofe, and that may many rue.
My life doth cry it out, my death doth try it true:
Wherof I will in briefe, rehearce the heauy hap,
That Baldwin in his woful warp, my wretchednes may wrap

In Windsore borne I was: and bare my fathers name,
Who won by war all Fraunce to his eternall fame:
And left to me the crown, to be receiude in peace   (decease.
Through mariage made with Charls his heyre vpon his lyfes

Which shortly did ensue, yet died my father furst,
And both the realmes were myne ere I a yeare were nurst:
Which as they fell to fone, so faded they as fast,   (past:
For Charles and Edward got them both or forty yeares were

This Charles was eldest sonne of Charles my father in lawe.
To whome as heire of Fraunce, the Frenchmen did them draw
But Edward was the heyre of Richard Duke of Yorke,
The heyre of Roger Mortymer: slaine by the kerne of Korke.
                                        Before

K. Henry the sixt.

Before I came to age Charles had recoured Fraunce,
And kild my men of war so lucky was his chaunce:
And through a mad contract I made with Rayners doughter
I gaue and lost all Normandy, the cause of many a slaughter.

First of mine vncle Humfrey, abhorring sore this act,
Because I therby brake a better precontract:
Than of the flattering Duke that first the mariage made,
The iust reward of such as dare their princes ill perswade.

And I pore sely wretch abode the brunt of all,
My mariage lust so swete was mixt with bitter gall.
My wife was wise, and good, had she ben rightly sought,
But our vnlawful getting it, may make a good thing nought.

Wherfore warne men beware, how they iust promise breake,
Least proofe of painfull plagues do cause thē wail the wreake,
Aduise well ere they graunt, but what they graūt perfourme.
For God wil plague al doublenes although we fele no worme.

I falsly borne in hand, belcued I did well,
But all thinges be not true that learned men do tell:
My cleargy said a prince was to no promise bound,
Whose words to be no gospell tho I to my grief haue found.

For after mariage ioynde Queue Margaret and me,
For one mishap afore, I dayly met with three,
Of Normady and Fraunce Charles got away my crowne,
The Duke of Yorke & other sought at home to put me downe.
            K.iiii.   Bellona

K. Henry the sixte.

Bellona rang the bell at home and all abrode,
With whose mishaps amaine fell Fortune did me lode:
In Fraunce I lost my forts, at home the foughten field,
My kinred slaine, my frendes opprest, my selfe enforst to yeeld.

Duke Richard tooke me twise, and forst me to resyne
My crowne and titles due vnto my fathers lyne:
And kept me as a warde, did all things as him list,
Till that my wife through bloudy sword had tane me fro his fist

But though we slew the Duke my sorrowes did not slake,
But like to Hyders head still more and more awake:
For Edward through the ayd of Warwicke and his brother,
From one field draue me to the Scots, & toke me in another.

Then went my frends to wracke, for Edward ware the crown
For which for nine yeares space his prison held me down:
Yet thence through Warwicks worke I was againe releast,
And Edward driuen fro þ realme to seke his frendes by East.

But what preuaileth pain or prouidence of man
To helpe him to good hap, whom desteny doth ban:
Who moyleth to remoue the rocke out of the mud,
Shall myer himselfe, & hardly scape the swelling of the flud.

This all my frendes haue founde, and I haue felt it so.
Ordaynd to be the touth of wretchednesse and woe,
For ere I had a yeare possest my seate againe,
I lost both it and liberty, my helpers all were slaine.

For

For Edward first by stelth, and sith by gathred strength,
Arryude and got to Yorke and London at the length:
Tooke me and tyed me vp, yet Warwicke was so stout,
He came with power to barnet field, in hope to help me out,

And there alas was slaine, with many a worthy knight.
O Lord that euer such lucke should hap in helping right:
Last came my wife and sonne, that long lay in exile,
Defyed the King, & fought a field, I may bewayle the while.

For there myne onely son, not thirtene yeare of age,
Was tane, and murdered streight by Edward in his rage:
And shortly I my selfe to stint all furder strife,
Stabde with his brothers bloudy blade in prison lost my lyfe.

Lo here the heauy haps which hapned me by heape,
Se here the pleasaunt fruites that many princes reape,
The painful plagues of those that breake their lawful bands.
Their mede which may & wil not saue their freds fro bloudy
(handes.

God graunt my wofull haps, to greuous to rehearce,
May teach all states to know how depely daungers pearce:
How fraple all honours are, how brittle worldly blisse,
That warned through my fearful fate they feare to do misse.
This

FINIS.

George Plantagenet

His tragedy ended, an other sayd: either you or king Hery are a good philosopher so narrowly to argue the causes of mysfortunes: but ther is nothing to experiēce which taught, or might teach the king this lesson. But to procede in our matter, I finde mencion here shortlye after the death of this kinge, of a Duke of Excester found dead in the sea betwene Douer and Calays, but what hee was, or by what aduenture he dyed, maister Fabian hath not shewed, and master Hall hath ouerskipped him: so that except wee be frendlyer vnto him, he is lyke to be double drowned, both in sea, and in the gulfe of forgetfulnes About this matter was much talke, but because on tooke vpon him to seeke out that story, that charge was committed to him.

And to be ocupied in the meane while I haue foūd the storye of one drowned lykwise and that so notably, though priuely, that all the worl d knew of it: wherfore I sayd: because night approcheth, and that wee wyll loose no tyme, ye shall heare what I haue noted concerning the Duke of Clarence, kyng Edwardes brother, who all to be washed in wyne, maye bewayl his infortune after this maner.

Duke of Clarence.

How George Plātagenet third sonne of the Duke of Yorke, was by his brother King Edward wrongfullye imprisonned, and by his brother Richard myserablye murdered, the 11. of Ianuary. Anno. 1478.

The foule is fowle men say, that fyles the nest,
Which makes me loth to speke now, might I chuse,
But seing tyme vnburdend hath her brest,
And fame blowne vp the blast of all abuse,
My silence rather might my lyfe accuse
Than shroude our shame, though faine I would it so:
For truth will out, although the world say no.

And therfore Baldwyn hartely I the beseech
To pause a while vpon my heauy plaint,
And vnneth though I vtter spedy spech,
No fault of wit nor folly makes me faint:
No heady drinks haue geuen my toung attaint
Through quaffing craft, yet wine my vitals confound
Not of which I dranke, but wherin I drownd.

What prince I am although I nede not shew,
Because my wine bewrayes me by the smell,
For neuer creature was soust in Bacchus dew
To death but I through Fortunes rigour fell:
Yet that thou maist my story better tell,
I will declare as briefly as I may,
My welth, my wo, and causers of decay.

The

George Plantagenet

The famous house surnamde Plantagenet,
Wherat dame Fortune frowardly did frowne,
While Bolenbroke vniustly sought to set:
His Lord King Richard quite besyde the crowne,
Though many a day it wanted due renowne,
God so preserd by prouidence and grace,
That lawfull heires did neuer fayle the race.

For Lionell King Edwards eldst child,
Both came and heir to Richard pʃulesse,
Begot a daughter Philip, whom vndefylde
The Earle of March espousd, and God did blesse
With fruit assinde the kingdome to possesse:
I meane syr Roger Mortimer, whose heyre
The Earle of Cambridge maried Anne the fayre.

This Earle of Cambridge Richard clept by name,
Was son to Edmund Langley Duke of Yorke:
Which Edmund was sift brother to the same
Duke Lionell that all this lyne doth korke:
Of which two houses ioyned in a forke,
My father Richard prince Plantagenet
True Duke of Yorke, was lawfull heire begot.

Who tooke to wife as ye shall vnderstand
A mayden of a noble house and olde,
Raulfe Neuils daughter Earle of Westmerland:
Whose sonne Earle Richard was a baron bolde,
And had the right of Salisbury in holde,
Through mariage made with good Earle Thomas hayre,
Whose earned prayses neuer shall appayre.

The

Duke of Clarence.

The Duke my father had by this his wyfe
Fower sonnes, of whome the eldest Edward hight,
The second Eadmund who in youth did lose his lyfe,
At wakefield slaine by Clifford cruell knight,
I George am third of Clarence Duke by right.
The fowerth borne to the mischief of vs all,
Was Duke of Glocester whom men did Richard call.

Whan as our sier in sute of right was slaine,
(Whose lyfe and death himselfe declared earst)
My brother Edward plied his cause amaine,
And got the crowne as Warwicke hath rehearst:
The pride wherof so depe his stomacke perst
That he forgot his frendes, dispysed his kin,
Of oth or office passing not a pyn.

Which made the Earle of Warwicke to maligne
My brothers state, and to attempt a way,
To bring from prison Henry selp King,
To help him to the kingdome if he may,
And knowing me to be the chiefest stay,
My brother had, he did me vndermine
To cause me to his treasons to encline.

Wherto I was prepared long before,
My brother had ben to me so vnkinde:
For sure no cankar fretteth flesh so sore,
As vnkynde dealing doth a louing mynde.
Loues strongest bandes vnkindenes doth vnbynde,
It moueth loue to malice, zeale to hate,
Chiefe frendes to foes, and bretherne to debate,

And

George Plantagenet.

And though the Earle of Warwicke subtile sire,
Perceiude I bare a grudge against my brother,
Yet towarde his feate to set me more on fire,
He kindled vp one firebrand with another:
For knowing fancy was the forcing rother
Which stirreth youth to any kynde of strife,
He offred me his daughter to my wyfe.

Where through and with his crafty filed tonge,
He stale my hart that earst vnsteady was:
For I was witlesse, wanton, fond, and yonge,
Whole bent to pleasure, brittle as the glasse:
I cannot lye, In vino veritas.
I did esteme the bewty of my bryde
Aboue my selfe and all the world besyde.

These fond affections ioynt with lacke of skill,
(Which trap the hart and blinde the eyes of youth,
And prickt the mynde to practise any yll)
So tickled me that voyde of kindely truth:
(Which if it want all wretchednesse ensueth).
I stinted not to persecute my brother,
Tyll time he left his kingdome to another.

Thus carnall loue did quench the loue of kynde,
Tyll lust were lost through fancy fully fed:
But whan at length I came vnto my mynde,
I saw how lewdly lightnesse had me led,
To seke with payne the peril of my hed:
For had King Henry once ben setled sure,
I was assurde my dayes could not endure.

And

Duke of Clarence.

And therfore though I bound my selfe with oth
To help King Henry all that euer I might,
Yet at the trety of my brethern both,
Which reason graunted to requyre but right,
I left his part wherby he perisht quite:
And reconcilde me to my bretherne twayne,
And so came Edward to the crowne agayne.

This made my father in law to fret and fume,
To stamp and stare, and call me false forsworne,
And at the length with all his power presume,
To help King Henry vtterly for lorne.
Our frendely profers still he tooke in scorne,
Refused peace and came to Barnet field,
And there was kild because he would not yeelde:

His brother also there with him was slaine,
Wherby decayd the keyes of chiualrye.
For neuer liued the matches of them twayne,
In manhood power, and martiall pollicy,
In vertuous thewes, and frendly constancy,
That would to God if it had bene his wyll
They might haue tournde to vs and liued still.

But what shalbe shal be: there is no choise,
Things nedes must driue as desteny decreeth,
For which ought in all our haps reioyse,
Because the eye eterne all thing for seeth
Which to no yll at any tyme agreeth,
For yls to yll to vs, be good to it,
So far his skils excede our reach of wit.

George Plantagenet

The wounded man which must abyde the smart,
Of stitching vp, or searing of his sore,
As thing to bad, reproues the Surgeons art
Which notwithstanding doth his health restore,
The childe likewise to science plied sore,
Countes knowledge ill, his teacher to be wood,
Yet Surgery and sciences be good.

But as the pacyents griefe and scholers paine,
Cause them deme bad such things as sure be best,
So want of wisdome causeth vs complayne
Of euery hap, wherby we seme opprest:
The pore do pine for pelfe, the rich for rest,
And whan as losse or sicknesse vs assaile
We curse our fate, our Fortune we bewayle.

Yet for our good, God worketh euerything:
For through the death of these two noble peres
My brother liued and raygned a quiet King,
Who had they lyued perchaunce in course of yeares
Would haue deliuered Henry fro the breres,
Or holp his son t'enioy the carefull crowne,
Wherby our line should haue ben quite put downe.

A carefull crowne it may be iustly named,
Not onely for the cares therto annext,
To se the subiect well and duly framed,
With which good care few Kings are greatly vext,
But for the dred wherwith they are perplext,
Of losing Lordship, liberty, or lyfe:
Which wofull wracks in kingdoms happen ryfe.

The

Duke of Clarence.   Folio.75

That which to shun while som to sore haue sought
They haue not sparde all persons to suspect:
And to destroy such as they gilty thought,
Though no apparaunce proued them infect.
Take me for one of this wrong punisht sect,
Imprisonde first, accused without cause,
And done to death no processe had by lawes.

Wherin I note how vengeaunce doth acquite
Lyke yll for yll, how vices vertue quell:
For as my mariage loue did me excite
Against the King my brother to rebell,
So loue to haue his children prosper well,
Prouoked him against both law and right,
To murder me, his brother and his knight.

For by his quene two princelyke sonnes he had,
Borne to be punisht for their parents synne:
Whose Fortunes kalked made the father sad,
Such wofull haps were found to be therin:
Which to auouch, writ in a rotten skin
A prophesy was found, which said a G,
Of Edwards children should destruction be.

Me to be G, because my name was George
My brother thought, and therfore did me hate.
But wo be to that wicked heads that forge
Such doubtfull dreams to brede vnkynde debate:
For God, a Gleue, a Gibbet, Grate, or Gate,
A Gray, a Griffeth, or a Gregory,
As well as George are written with a G.
                                    L.i.   Such

George Plantagenet.

Such doutfull ridles are no prophecies.
For prophecies, in writyng though obscure,
Are plaine in sence, the darke be very lies:
What God foreshewerh is euident and pure,
Truth is no harold nor no Sophist sure:
She noteth not mens names, their shieldes nor creasts,
Though she compare them vnto byrds and beasts.

But whome she doth forshewe shall rayne by force,
She tearms a Wolfe, a Dragon or a Beare:
A wilfull prince a raynlesse raging horse.
A bolde a Lyon: a Coward much in feare
A Hare or Hart: a crafty, pricked eare:
A Lecherous, a Bull, a Goate, a Foale:
An vndermyner a Moldwarpe, or a Mole.

By knowen beasts thus truth doth plaine declare
What men they be of whom she speakes before,
And who so can mens properties compare
And marke what beast they do resemble more,
Shall soone discerne who is the griesly bore.
For God by beasts expresseth mens condicions,
And not their badges, harroldes supersticions.

And learned Merlyne whom God haue the spryte,
To know and vtter princes acts to come,
Lyke to the Iewish prophets, did recite
In shade of beasts their doings all and some,
Expressyng playne by maners of the dome,
That kings and lords such properties should haue
As haue the beasts whose name he to them gaue.

Which

Duke of Clarence.

Which while the folyſh did not well conſider,
And ſeing princes gaue for difference
And knowledge of their iſſues mixt together,
All maner beaſts, for badges of pretence,
Ther tooke thoſe badges to expreſſe the ſence
Of Merlynes mynde, and thoſe that gaue the ſame,
To be the princes noted by their name.

And hereof ſprang the falſe named propheceies,
That go by letters, ſiphers, armes or ſynes:
Which all be foliſh falſe and crafty lies
Deuyſde by geſſe, or guiles vntrue deuines:
For whan they ſaw that many of many lynes
Gaue armes alyke, they wiſt not which was he,
Whome Merlyne meant the noted beaſt to be.

For all the broode of warwickes gaue the Beare,
The Buckinghams do lykewyſe geue the Swan.
But which Beare bearer ſhould the Lyon teare.
They were as wiſe as Gooſe the fery man:
Yet in their ſkill they ceaſed not to ſcan:
And to be demed of the people wyſe,
Set forth their gloſes on propheceies.

And whome they douted openly to name
They darkely tearmed or by ſome letter ment,
For ſo they thought how euer the world did frame,
Preſerue them ſelues from ſhame or being ſhent.
For how ſoeuer contrary it went,
They might expound their meaning otherwyſe,
As haps in things ſhoulde newly ſtill ariſe.

L.iiii. And

George Plantagenet

And thus there grew of a mistaken truth,
An art so false as made the tru suspect:
Wherof hath come much mischiefe, more the ruthe,
That errours should our mynds so much infect.
True prophets haue fowly ben reiect:
The false which brede both murder war and strife,
Beleued to the losse of many a good mans lyfe.

And therfore Baldwin teach men to discerne,
Which prophecies be false and which be true:
And for a ground this lesson let them learne,
That all be false which are deuised new
The age of things is iudged by the hue.
All riddels made by letters, names or armes,
Are yonge and false, far worse than witches charms.

I know thou musest at this lore of myne,
How I no studient, should haue learned it:
And dost impute it to the fume of wyne
That stirs the tongue, and sharpneth vp the wit,
But harke, a frende did teach me euery whit.
A man of myne in all good knowledge rise,
For which he giltlesse lost his learned lyfe.

This man abode my seruaunt many a day,
And stil in study set his hole delight:
Which taught me more then I could beare away
Of euery arte: and by his searching sight
Of things to come he would foreshew as right,
As I rehearse the pageants that were past:
Such perfectnes God gaue him at the last.

Duke of Clarence

He knew my brother Richard was the Bore,
Whose tuskes should teare my brothers boyes and me,
And gaue me warning therof long before.
But wit nor warning can in no degree
Let things to hap, which are ordaind to be.
Witnesse the painted Lyonesse, which slue
A prince imprisoned, Lyons to eschewe.

He told me eke my yooke fellow should dy,
(Wherin would God he had ben no deuyne)
And after her death I should woe earnestly
A spouse, wherat my brother would repine:
And fynde the means she should be none of myne.
For which such malice should among vs ryse,
As saue my death no treaty should decise.

And as he said so all things came to passe:
For whan King Henry and his sonne were slaine,
And euery brople so throughly quenched was,
That the King my brother quietly did raigne,
I, reconsiled to his loue agayne,
In prosperous health did leade a quiet lyfe,
For fiue yeares space with honours laden rife,

And to augment the fulnesse of my blisse,
Two louely children by my wyfe I had:
But froward hap whose maner euer is
In chiefest ioye to make the happy sad,
Bemixt my sweete with bitternes to bad:
For while I swam in ioyes on euery syde,
My louing wife, my chiefest Iewell dyed

L.iii. Whose

George Plantagenet

Whose lacke, whan sole I had bewayled a yeare,
The Duke of Burgoins wyfe dame Margarete
My louing sister willing me to cheare,
To mary agayne did kyndely me intreate:
And wisht me matched with a mayden nete
A step daughter of hers Duke Charls hayre,
A noble damsell, yong, discrete and fayre.

To whose desire because I did enclyne,
The King my brother douting my degree
Through prophecies, against vs did repyne:
And at no hand would to our wills agree.
For which such rancour pearst both him and me
That face to face we fell at flat defiaunce,
But were appeased by frends of our aliaunce.

Howbeit my mariage vtterly was dasht:
Wherin because my seruant sayd his mynde,
A meane was sought wherby he mought be lasht.
And for they could no cryme agaynst him fynde,
They forgde a fault the peoples eyes to blynde,
And told he should by sorceries pretend,
To bring the King vnto a spedy ende.

Of all which points he was as innocent
As is the babe that lacketh kyndely breth:
And yet condemned by the Kings assent,
Most cruelly put to a shamefull death.
This fyerd my hart, as foulder doth the heath:
So that I could not but exclame and cry,
Against so great and open iniury,

For

Duke of Clarence.

For this I was comaunded to the tower,
The King my brother was so cruell harted:
And whan my brother Richard saw the hower
Was come, for which his hart so sore had smarted,
He thought it best take the tyme before it parted.
For he endeuoured to attain the crown,
From which my life must nedes haue held hym down.

For though the King within a while had dyed,
As nedes he must he surfayted so oft,
I must haue had his children in my guyde
So Richard should besyde the crowne haue cost:
This made him ply the while the waxe was soft,
To fynde a meane to bring me to an ende,
For realmrape spareth neyther kin nor frend.

And whan he saw how reason can asswage
Through length of tyme my brother Edwards yre,
With forged tales he set him newe in rage,
Tyll at the last they did my death conspyre.
And though my truth sore troubled their desyre,
For all the world did know myne innocence,
Yet they agreed to charge me with offence,

And couertly within the tower they calde,
A quest, to geue such verdite as they should.
Who what with feare and what with fauour thralde,
Durst not pronounce but as my brethern would.
And though my false acusers neuer could
Proue ought they said, I giltlesse was condemned:
Such verdites passe where iustice is contemned.

L iiii. This

George Plantagenet

This feate atchiued yet could they not for shame
Cause me be kilde by any common way,
But like a Wolfe the tyraut Richard came,
(My brother, nay my butcher I may say)
Unto the tower when all men were away,
Saue such as were prouided for the feate:
Who in this wise did straungely me entreate.

His purpose was with a prepared string
To strangle me: but I bestird me so,
That by no force they could me therto bring,
Which caused him that purpose to forgo.
Howbeit they bound me whether I would or no.
And in a but of malmesy standing by,
New christened me because I should not crie.

Thus drownd I was yet for no due desert,
Except the zeale of iustice be a cryme:
False prophecies bewitcht King Edwards hart.
My brother Richard to the crowne would clyme.
Note these three causes in thy rufull ryme:
And boldly say they did procure my fall
And death of deaths most straunge and hard of all.

And warne all princes prophecies to eschue
That are to darke and doutfull to be knowen:
What God hath said, that cannot but ensue,
Though all the world would haue it ouerthrowen.
When men suppose by fetches of their owne
To flye their fate, they furder on the same
Like quenching blasts which oft reuiue the flame.

Will princes therfore not to thinke by murder
They may auoyde what prophecies behight,
But by their meanes their mischiefs they may furder,
And cause Gods vengeaunce heuier to alight:
Wo worth the wretch that striues with Gods foresight.
They are not wise, but wickedly do arre.
Which thinke yll deedes, due destenies may barre.

For if we thinke that prophecies be true,
We must beleue it cannot but betyde,
Which God in them forsheweth shall ensue:
For his decrees vnchaunged do abide.
Which to be true my brethern both haue tried.
Whose wicked warkes warne princes to detest,
That others harmes may kepe them better blest.

FINIS.

K. Edward the fourth.

By that this tragedye was ended, nighte was so nere com that we could not conueniently tary thgether any longer: and therfore said mayste Ferrers: It is best my maisters to stay here. For we be now com to the end of Edward the fourths raigne. For ye last whom we fynde vnfortunate therein, was this Duke of Clarence: in whose behalfe I commend much ye which hath be noted,

Let vs therfore for vhys tyme leaue to him, & this day seuen nyghts hence, if youy busines will so suffer, let vs all mete here together agayne. And you shal se that in the meane season I will not onely deuise vppon this my selfe, but cause dyuers other of my acquaintaunce which can do very well, to helpe vs forward with the rest. To this euery man gladlye agreed, howebeit (saide another) seing we shall ende at Edwarde the fourths ende let himselfe make an ende of oure dayes labour with the same oration whiche mayster Skelton made in his name, the tenour wherof so far as I remember is as foloweth.

K. Edward the fourth.

Howe Kinge Edwarde the fourth through his surfetinge and vntemperate lyfe, sodainlye dyed in the midst of his prosperity, the nynth of Aprill. Anno. 1483.

Iseremini mei ye that be my frends,
This world hath formed me downe to fall:
How may I endure whan that euery thing ends?
What creature is borne to be eternall?
Now there is no more but pray for me all,
Thus say I Edward that late was your King,
And xxii. yeares ruled this imperiall:
Some vnto pleasure and some to no lyking:
Mercy I aske of my misdoing,
What auayleth it frends to be my foe?
Sith I cannot resist, nor amend your complayning,
Quia ecce nunc in puluere dormio.

I slepe now in mold as it is naturall,
As earth vnto earth hath his reuerture:
What ordayned God to be terrestriall,
With out recourse to the earth by nature,
Who to lyue euer may himselfe assure?
What is it to trust to mutability,
Sith that in this world nothing may endure?
For now am I gone that was late in prosperity.
To presume theruppon it is but vanity,
Not certaine, but as a chery faire full of wo,
Rayned not I of late in greate prosperity,
Et ecce nunc in puluere dormio.

Where

K. Edward the fourth.

Where was in my lyfe such an one as I,
While Lady Fortune with me had continuaunce:
Graunted not she me to haue victory,
In England to reigne and to contribute Fraunce,
She tooke me by the hand and led me a daunce,
And with her sugred lyps on me she smyled,
But what for dissembled countenaunce,
I could not beware tyll I was beguyled.
Now from this world she hath me exilde,
Whan I was lothest hence for to go,
And am in age who saith but a chylde.
Et ecce nunc in puluere dormio.

I had ynough I held me not content,
Whithout remembraunce that I should dye:
And moreouer to encroch redy was I bent,
I knew not how long I should it occupye,
I made the tower strong I wist not why.
I knew not to whom I purchased Tattersall.
I mended Douer on the mountaine hye,
And London I prouoked to fortify the wall,
I made Notingham a place full royall.
Wyndsore, Eltam, and many other mo,
Yet at the last I went from them all
Et ecce nunc in puluere dormio.

Where is now my conquest and victory?
Where is my riches and royall array?
Where be my coursers and my horses hye?
Where is my myrth, my solace, and my play?
As vanity to nought all is wythred away:
O Lady Bes long for me may you call,

F.iij

K. Edwarde the fourth.

For I am departed vntill domes daye:
But loue you that Lord that is soueraine of all.
Where be my Castels and buildings royall?
But Wyndsore alone now haue I no moe,
And of Eton the prayers perpetuall,
Et ecce nunc in puluere dormio.

Why should a man be proud or presume hye
Saint Bernard therof nobly doth treate,
Saying aman is but a sacke of stercory,
And shall retourne vnto wormes meate:
Why what became of Alexander the greate?
Or els of strong Sampson, who can tell,
Were not worms ordaynde their flesh to freate:
And of Salomon that was of wit the well,
Absolon profered his heere for to sell,
Yet for his bewty worms eate him also,
And I but late in houours did excell,
Et ecce nunc in puluere dormio.

I haue played my pageant, now am I past,
Ye wote well all I was of no greate elde,
Thus all thing concluded shall be at the last,
Whan death approcheth then lost is the field:
Than seeyng this world me no lengar upholde,
For nought would conserue me here in this place,
In manus tuas domine my sprite vp I yelde,
Humbly beseching the O God of thy grace.
O you curteous commons your hartes embrace
Beningly now to pray for me also,
For right well ye know your King I was.
Et ecce nunc in puluere dormio.

FINIS.

Whan

Sir Anthony Woduile

When thys was saide, euery man for ÿ time tooke his leaue of other, and departed (for thē it wared darke) appointing a new day of meting which being come, wee met all together againe. And when wee had saluted one an other, then one tooke the booke and began to reade ÿ storye of king Edward the fift: (for there wee left) and when he came to ÿ apprehēding of ÿ Lorde Riuers: stay ther I pray you (said I) for here is his complaint. For the better vnderstanding wherof, you must ymagin ÿ he was accompanied w the Lord Richard Gray, Hawte & Clapeham, whose infortunes he bewaileth after this maner.

How Syr Anthonye Woduile Lorde Riuers and Scales, Gouernour of prince Edward, was wyth his Nephue Lord Richard Gray & other causeleffe imprisoned and cruelly murdered. Anno. 1483.

As sely suiters letted by delayes
To shew their prince the meaning of their mynde,
That long haue bought their brokers yeas and nays
And neuer the nyer: do dayly wayte to fynde
The princes grace, from waighty affaires vntwynde:
Which tyme attayned, by attending all the yeare,
The weried prince will than no suters heare:

                                            My cast

Lord Riuers.

My case was such not many dayes agoe,
For after bruite had blazed all abroade
That Baldwin through the ayd of other moe,
Of fame or shame fallen princes would vnloade,
Out from our graues we got without abode,
And preaced forward with the rufull rout,
That sought to haue their doings bulted out.

But whan I had long tended for my turne
To tell my tale as dyuers other dyd:
In hope I should no lengar while soiourne
But from my suites haue spedyly ben ryd,
Whan course and place both orderly had bid
Me shew my mynde, and I prepard to saye,
The hearers paused arose and went their way.

These doubtfull doings draue me to my dumps,
Uncertaine what should moue them so to do:
I feared least affections lothly lumps
Or inward grudge had driuen them therto,
Whose wicked stings all stories truth vndo,
Oft causing good to be reported yll,
Or dround in suds of Læthes muddy swill.

For hitherto sly wryters wyly wits
Which haue engrossed princes chiefe affayrs,
Haue bene lyke horses snaffled with the bits
Of fancy, feare, or doute full depe dispayrs,
Whose rains enchained to the chiefest chayrs,
Haue so ben strayned of those that bare the stroke
That truth was forst to chow or els to choke.

This

Sir Anthony Woduile

This caused such as lothed lowd to ly,
To passe with silence sundry princes lyues.
Lesse fault it is to leaue, then leaue awry:
And better drownd, than euer bound in gyues.
For fatall fraud this world so fondly driues,
That what so euer writers brains may brue
Be it neuer so false, at length is tane for true.

What harme may hap by help of lying penns
How written lies may lewdly be maintaynde.
The lothly rites, the deuilysh ydoll denns
With giltlesse bloud of vertuous men bestainde,
Is such a proofe as all good harts haue plainde.
The taly grounds of stories throughly tries,
The death of martirs vengeance on it cries.

Far better therfore not to write at all
Than stayne the truth for any maner cause,
For this they meane to let my story fall
(Thought I) and ere my time my volume clause.
But after I knew it onely was a pause,
Made purposely, most for the readers ease,
Assure thee Baldwin, highly it did me please.

For freshest wits, I know will sone be weary,
In reading long what euer booke it be,
Except it be vaine matter, straunge or mery,
Well saust with lies, and glared all with glee,
With which because no graue truth may agree,
The closest stile for stories is the metest,
In rufull moans the shortest fourme is swetest,

Lord Riuers.

And sith the playnts already by thee penne,
Are brief ynough, the nomber also small,
The tediousnesse I thinke doth none offend,
Saue such as haue no lust to learne at all,
Regarde none such: no matter what they brall.
Warne thou the wary least they hap to stumble.
As for the carelesse, care not what they mumble.

My lyfe is such as (if thou note it well)
May cause the witty welthy to beware.
For their sakes therfore plainly will I tell,
How false and combrous worldly honours are,
How cankred foes, bring carelesse folke to care.
How tyrantes suffered and not queld in tyme
Do cut their throats that suffer them to clyme.

Neither will I hyde the chiefest point of all
Which wisest rulers least of all regarde,
That was and will be cause of many a fall.
This cannot be to ernestly declarde
Because it is so seeld, and slackly heard.
The abuse and scorning of Gods ordinaunces,
Is chiefest cause of care and wofull chaunces,

Gods holy orders highly are abused
Whan men do chaunge their ends for straunge respects:
They scorned are, whan they be cleane refused
For that they can not serue our fond affects.
The one our shame, the other our sin detects.
It is a shame for christians to abuse them,
But deadly sinne for scorners to refuse them.

M i. I meane

Sir Anthony Woduile

I meane not this all onely of degrees
Ordaind by God for peoples preseruation,
But of his law, good orders, and decrees,
Prouided his creatures conseruation.
And specially the state of procreation
Wherin we here the number of them encrease
Which shall in heauen enioy eternall peace.

The onely end why God ordayned this,
Was for the encreasing of that blessed number
For whome he hath prepard eternall blisse.
They that refuse it for the care or cumber
Being apt therto, are in a sinfull slumber:
No fond respect, no vaine deuised vowes
Can quit or bar what God in charge allowes.

It is not good for man to liue alone
Sayd God: and therfore made he him a make:
Sole life said Christ is graunt: d few or none,
All seed sheders are bound lyke wiues to take:
Yet not for lust, for lands, or riches sake,
But to beget and foster so their frute
That heauen and earth be stored with the suite.

But as this state is damnably refused
Of many apt and able therunto,
So is it likewyse wickedly abused
Of all that vse it as they should not doe:
Wherin are gilty all the greedy who
For gaine, for frendship, lands or honors wed,
And these pollute the vndefyled bed.

            And

Lord Riuers.

And therfore God through iustice cannot cease
To plague these faults with sundry sorts of whips:
As disagrement, healths or welths decrease,
Or lothing sore the neuer liked lips.
Disdaine also with rigour somtyme nips
Presuming mates, vnequally that match:
Some bitter leauen sowers the musty batch.

We worldly folke acount him very wise
That hath the wit most welthily to wed.
By all meanes therfore alwaies we deuise
To see our issue rich in spousals sped.
We buy and sell rich orphans: babes scant bred
Must mary ere they know what mariage means
Boyes marry old trots, old fooles wed yong queans.

We call this wedding which in any wise
Can be no mariage, but pollucion plaine.
A new found trade of humane marchandise,
The deuils net, a filthy fleshly gayne:
Of kinde and nature an vnnaturall staine,
A fowle abuse of Gods most holy order,
And yet alloud almost in euery border.

Would God I were the last that shall haue cause
Against this creping cancar to complaine,
That men would so regard their makers lawes,
That all would leaue the lewdnes of their braine,
That holy orders holy might remaine.
That our respects in wedding should not choke
The end and fruite of Gods most holy yoke.

The sage

Sir Anthony Woduile

The sage King Solon after that he saw,
What mischiefs folowe missought mariages,
To barre all baits, established this law.
No frend nor father shall geue herytages,
Coyne, cattell, stuffe, or other cariages
With any mayd for dowry or wedding sale,
By any meane on pain of banning bale.

Had thys good law in England been in force
My father had not so cruelly been slaine.
My brother had not causles lost his corps.
Our mariage had not bred vs such disdayne,
My selfe had lackt great part of greuous paine,
We wedded wiues for dignity and lands,
And left our liues in enuies bloudy hands.

My father hight Syr Richard Woduile: he
Espousde the Duches of Bedford, and by her
Had issue males my brother John, and me
Called Anthony, King Edward did prefer
Us far aboue the state wherin we were.
For he espoused our sister Elizabeth,
Whome Sir John Gray made wydow by his death.

How glad were we, thinke you of this alyaunce,
So nercely coupled with so noble a King.
Who durst with any of vs be at defiaunce
Thus made of might the mightiest to wring:
But fye what cares do highest honours bring,
What carelesnes our selues or frends to know,
What spyte and enuy both of high and lowe.

Because

Lorde Riuers.

Because the King had made our sister Quene
It was his honor to prefer her kin.
And sith the rediest way, as wisest ween,
Was first by wedding welthy heyrs to win,
It pleased the prince by lyke meane to begin.
To me he gaue the rich Lord Scales his heir,
A vertuous maid in myne eye very fayre.

He ioyned to my brother Iohn, the olde
Duches of Northfolke notable of fame.
My nephue Thomas (who had in his holde
The honor and right of Marquis Dorcets name)
Espoused Cicelie a right welthy dame,
Lord Bonuiles heyre: by whome he was possest
In all the rites wher through that house was blest.

The honors that my father attaind were dyuers
First Chamberlain, than Constable he was.
I do omit the gainfullest, Earle Riuers.
Thus glistred we in glory clere as glas.
Such myracles can princes bring to passe
Among their lieges whom they mynde to heaue
To honors false, who all their gests deceiue.

Honors are lyke that cruell King of Thrace,
With new com gests that fed his hungry horses.
Or lyke the tirant Busiris whose grace
Offred his Gods all straungers strangled corses.
To forreiners so hard false honors force is
That all her bourders, straungers either gealts
She spoiles to feede her Gods and gredy beasts.

M iii.

Sir Anthony Woduile

Her Gods be those whom God by law or lot,
Or kinde by birth, doth place in highest roumes,
Her beasts be such as gredely haue got
Office or charge to guide the sely gromes.
These officers in law or charge are bromes,
That swepe away the sweete from simple wretches,
And spoile the enriched by their crafty fetches.

These plucke downe those whom princes set aloft,
By wresting lawes, and false conspiracies:
Yea Kings themselues by these are spoiled oft.
Whan wilfull princes carelessly despise
To heare th' oppressed peoples heauy cries,
Nor will correct their polling theues, than God
Doth make those reues the rechles princes rod.

The second Richard is a proofe of this
Whom crafty Lawyers by their lawes deposes.
An other patern good King Henry is
Whose right by them hath diuersly been glosed,
Good while he grew, bad whan he was vnrosed,
And as they foadred these and diuers other
With like deceit they vsed the King my brother.

While he preuailed they said he owed the crown,
All lawes and rights agreed with the same:
But whan by drifts he seemed to be down,
All lawes and right extremely did him blame
Noughtsaue vsurping traytour was his name.
So constantly the Judges construe lawes,
That all agree still with the stronger cause.

Lord Riuers.

These as I said, and other lyke in charge
Are honors horses whom she sedes with gests.
For all whom princes franckly do enlarge
With dignities, these bark at in their breasts:
Their spight, their might, their falsehood neuer rests
Till they deuour them: sparing neither bloud,
Ne limne life, and all to get their good.

The Earle of Warwicke was a praunsing courser
The hauty hart of eis could beare no mate:
Our welth through him waxt many a tyme the worser
So canckardly he had our kin in hate.
He troubled oft the Kings vnsteady state
And that because he would not be his warde
To wed and worke, as he should list award.

He spited vs because we were preferd
By mariage to dignities so great,
But craftely his mallice he deferd
Tyll traitorosly he found means to entreate
Our brother of Clarence to assist his feat:
Whome whan he had by mariage to him bound
Than wrought he straight our linage to confound.

Through slaunderous brutes he bruted many a brople
Through out the realme against the King my brother:
And raysed trayterous rebels thirsting spoile
To murder men: of whome among all other
One Robin of Riddesdale many a soule did smother
His rascall rable at my father wroth
Tooke sier and sonne, and quicke beheaded both.

Sir Anthony Woduile

This hainous act although the King detested,
Yet was he faine to pardon: for the rout
Of rebels all the realme so sore infested,
That euery way assaild, he stoode in doubt:
And though he were of courage high and stout,
Yet he assaied by fair meanes to asswage
His enemies ire, reueild by rebels rage.

But Warwicke was not pacified thus,
His constant rancor causles was extreme,
No meane could serue the quarell to discus,
Till he had driuen the King out of the realme.
Neither would he then be waked from his dreame.
For whan my brother was com and placed again,
He stinted not til he was stoutly slaine.

Than grew the King and realme to quiet rest,
Our stocke and frends still flying higher and higher:
The Quene with children fruitfully was blest:
I gouernd them, it was the Kings desier.
This set their vncles furiously on fier,
That we the Quenes bloud were assigned to gouerne
The prince, not they, the Kings own bloud and brethern

This caused the Duke of Clarence so to chafe
That with the King he brainles fell at bate:
The counsaile warely for to kepe him safe
From raising tumults as he did of late,
Imprisoned him: where through his brothers hate
He was condemnde, and murdred in such sort
As he him selfe hath truly made report.

Was

Lorde Riuers.

Was none abhorred these mischiefs more than I,
Yet could I not be therewith discontented,
Considering that his rancour touched me ny.
Els would my conscience neuer haue consented
To wish him harme, could he haue ben contented.
But feare of hurt, for sauegard of our state
Doth cause more mischiefe than desert or hate.

Such is the state that many wish to beare,
That either we must with others bloud be stained,
Or leade our liues continually in feare.
You mounting myndes behold here what is gaynde
By combrous honour, painfully attainde:
A damned soule for murdringe them that hate you,
Or doutfull lyfe, in daunger lest they mate you.

The cause (I thinke) why some of high degree
Do deadly hate all sekers to ascend,
Is this: The cloyne contented can not be
With any state, tyll tyme he apprehend
The highest top: for therto clymers tend.
Which seldom is attaind without the wracke
Of those betwene, that stay and beare him back.

To saue them selues they therfore are compeld
To hate such climers, and with wit and power
To compasse meanes where through they may be queld,
Ere they ascend their honours to deuour.
This causde the Duke of Clarence frowne and lowre
At me and other, whome the King promoted
To dignities: wherin he madly doted.

For seing

Sir Anthony Woduile

For seing we were his dere allied frends,
Our furderaunce should rather haue made him glad
Than enmy like to wish our wofull ends.
We were the nerest kinsfolke that he had.
We ioy'd with him, his sorrow made vs sad:
But he estemed so much his painted sheath
That he disdaind the loue of all beneath.

But se how sharply God reuengeth sinne:
As he maligned me and many other
His faithfull frends, and kindest of his kin,
So Richard Duke of Glocester, his very brother,
Maligned him and beastly did him smother.
A deuelish dede, a most vnkindly part,
Yet iust reuenge for his vnnaturall hart.

Although this brother queller, tirant fell
Enuied our state as much and more than he:
Yet did his cloaking flattery so excell
To all our frends ward chiefly vnto me,
That he appeard our trusty stay to be:
For outwardly he wrought our state to furder,
Where inwardly he mynded nought saue murder.

Thus in appearaunce who but I was blest:
The chiefest honors heaped on my head:
Beloued of all, enioying quiet rest.
The forward prince by me alone was led,
A noble impe, to all good vertues bred:
The King my liege without my counsaile knowne
Agreed nought: though wisest were his owne.
             But quiet

Lorde Riuers.

But quiet blisse in no state lasteth long
Assailed still by mischief many wayes:
Whose spoiling battry glowing hote and strong,
No flowing welth, no force nor wisdome staies
Her smoakeles poulder beaten souldiers slaies.
By open force foule mischief oft preuails,
By secret sleight, she seeld her purpose fails.

The King was bent to much to foolish pleasure,
In banqueting he had so greate delight:
This made him grow in grosnes out of measure,
Which, as it kindleth carnall appetite,
So quencheth it the liuelynes of the spzite.
Wherof ensue such sicknes and diseases
As none can cure saue death that all displeases.

Through this fault furdered by his brothers fraud
(Now God forgyue me if I iudge amisse)
Or through that beast his ribald or his baud
That larded still thse sinfull lusts of his,
He sodainly forsooke all worldly blisse.
That loathed leach, that neuer welcome death,
Through spasmous humours stopped vp his breath.

That tyme lay I at Ludloe Wales his border.
For with the prince the King had sent me thyther
To stay the robberies, spoile, and foule disorder,
Of diuers outlawes gathered there together:
Whose banding tended no man wist well whither
Whan these by wisdome saftly were supressed,
Came wofull newes, our soueraigne was deceassed.

The griefe

Sir Anthony Woduile.

The grief wherof whan reason had asswaged,
Because the prince remained in my guide,
For his defend great store of men I waged,
Doubting the stormes which at such tyme betyde.
But while I there thus warely did prouide,
Commaundement came to send them home againe
And bring the King thence with his houshold traine.

This charge sent from the counsaile and the Quene
Though much against my mynde I beast obayed:
The deuill him selfe wrought all the drift I wene,
Because he would haue innocents betrayed:
For ere the King were halfe his way conuayed,
A sort of traitors falsely him betrapt
I caught afore, and close in prison clapt.

The Duke of Glocester that incarnate deuill
Confedred with the Duke of Buckingham,
With eke Lord Hastings, hasty both to euill
To meete the King in mourning habit came,
(A cruell Wolfe though clothed lyke a Lambe)
And at Northampton, where as than I bayted
They tooke their inne as they on me had wayted.

The King that night at Stonystratford lay,
A towne to small to harbour all his trayne:
This was the cause why he was gone away
While I with other did behinde remaine.
But will you see how falsely frends can faine?
Not Sinon sly, whose fraude best fame rebukes,
Was halfe so suttle as these double Dukes.

         First to

Lorde Riuers.

First to myne Inne, commeth in my brother false
Embraceth me: well met good brother Scales,
And wepes withall: the other me enhalse
With welcome cosin, now welcome out of Wales
O happy day, for now all stormy gales
Of strife and rancour vtterly are swaged,
And we our own to liue or dye vnwaged.

This proferde seruice saust with salutacions
Immoderate, might cause me to suspect:
For commonly in all dissimulations
Th'exces of glauering doth the guile detect:
Reason refuseth falsehode to dyrect:
The will therfore for feare of being spied
Exceedeth mean, because it wanteth guyde.

This is the cause why such as fayne to wepe
Do howle outright, or wayling cry ah,
Tering themselues, and straining sighs most depe.
Why such dissemblers as would seme to laugh
Breth not tihhee, but braye out, hah hah hah.
Why beggers fayning brauery are the proudst
Why cowards bragging boldenesse, wrangle loudst.

For commonly all that do counterfayte
In any thing, excede the naturall mean,
And that for feare of fayling in their feat.
But these conspyrers couched all so cleane,
Though close demeanour, that their wyles did weane
My hart from douts, so many a false deuice
The forged fresh, to hyde their enterprise.

They

Sir Anthony Woduile.

They supt with me, propounding frendly talke
Of our affayrs, still geuing me the prayse.
And euer among the cups to me ward walke:
I drinke to you good Cuz ech traytour saies:
Our banquet done when they should go their wayes
They tooke their leaue, oft wishing me good night
As hartely as any creature might.

A noble hart they say is Lyon like,
It can not couche, dissemble, crouch nor fayne.
How villanous were these, and how vnlyke?
Of noble stocke the most ignoble stayne.
Their woluish harts, their trayterous forly braine
Either proue them base, of rascall race engendred
Or from hault lynage bastardlike degendred.

Such polling heads as prayse for prudent pollicy
False practises, I wish were pact on poales.
I meane the bastard law broode, which can molifye
All kinde of causes in their crafty nolles.
These vndermine all vertue, blynde as molles,
They bolster wrong, they racke and strain the right
And prayse for law both malice, fraud, and might.

These quench the worthy flames of noble kynde,
Prouoking best borne to the basest vices,
Through crafts they make the bouldest courage blinde,
Disliking highly valiant enterpryses:
And praysing vily villanous deuices.
These make the Bore a Hog, the Bull an Oxe.
The Swan a Goose, the Lyon a Wolfe or Foxe.

The

Lord Riuers.

The Lawyer Catesby and his crafty feers
A rout that neuer did good in any realme,
Are they that had transformed these noble peers:
They turnde their bloud to melancholicke fleume.
Their courage hault to cowardise extreame
Their force and manhode into fraud and malice,
Their wit to wyles: stout Hector into Paris.

These glauerers gone, my selfe to rest I layde,
And doubting nothing soundly fell a slepe:
But sodainly my seruants sore afrayde
Awaked me: and drawing sighes full depe,
Alas (quoth one) my Lord we are betrayde.
How so (quoth I) the Dukes are gone their waies
They haue barred the gates, and borne away the keyes.

While he thus spake, there came into my mynde
This fearfull dreame, wherout I waked was:
I saw a riuer stopt with stormis of winde
Where through a Swan, a Bull and Bore did passe,
Fraunching the fysh and fry, with teath of brasse,
The riuer dryed vp saue a litle streame
Which at the last did water al the realme.

Me thought this streane did drown the cruell Bore
In litle space, it grew so depe and brode:
But he had kild the Bull and Swan before.
Besides all this I sawe an ougly tode
Crall toward me, on which me thought I trode:
But what became of her, or what of me
My sodaine waking would not let me see.

Their

Sir Anthony Woduile

These dreames considered with this sodain newes
So dyuers from their doings ouer night,
Dyd cause me not a litle for to muse,
I blest me, and ryse in all the hast I might.
By this, Aurora spred abroade the light
Which fro the ends of Phebus beams she tooke
Who than the Bulls chief gallery forsooke.

When I had opened the window to looke out
There might I se the stretes ech where beset,
My inne on ech side compassed about
With armed watchmen, all escapes to let
Thus had these Neroes caught me in their net.
But to what ende, I could not throwly gesse,
Such was my plainnes, such their doublenesse.

My conscience was so clere I could not doubt
Their deadly drift, which lesse apparaunt lay,
Because they causde their men retourne the rout
That yode toward Stonystratford as they say,
Because the Dukes will fyrst be there to day:
For this (thought I) they hinder me in ieast,
For giltlesse myndes do easely deeme the best.

By this the Dukes were come into myne inne
For they were lodged in an other by.
I gote me to them thinking it a sime
Within my chamber cowardly to lye.
And merely I asked my brother why
He vsed me so: he sterne in euill sadnes
Cryed out: I arrest thee traytour for thy badnes.

Lord Riuers.

How so (quoth I) whence riseth your suspicion?
Thou art a traitour (quoth he) I the arrest.
Arrest (quoth I) why where is your commission?
He drew his weapon so did all the rest
Crying: yeld the traitour. I so sore distrest
Made no resistaunce: but was sent to ward
None saue their seruaunts assigned to my gard.

This done they sped him to the King in poste,
And after their humble reuerence to him done,
They traiterously began to rule the roste
They picked a quarell to my sisters sonne
Lord Richard Gray: the King would not be wonne
To agree to them, yet they against all reason,
Arrested him they said for hainous treason.

Sir Thomas Uaughan and Syr Richard Hault
Two worthy knights were likewise apprehended,
These all were gilty in one kynde of fault,
They would not like the practise then pretended:
And seing the King was herewith sore offended,
Backe to Northampton they brought him againe
And thence discharged most part of his traine.

There lo Duke Richard made himselfe protector
Of King and realme by open proclamation,
Though neither King nor Quene were his elector,
Thus he presumed by lawlesse vsurpation.
But will you see his deepe dissimulation?
He sent me a dish of deinties from his borde
That day, and with it, this false frendly worde.

N i.   Commende

Sir Anthony Woduile

Commend me to him all things shalbe well,
I am his frend, bid him be of good chere:
These newes I prayed the messanger go tell
My Nephue Richard, whome I loued full deare.
But what he ment by well, now shall you heare:
He thought it well to haue vs quickly murdred
Which not long after thorowly he furdered.

For strait from thence we closely were conuayed
From iayle to iayle Northward we wist not whither:
Where after we had a while in sunder strayed,
At last we met at Pomfret all together.
Syr Richard Ratcliffe bad vs welcome thither,
Who openly, all law and right contemned
Beheaded vs before we were condemned.

My cosin Richard could not be content
To leaue his lyfe, because he wist not why,
Good gentleman that neuer harme had ment,
Therfore he asked wherfore he should dye:
The priest his ghostly father did replye
With weping eyes: I knowe one wofull cause.
The realme hath neyther righteous Lords nor lawes.

Sir Thomas Vaughan chafing cryed still:
This tyrant Glocester is the gracelesse G.
That will his brothers children beastly kill.
And least the people through his talke might see
The mischiefs toward, and therto not agree
Our tormentour that false periured knight
Bad stop our mouths, with words of high dispight.

Thus died

Thus dyed we giltlesse processe hard we none,
No cause alleagde, no Iudge, nor yet accuser,
No quest empaneld passed vs vppon.
That murdrer Ratcliffe, law and rights refuser,
Did all to flatter Richard his abuser.
Vnhappy both that euer they were borne,
Through giltlesse bloud that haue their soules forlorne.

In part I graunt I well deserued this,
Because I caused not spedy execution
Be done on Richard for that murder of his,
When first he wrought King Henries close confusion.
Not for his brothers hatefull persecution.
These cruell murders painfull death deserued
Which had he suffred, many had ben preserued.

Warne therfore all that charge or office beare
To see all murdrers spedely executed:
And spare them not for fauour or for feare:
By guiltles bloud the earth remaines polluted.
For lacke of Iustice kingdomes are transmuted.
They that saue murdrers from deserued paine,
Shall through those murdrers miserably be slaine.

FINIS.

N ii. Whan

The Lord Haſtings.

Whā I had read this, they liked it very wel. one wiſhed ẏ the combat which he fought with the baſtard of Burgoine, and the honour which he wan both with ſpeare and axe ſhold not be forgotten Another moued a queſtion about a greate matter, & that is the variaunce of the chronicles about the Lorde Thomas Graye Marquiſe Dorcet: whō Fabian euery where calleth ẏ quenes brother. ſir Thomas More and and Hall call hym the quenes ſon as he was in very dede. Fabian ſaith he was gouernour of the prince, and had ẏ conueiaunce of him from Ludlo towards London. The other (whome we follow) ſay he was than at Lōdon with the quene prouiding for the kings coronacion, and tooke ſanctuary with her as ſoone as hee harde of the apprehendinge of his vncle. This diſagreing of writers is a great hindraunce of ẏ truth, and no ſmall cumbraunce to ſuch as be diligent readers, beſides the harme that maye happen in ſucceſſion of heritages. It were therefore a worthye and good dede for the nobility, to cauſe all the recordes to be ſought, and a true and perfect chronicle therout to be writen. Unto which we refer ẏ deciding of this & of all other like controuerſies, geuing this to vnderſtand in the mean tyme, that no man ſhall thinke his title either better or worſe by any thinge that is written in any part of this treatiſe. For the onely thing which is purpoſed herein, is by example of others miſeries, to diſſwade all men frō all ſinns and vices. If by the way we touch any thinge con‑
cerning

The Lorde Haſtings.

cerning titles, we followe therin Halles chronicle. And where we ſeme to ſwarue from his reaſons & cauſes of dyuers doings, there we gather vpon cõiecture ſuch things as ſeme moſt probable, or at the leaſt moſt conuenient for the furderance of our purpoſe. Whan the reader would haue proceded in ye cronicle which ſtraighte intreateth of the vilanous deſtruction of the Lord Haſtings, I willed him to to ſurceas, becauſe I had there his tragedye verye learnedly penned. For the better vnderſtandinge whereof, you muſte ymagin that you ſee him newly crept out of hys graue, and ſpeakynge to me as followeth.

How the Lord Haſtings was betrayed by truſtinge to much to his euill counſailour Cateſby, and vilanouſly murdered in the tower of Londõ by Richard Duke of Gloceſter. the 13. of Iune. Anno. 1483.

Aſtings I am, whoſe haſtned death who knewe, My lyfe with prayſe, my death with plaint purſue. With others fearing leaſt my headleſſe name Bewrongd, by partiall bruite of flattering fame: Cleauing my tombe the way my fame forewent, Though bared of loyns which body and Fortune lent Erſt my proud vaunt: preſent preſent to thee My honour, fall, and forced deſtenye.

N iii.   Ne feare

The Lorde Hastings

Ne feare to staine thy credit by my tale.
In Læthes floud, long since, in Stigian vale
Selfe loue I dreint. what tyme hath fyned for true,
And ceasseth not, (though stale) still to renewe:
Recount I wil. wherof be this the proofe.
That blase I will my prayse, and my reproofe.
We naked ghosts are but the very man
Ne of our selues more than we ought we scan.

But doute distracteth me, if I should consent
To yeeld myne honourd name a martyrde sayut.
Yf Martirdoine rest in the mysers lyfe
Through torments wrongly reft by fatall knyfe:
How Fortunes nurslyng I, and dearest babe,
Ought therto stope, none may me weill perswade.
For how may myser martirdoine betyde,
To whom in cradell Fortune was affyed?

See how this grossest aire infecteth me since,
Forgot haue I, of loyalty to my prince.
My happy mede is, Martir to be named?
And what the heauens embrace, the world ay blamed:
For mens vniustice wreaked but Gods iust ire,
And by wrong end, turnd wreake to Iustice hire.
O iudgements iust, by vniustice iustice dealt,
Who douts of me may learne, the truth who felt.

So therfore, as my fall may many stay:
As well the prince, from violent headlong sway,
Of noble peeres, from honors throne to dust,
As nobles lesse in title state to trust:

         Shonning

The Lorde Hastings.

Shonning those sinns, that shake the golden leaues
Perforce from boughs, ere nature bare the greaues:
So, what my lyfe profest, my death here teacheth,
And, as with word so with example preacheth

The hilly heauens, and valey earth belowe,
Yet ring his fame, whose dedes so great did growe.
Edward the fourth ye know vnnamde I meane.
Whose noble nature to me so did leane,
That I his staffe was, I his onely ioye,
And euen what Pandare was to him of Troy.
Which moued him first, to create me chamberlayne.
To serue his sweetes, to my most sower payne.

Wherein, to iustly prayfed for secretnesse
(For now my guilt with shriking I confesse)
To him to true, to vntrue to the Quene,
Such hate I wan, as lasted long betwene
Our familyes. Shores wife was my nyce cheate.
The holy hore, and eke the wyly peat.
I fed his lust with louely peces so,
That Gods sharpe wrath I purchast my iust woe,

Se here of nobles new the diuers sourse.
Some vertue rayseth, some clyme vp sluttish sortg.
The fyrst, though onely of themselues begon,
Yet circlewise into themselues do ron.
Within their fame their force vnited so,
Both endlesse is, and stronger gainst their foe.
For, when endeth hit that neuer hath begon:
Or what by force, may circled knot be vndone?

N iiii. Thother

The Lorde Haſtings

Th'other as by wicked meanes they grew,
And raigned by flattery or violence: so sone rue.
First tombling step from honours old, is vice.
Which once discend, some linger, none arise
To former type. But they catch vertues spray,
Which mounteth them that clyme by lawfull way.
Beware to rise by seruing princely luſt.
Surely to ſtand, one mean is riſing iuſt.

Which learne by me, whome let it helpe to excuſe,
That ruthfull now my ſelfe I do accuſe
And that my prince I euer pleaſed with ſuch,
As harmed none, and him contented much.
In vice, some fauour, or leſſe hate let win,
That I ne wryed to worſer end my ſin.
But vſed my fauour to the ſafety of ſuch,
As fury of later war to lyue did grutch.

For as one durt(though durty ſhyneth the ſonne:
So, euen amids my vice, my vertue ſhoane.
My ſelfe I ſpared with any his cheate to ſtaine,
For loue and reuerence ſo I could refrayne.
Giſippus wife erſt Titus would deſpye
With frendſhipd breach. I quencht that brutiſh fyre.
Manly hit is, to loth the fawning luſt.
Small vaunt to flye, what of conſtreint thou muſt.

Theſe therfore raſed, if thou myne office ſkan,
Lo none I hurt but furdred euery man.
My chamber England was, my ſtaffe the law:
Wherby ſauns rygour, all I held in awe.

                                         So louing

The Lorde Hastings.

So louing to all, so beloued of all,
As, (what ensued vppon my bloudy fall
Though I ne felt) yet suerly this I thinke.
Full many a trickling teare their mouths did drinke.

Disdayne not princes easie accesse, meeke cheare.
We knowe, then Angels statelier port ye beare
Of God himselfe: to masty a charge for sprites.
But then, my Lords, consid're, he delights
To vayle his grace to vs pore earthly wants,
To simplest shrubs, and to the dunghill plants.
Expresse him then, in might and mercies meane.
So shall ye winne, as now ye weld, the realme.

But all to long I feare I do delaye
The many means, wherby I did bewray
My zealous will, to earne my princes grace.
Least thou differ, to thinke me kynde percase.
As nought may last, so Fortunes weathry cheare
With powting lookes gan lower on my sire,
And on her wheele, aduaunst hye in his roome
The Warwicke Earle, mase of Christendome,

Besides the tempting prowesse of the foe,
His traytour brother did my prince forgo.
The cause was liked, I was his linked allye.
Yet nor the cause, nor brothers trechery,
Nor enmies force, ne band of mingled bloud:
Made Hastings beare his prince other mynde then good,
But tane and scaped from Warwicks griping pawes,
With me he fled through fortunes frowardst flawes.

To London

The Lorde Hastings.

To London come, at large we might haue seemed,
Had not we then the realme a prison deemed.
Ech bush a barre, ech spray a banner splayed,
Ech house a fort our passage to haue staied.
To Linne we leape, where while we awayte the tyde,
My secret frends in secret I supplied,
In mouth to mainteine Henry sixt their King,
By dede to deuoyre Edward to bring in.

The restles tyde, that bare the empty bay,
With waltryng waues roames wambling forth. Away
The mery mariner hales. The bragging boy,
To masts hye top vp hies. In signe of ioy
The wauering flag is vaunst. The suttle seas
Their swelling ceasse: to calmest euen peace
Sinkth down their pryde. With dronkennes gainst all care
The seamen armed, awayt their noble fare.

On bord we come. The massy anchors wayde,
One English shyp, two hulkes of Holland, ayde
In such a pinch. So small tho was the trayne,
Such his constraint, that now, that one with payne
Commaund he might, who erst might many moe:
Then brought the ghastly Greekes to Tenedo.
So nought is ours that we by hap might lose,
What nearest semes, is farthest of in woes.

As banished wights, such ioyes we mought haue made,
Eased of aye threatning death, that late we dradde.
But once our countreis sight (not care) exempt,
No harbour shewing, that mought our feare relent,
                                                No couert

The Lorde Hastings.

No couert caue, no shrub to shroud our lyues,
No hollow wood, no flyght, that oft depriues
The mighty his pray, no sanctuary left
For exiled prince, that shroudes ech slaue from theft:

In prison pent, whose woody walles to passe
Of no lesse perill than the dying was:
With the Ocean moated, battred with the waues,
(As chaind at oares the wretched Galley slaues,
At mercy sit of sea and enmies shot,
And shonne with death what they with flight may not)
But grenish waues, and desert lowring skies
All comfort els forclosed our exiled eyes:

Loe loe from highest top, the slauish boy
Sent vp with sight of land our harts to ioye:
Descries at hand whole flete of Easterlings,
As than whose enmies of the British Kings.
The mouse may somtyme helpe the Lyon in nede
The byttle bee once spilt the Aegles brede.
O Princes seke no foes. In your distresse,
The earth, the seas, conspyre your heauinesse.

Our foe discryed by flight we shon in hast,
And lade with Canuas now the bending mast.
The ship was rackt to try her sapling then,
As Squirels clyme the troupes of trusty men.
The steresman sekes a redier course to ronne,
The souldier stirs, the gonner hies to gonne.
The Flemings sweate, the English shyp disdains
To wait behinde to beare the Flemings trains.

Forth flyeth

The Lorde Haſtings.

Forth flyeth the barke, as from the violent goonne
The pellet pearſeth all ſtaies and ſtops eft ſoone.
And ſwyft ſhe ſingeth, as oft in ſunny day
The Dolphin fleetes in ſeas in mery May.
As we for lyues, ſo Th'eaſterlings for gaine,
Thwack on the ſayles, and after make amayne.
Though laden they were, and of burthen great:
A King to maſter yet, what Swyne nold ſweat:

So mid the vale the greyhound ſeing ſtert
His fearfull foe, purſueth. Before ſhe fleteth.
And where ſhe turnth, he turnth her there to beare.
The one pray pricketh, the other ſafties feare.
So were we chaſed, ſo fled we afore our foes.
Yet flight then fight in ſo vneuen cloſe.
I end. Some thinke perhaps, to long he ſtaieth
In perill preſent ſhewing his fyxed faith.

This ventred I, this dread I did ſuſtaine,
To try my truth, my life I did diſdaine.
But, loe, lyke tryall againſt his ciuill foe.
Faiths worſt is tryail, which is reſerued to woe.
I paſſe our ſcape, and ſharpe retourning home,
Where we were welcomd by our wonted fone.
To battaile mayne diſcends the empyres right.
At Barnet ioyne the hoaſts in bloudy fight.

There ioynd three battayles ranged in ſuch array,
As mought for terrour Alexander fray.
What ſhould I ſtay to tell the long diſcourſe?
Who wan the palme? who bare away the worſe?

The Lord Hastings.

Suffyseth to say by my reserued band,
Our enemies fled, we had the vpper hand.
My iron army held her steady place,
My prince to shield, his feared fo to chase.

The like successe befell me in Tewkesburie field,
My furious force, there for so perforce, to peeld
The traitour foe: and render to my king
Her onely son, least he more bate might bring.
Thus hast thou a mirrour of a subiects mynde,
Such as perhaps is rare againe to fynde:
The caruing cuts, that cleaue the trusty steele,
My faith, and due allegiaunce, could not fyle.

But out alas, what praise may I recount,
That is not spiced with spot, that doth surmount
My greatest vaunt? for bloudy war to feete
A Tyger was I, all for peace vnmeete,
A Souldiers hands must oft be dyed with goare,
Least starke with rest, they sinewd war and hoare.
Peace could I win by war, but peace not vse.
Few dayes enioy he, who warlike peace doth chose.

When Crofts a knight presented Henries heir
To this our prince, in furious moode enquere
Of him began, what folly or phrensy vaine,
With arms forst him to inuade his realme?
Whome answering, that he claimd his fathers right:
With gauntlet smit, commaunded from his sight:
Clarence, Glocester, Dorcet, and I Hastings slue.
The guilt wherof we shortly all did rue.

Clarence

The Lorde Hastings.

Clarence, as Cirus, drowud in bloudlike wyne,
Dorcet I furthered to his spedy pyne.
Of me, my selfe am speaking president,
Nor easier fate the bristled Boare is lent.
Our blouds haue payd the vengeaunce of our guilt,
His fryed bones, shall broyle for bloud he hath spilt.
O waltsome murther, that attainteth our fame.
O horrible traitours wanting worthy name.

Who more mischieuously of all states deserue,
As better they, who such did first preserue.
If those, for gifts, we recken heauenly wights,
These may we well deeme fends, and damned sprites.
And while on earth they walke, disguysed deuils,
Sworne foes of vertue, factours for all euils.
Whose bloudy hands torment their goared harts.
Through bloudsheds horrour, in soundest sleye he sterts.

O happy world were the Lyons men:
All Lyons should at least be spared then.
No suerty now, no lasting league is bloud.
A meacocke is, who dreadth to see blud shed.
Stale is the paterne, the fact must nedes be rife.
While.ii. were armies ii. the issues of first wife,
With armed hart and hand, the one bloudy brother,
With cruell chase pursueth and murdreth th'other.

Which who deñeth not: yet who ceaseth to sue?
The bloudy Caynes their bloudy fyre renewe.
The horrour yet is like in common frayes.
For in ech murther, brother brother slayes.

Traytours

The Lorde Hastings.

Follo. 98

Traitours to nature, countrey kin and kynde.
Whome no band serueth in brothers scale to bynde.
O simple age, when slaunder slaughter was.
The tonges small euill, how doth this mischiefe passe?

Hopest thou to cloake couert thy mischief wrought?
Thy conscience, Captif, shall proclaime thy thought.
A vision, Chaucer sheweth, diseldasd thy cryme.
The foxe descry the crowes and chattring pyen.
And shall thy felow felons, not bewray
The guiltlesse death, whome guilty hands do slay?
Unpunished scapes for haynous cryme some one,
But vnadvenged, in mynde or body, none.

Vengeaunce on my mynde, the freating furies take.
The sinfull coarse, lyke earthquake agewes shake.
Their frowning lookes, theyr frounced myndes bewray.
In hast they run, and mids their race they stay,
As gidded roe. Amids their speach they whist,
At meate thy muse. No where they may persist
But some feare netleth them. Ay hang they so.
So neuer wanteth the wicked murtherer wo.

An infant rent with Lyons ramping pawes?
Why slaunder I Lyons? They feare the sacred lawes
Of princes bloud. Ay me more brute than beast,
With princes sides, (Licaons ype) to feast?
O tyrant Tigris, O insatiable wolues,
O English curtesie, monstrous mawes and gulfes.
My death shall forthwith preach my earned meede.
Yf fyrst to one lyke murther I proceede.

Whyle

The Lorde Hastings

While Edward liued, dissembled discord lurked:
In double harts yet so his reuerence worked.
But when succeding tender feble age,
Gaue open gap to tirants rushing rage:
I holpe the Boare, and Buck, to captiuate
Lord Riuers, Gray, Sir Thomas Vaughan and Hawte.
Yf land would help the sea, well earnd that ground
Hit selfe, to be with conquering waues surround.

Their spedy death by priuy dome procured,
At Pomfret: their my life short while endured.
My selfe I slue, when them I damned to death.
At once my throate I riued, and reft them breath.
For that selfe day, afore or neare the hower
That whithred Atropos nipt that springing flower
With vyolent hand, of their forth running lyfe:
My head and body, in Tower twynd lyke knyfe.

By this my paterne, all ye peers beware.
Oft hangeth he him selfe, who others weenth to snare.
Spare to be ech others butcher. Feare the Kite,
Who soareth aloft, while frog and mouse do fight.
In ciuill combat, grappling void of feare
Of foreyne foe at once all both to beare.
Which plainer by my pytied plaint to see,
A while anew your listning lend to me.

To true it is, two sondry assemblies kept,
At Crosbies place, and Baynards Castell set.
The Dukes at Crosbies, but at Baynards we.
The one to crowne a King, the other to be.

Suffolk

The Lorde Hastings.

Suspicious is secession of foule frends,
When eythers drift to others mischif tends,
I feared the end, my Catesbies being there
Discharged all douts. Hym held I most entyre.

Whose great preferment by my means, I thought
Some spurre, to pray the thankfulnes he ought.
The trust he ought me, made me trust him so
That priuy he was both to my weale and woe.
My harts one halfe, my chest of confidence,
My tresures trust, my ioye dwelt in his presence.
I loued him Baldwin, as the apple of mine eye.
I lothed my life when Catesby would me dye.

Flye from thy chanell Thames, forsake thy streames,
Leaue the Adamannt Iron, Phœbus lay thy beames:
Ceasse heauenly Sphears at last your weary warke,
Betray your charge, retourne to Chaos darke.
At least, some ruthles Tiger hang her whelpe,
My Catesbies so with some excuse to help.
And me to comfort, that I alone, ne seme
Of all dame natures workes least in extreme.

A Golden treasure is the tryed frend.
But who may Gold from counterfaits defend?
Trust not so soone, ne all to light mistrust.
With th'one thy selfe with th'other thy frend thou hurtst.
Who twyneth betwixt, and steareth the golden meane,
Nor rashly loueth, nor mistrusteth in vayne.
For frendship poyson, for safety mithridate
Pitis, thy frend to loue as thou wouldest hate.

D i.   Of tickle

The Lorde Haſtings

Of tickle credit ne had ben the miſchief,
What neded Virbius miracle doubled life?
Credulity ſurnamed firſt the Aegean ſeas.
Miſtruſt, doth treſon in the truſtieſt rayſe.
Suſpicions Romulus, ſtaind his walls firſt reard
With brothers bloud, whome for light leape he feard.
So not in brotherhood ielouſie may be borne,
The iealous cuckold weares the infamous horne.

A beaſt may preach by tryall, not foreſight.
Could I haue ſhond this credit, nere had light
The dreaded death, vpon my guilty head.
But fooles are wont to learne by after reade.
Had Cateſby kept vnſtain, the truth he plight,
Yet had ye enioy'd me, and I yet the light
All Derbies douts I clered with his name.
I knew, no harme could hap vs, ſauns his blame.

But ſee the fruites of fickle light beliefe.
The ambitious Dukes corrupt the traitour theſe,
To groape me, if allured I would aſſent,
To bin a partner of their curſde entent.
Wherto, when neither force nor frendſhip vaylde,
By tirant force their purpoſe they aſſailde.
And ſummond ſhortly a counſaile in the tower,
Of June the fiftenth, at apointed hower.

Alas, are counſels wryed to catch the good?
Is no place now exempt from ſheading bloud.
Sith counſels, that were carefull to preſerue
The guiltleſſe good, are meanes to make them ſtarue.

What may

The Lord Haſtings.

What may not miſchief of mad man abuſe:
Religious cloake ſome one to vice doth chuſe,
And maketh God protectour of his cryme.
O monſtrous world, well ought we wiſh thy fyne.

The fatall ſkies, roll on the blackeſt day,
When doubled bloudſhed, my bloud muſt repay.
Others none forceth. To me ſir Thomas Haward
As ſpurre is buckled, to prouoke me forward.
Derbie who feared the party ſittings pore.
Whether, much more he knew by experience hoare,
Or vnaffected, clearer truth could ſee:
At midnight darke this meſſage ſends to me.

Haſtings away, in ſlepe the Gods foreſhew
By dreadfull dreame, fell fates vnto vs two.
He thought a Boare with tuſke ſo raſed our throats,
That both our ſhoulders of the bloud did ſmoake.
Ariſe to horſe, ſtraight homeward let vs hye.
And ſith our foe we may not mate, O flye.
Of Chaunteclere you learne dreames ſoth to know
Thence wiſe men conſter, more then the cocke doth crow.

While thus he ſpake, I held with in myne arme
Shores wyfe, the tender peece, to kepe me warme.
Fye on adultery, fye on lecherous luſt.
Marke in me ye nobles all, Gods iudgements iuſt.
A Pandare, Murtherer, and Adulterer thus,
Onely ſuch death I dye, as I ne bluſhe.
Now leaſt my dame mought feare appall my hart:
With eger moode vp in my bed I ſtart.

      O ii.   And, is

The Lorde Hastings

And, is thy Lord (quoth I) a sorcerer?
A wise man now become a dreame reader?
What though so Chaunteclere crowed? I reke it not.
On my part pleadeth as well dame Partelot.
Uniudgde hangth yet the case betwixt them tway.
Ne was his dreame cause of his hap I say.
Shall dreming douts from prince my seruing slacke?
Nay, then mought Hastings lyfe and liuing lacke.

He parteth. I sleepe. my mynde surcharged with sinne,
As Phœbus beames by misty cloud kept in,
Ne could misgeue, ne dreame of my mishap.
As blocke I tumbled to myne enemies trap.
Security causles through my carelesse frende,
Reft me foresight of my approching end.
So Catesby clawed me, as when the Cat doth play
Dalieng with mouse whome straight she myndes to slay.

The morow come, the latest light to me,
On palfray mounted, to the tower I hye.
Accompanied with that Haward my mortall foe,
To slaughter led. thou God wouldst haue it so.
(O depe dissemblers, honouring with your cheare,
Whome in hid hart ye trayterously teare.)
Neuer had realme so open signs of wracke,
As I had shewed me of my heauy hap.

The vision first of Stanley, late descryed.
Then mirth so extreme, that neare for ioy I dyed.
Were hit, that Swanlike I foresong my death,
Or mery mynde foresaw the loose of breath

          That long

The Lorde Hastings.

That long it coueited, from this earths annoye.
But euen as siker as th'end of woe is ioye,
And glorious light to obscure night doth tend:
So extreame mirth in extreme moane doth end.

For why, extreames are haps rackt out of course,
By vyolent might far swinged forth perforce.
Whiche as they are pearcingst while they violenst moue,
For nearest they cleaue to cause that doth them shoue:
So soonest fall from that their highest extreame,
To th'other contrary that doth want of meane.
So lawghed he erst, who lawghed out his breath,
So lawghed I, whan I lawghd my selfe to death.

The pleasingst means boade not the luckiest ends.
Not aye, found treasure to like pleasure tends.
Mirth meanes not mirth all tyme, thryse happy hyre
Of wit, to shun the excesse that all desyre.
But this I passe. I hye to other like:
My palfrey in the plainest paued streete,
Thrise bowed his boanes, thrise kneled on the flower,
Thrise shond (as Balams asse) the dreaded tower.

What? should I thinke he had sence of after haps?
As beasts foreshew the drought or rainy drops,
As humours in them want or els abound,
By influence from the heauens, or chaunge of ground,
Or do we interpret by successe ech sygne?
And as we fancy of ech hap deuyne?
And make that cause, that kin is to th'effect?
Not hauing ought of consequence respect?

D. iii.   Bucephalus

The Lorde Hastings.

Bucephalus kneeling onely to his Lorde,
Shewed onely, he was, monarche of the world.
Why may not then, the steede foreshewe by fall,
What casuall hap the sitter happen shall:
Darius horse by brayinge brought a realme.
And what letteth, why he ne is (as the asse) Gods meane,
By speaking signe, to shew his hap to come,
Who is deafe hearer of his speaking domme?

But forward yet. In tower streete I stayed
Where (could I haue seene) loe Haward all bewrayed
For as I commond with a priest I met:
A way my Lord quoth he, your tyme is ne yet
To take a priest. Loe, Synon might be seene,
Had Troyans eares, as they had hares foole eyen.
But, whom thou God allotted hast to dye
Some grace it is to dy with wimpled eye.

Ne was this all. For euen at Towerwharfe,
Neare to those walles within whose sight I starfe,
Where earst in sorow soust and depe distresse,
I emparted all my pyninge pensifenesse
With Hastings: (so my purseuaunt men call)
Euen there, the same to meete hit did me fall.
Who gan to me most dolefully renewe,
The wofull conferrence had erst in that Lieu.

Hastings (quoth I) according now thy fare,
At Pomfret this day dying, who caused that care.
My selfe haue all the world at my will,
With pleasures cloyed, engorged with the fill.
         God graunt

The Lorde Hastings.

God graunt it so quoth he, why doutest thou tho
Quoth I: and all in chafe to him gan shewe
In ample wise, our drift with tedious tale,
And entred so the tower to mpbale.

What should we thinke of signes they are but haps,
How may they then, be signes of afterclaps?
Doth euery chaunce foreshew or cause some other?
Or tending at it selfe, extendth no furder?
As th'ouerflowing floud some mount doth choake,
But to his ayde some other floud hit poake:
So if with signes thy sinns once ioyne, beware.
Els wherto chaunces tend, nere curious care.

Had not my sinne deserued my death as wreake,
What might my mirth haue hurt? or horses becke?
Or Hawards bitter scoffe? or Hastings talke?
What meane then foole Astrologers to calke,
When nature seemd to slow by arts sloape meane,
Conueyghed him sooner to his liues extreame.
Happy, in preuenting woes that after hapt,
In slumber swete his liuing lights he lapt.

Whose thus vntymely death, if any grieue:
Knowe he, he lyued to dye, and dyed to liue.
Vntymely neuer coms the liues last met.
In cradell death may rightly clayme his det.
Straight after birth due is the fatall beere.
By deaths permission the aged linger here.
Euen in the swathbands out commission goeth
To loose thy breath, that yet but pongly bloweth.

D iiii.   Happy

The Lorde Hastings.

Happy, thryse happy, who so loosth his breath,
As life he gayneth by his liuing death.
As Hastings here. Whome tyme and truth agree,
To engraue by fame in strong eternity.
Who spareth not spitting, if he spit but bloud:
Yet this our Lord, spared not for others good,
With one swete breath his present death to speake,
Against the vsurpour Bore, that hellish freake.

Worthy to lyue, but liued not for himselfe
But prised his fame more then this worldly pelfe.
Whose name and lyne, if any yet preserue,
We wish they liue like honour to deserue.
Whether thou seke by martiall prowesse prayse,
Or Pallas pollicie high thy name to rayse,
Or trusty seruice iust death to attaine:
Hastings foreled. Trace here his bloudy trayne.

FINIS. Maister. D.

Dohan

Maister Sackuils induction.

When I had read this, one saide it was very darke, and hard to be vnderstoode: except it were diligentlye and very leasurely conſydered. I lyke it the better (saide an other.) For that shall cause it to be the oftner read, and the better remembred. Consydering also that it is wrytten for the learned (for such all Magistrates are or shoulde be) it cannot be to harde, so longe as it is sound and learnedly written. Then saide the reader: The next here whome I fynde miserable are king Edwards two sonnes, cruellye murdered in the tower of London: Haue you their tragedy?

No surely (saide I) The Lord Vault vndertooke to pen it, but what he hath done therein I am not certayne, and therefore I lette it passe tyll I knowe farder.

I haue here the Duke of Buckingham, kinge Richards chiefe instrument, written by maister Thomas Sackuille. Reade it we praye you saide they: with a good will (quoth I) but first you shall heare his preface or induction. Hath hee made a preface (saide one) what meaneth he thereby, seinge none other hath vsed ye like order? I will tell you the cause thereof (said I) which is this: After that hee vnderstoode that some of the counsayl would not suffer the booke to be printed in such order as wee had agreed and determined, he purposed to haue gotten at my hands, all the tragedies that were before the Duke of Buckinghams, which he would haue preserued in one volume. And from ye tyme backward euen to

Maister Sackuils induction.

euen to the tyme of Wyllyam the Conquerour; hee determined to contynue and perfecte all the storye him selfe, in such order as Lydgate (folowing Bochas) had alreadye vsed. And therefore to make a meete induction into ye matter, he deuised this poesie: whiche in my iudgement is so well penned, that I would not haue any verse thereof left out of oure volume. Now that you know the cause & meaning of his doing, you shall also heare what he hath done. His Induction beginneth thus.

¶ THE INDVCTION.

The wrathfull winter proching on a pace,
With blustring blasts had all ybarde the treen,
And old Saturnus with his frosty face
With chilling cold had pearst the tender greene:
The mantels rent, wherein enwrapped bene
The gladsome groaues that now lay ouerthrown,
The tapets torne, and euery tree down blown.

The soyle that earst so seemly was to seen
Was all despoiled of her beauties hewe:
And soote fresh flowers (wherwith the somers queen
Had clad the earth) now Borcas blasts down blewe.
And small foules flocking, in their song did rewe
The winters wrath, wherwith ech thing defaste:
In wofull wise bewayd the somer past.

Hawthorne

Maister Sackuils Induction.

Hawthorne had lost his motley lyuery,
The naked twigs were shiuering all for cold:
And dropping downe the tears aboundantly,
Ech thing (me thought) with weping eye me tolde
The cruell season, bidding me withholde
My selfe within for I was gotten out
Into the fields wheras I walkt about.

When loe the night with misty mantles spred
Gan darke the day, and dim the azure skies,
And Venus in her message Hermes sped
To bloudy Mars, to will him not to ryse,
While she her selfe approcht in spedy wyse:
And Virgo hiding her disdainfull brest
With Thetis now had layd her downe to rest.

Whiles Scorpio dreading Sagittarius dart,
Whose bow prest bent in fight, the string had slipt,
Down slyd into the Ocean flud aparte,
The Beare that in the Irish seas had dipt
His griesly feete, with spede from thence he whipt:
For Thetis hasting from the Virgins bed,
Pursued the Beare, that eare she came was fled.

And Phaeton now neare reaching to his race
With glistring beams, gold streaming where they bent,
Was prest to enter in his resting place.
Erithius that in the cart fyrst went
Had euen now attaind his iourneis stent.
And fast declining hid away his head,
While Titan choucht him in his purple bed.

And pale

Maister Sackeuils induction.

And pale Cinthea with her borrowed light
Beginning to supply her brothers place,
Was past the none stede sixe degrees in sight
When sparkling stars amid the heauens face
With twinkling light shone on the earth apace,
That while they brought about the nights chare,
The darke had dimde the day ere I was ware.

And sorrowing I to se the sommer flowers,
The liuely grene, the lusty leafe forlorne,
The sturdy trees so shattred with the showers,
The fields so fade that florisht so beforne,
It taught me well all earthly things be borne
To dye the death for nought long tyme may last,
The somers beauty yelds to winters blast.

Then looking vpward to the heauens leames
With nights stars thicke powdred euery where,
Which erst so glistned with the golden streames
That chearfull Phœbus spred downe from his spheres,
Beholding darke oppressing day so neare:
The sodain sight reduced to my mynde,
The sundry chaunges that in earth we fynde.

That musing on this worldly wealth in thought,
Which coms and goes more faster than we see
The flickring flame that with the fyre is wrought,
My busie mynde presented vnto me
Such fall of piers as in the realme had be:
That oft I wisht some would their woes descryue,
To warne the rest whome Fortune left a liue.

          And strayt

Maister Sackuils Induction.

And strait forth stalking with redoubled pace
For that I sawe the night drew on so fast,
In blacke all clad there fell before my face
A piteous wight, whome wo had all fore wast,
Forth on her eyes the cristall teares out brast,
And sighing sore her hands she wrong and folde,
Tare all her heare that ruth was to behold.

Her body small forwithred and forspent,
As is the stalke that sommers drought opprest,
Her wealked face with wofull teares besprent,
Her coulour pale, (as it semed her best)
In wo and plaint reposed was her rest.
And as the stone that drops of water weares,
So dented were her chekes with fall of teares.

Her eyes swollen with flowing streames aflote,
Wherewith her lokes throwen vp full piteously,
Her forcelesse hands together oft she smote,
With dolefull shrikes, that eckoed in the skye:
Whose plaint such sighes did strait accompany,
That in my doome was neuer man did see
A wight but halfe so woe begone as she.

I stoode agast beho'lding all her plight,
Tweene dread and dolour so distreinde in hart
That while my heares vpstarted with the sight,
The tears out streamd for sorow of her smart:
But when I sawe no end that could appart
The deadly dewle, which she so sore did make,
With dolefull voice then thus to her I spake.

Vnwrappe

Maister Sackeuils induction.

Unwrap thy woes what euer wight thou be
And stint in tyme to spill thy selfe with plaint,
Tell what thou art, and whence, for well I see
Thou canst not dure with sorrow thus attaint.
And with that word of sorrow all forfaint
She loked vp, and prostrate as she lay
With piteous sound lo thus she gan to say.

Alas, I wretch whome thus thou seest distreyned
With wasting woes that neuer shall aslake,
Sorrowe I am, in endlesse torments payned,
Among the furies in the infernall lake:
Where Pluto God of Hell so griesly blacke
Doth holde his throane, and Lætheus deadly taste
Doth rieue remembraunce of ech thing forepast.

Whence come I am, the drery desteny
And luckelesse lot for to bemone of those,
Whome Fortune in this maze of miserie
Of wretched chaunce most wofull myrrours chose
That when thou seest how lightly they did lose
Their pompe, their power, and that they thought most
Thou maiest soone deme no earthly ioy may dure.

Whose rufull voice no soner had outbrayed
Those wofull words, wherewith she sorowed so,
But out alas she shright and neuer stayed,
Fell down, and all to dasht her selfe for woe.
The colde pale dread my lyms gan ouergoe
And I so sorrowed at her sorrowes eft,
That what with griefe and feare my wits were reft.

I stretcht

Maister Sackuils induction.

I stretcht my selfe, and strait my hart reuiues,
That dread and dolour erst did so appale,
Lyke him that with the feruent feuer striues
When sicknesse seekes his castell health to skale
With gathred sprites so forst I feare to auale.
And rearing her with anguish all fordone,
My sprits return'd, and then I thus begon.

O Sorrow, alas sith Sorrow is thy name,
And that to thee this drere doth well pertaine,
In vaine it were to seeke to cease the same:
But as a man himselfe with sorrow slaine,
So I alas do comfort the in paine,
That here in sorrow art forsonke so depe
That at thy sight I can but sigh and wepe.

I had no soner spoken of a stike
But that the storme so rumbled in her brest,
As Eölus could neuer roare the like,
And showers downe raind from her eies so fast,
That all bedreint the place, till at the last
Well easd they the dolour of her minde,
As rage of rayne doth swage the stormy winde.

For forth she paced in her fearfull tale:
Come, come, (quod she) and see what I shall showe,
Come heare the plaining, and the bitter bale
Of worthy men, by Fortune ouerthrowe.
Come thou and see them rewing all in rowe.
They were but shades that erst in mynde thou rolde.
Come, come with me, thine eyes shall them beholde.

What could

Maister Sackuils Induction.

What could these woordes but make me more agast?
To heare her tell whereon I musde whyle ere?
So was I mazde therewith: till at the last,
Musing vpon her wordes, and what they were,
All sodaynly well lessoned was my feare:
For to my mynde retourned how she teld
Both what she was, and where her wun she held.

Wherby I knewe that she a Goddesse was,
And therewithall resorted to my mynde
My thought, that late presented me the glas
Of brittle state, of cares that here we fynd,
Of thousand woes to sely men assynde:
And how she now bid me come and beholde
To see with eye that erst in thought I rolde.

Flat down I fell, and with all reuerence
Adored her, perceiuing now that she
A Goddesse sent by godly prouidence,
In earthly shape thus showd her selfe to me,
To wayle and rue this worlds certainty:
And while I honourd thus her godheds might,
With plaining voyce these wordes to me she shright.

I shall the guyde first to the griesly lake,
And thence vnto the blissfull place of rest.
Where thou shalt see and heare the plaint they make,
That whilome here bare swynge among the best.
This shalt thou see, but great is the vnrest
That thou must byde before thou canst attaine
Vnto the dreadfull place where these remaine.

         And with

Maister Sackuils induction.

And with these words as I vpraysed stood,
And gan to folowe her that straight forth paste,
Ere I was ware, into a desert wood
We now were come: where hand in hand imbraste,
She led the way, and through the thicke so traste,
As but I had bene guyded by her might,
It was no way for any mortall wight.

But loe, while thus amid the desert darke,
We passed on with steps and pace vnmete:
A rumbling roare confusde with howle and barke
Of Dogs, shoke all the ground vnder our feete,
And stroke the din within our eares so deepe,
As halfe distraught vnto the ground I fell,
Besought retourne, and not to visite hell.

But she forthwith vplifting me a pace
Remoued my dread, and with a stedfast mynde
Bad me com on, for heare was now the place,
The place where we our trauaile end should fynde.
Wherewith I rose, and to the place assynde
Astoinde I stalke, when straight we approched nere
The dreadfull place, that you will dread to here.

And hydeous hole all vaste, withouten shape,
Of endles depth, orewhelmde with ragged stone,
With ougly mouth, and griesly iawes doth gape,
And to our sight confounds it selfe in one.
Here entred we, and yeding forth, anone
An horrible lothly lake we might discerne
As blacke as pitch, that cleped is Auern.

P i.   A deadly

Maister Sackeuils induction.

A deadly gulfe where nought but rubbish growes,
With fowle blacke swelth in thickned lumps that lyes,
Which vp in th'ayre such stinking vapors throws
That ouer there, may flye no fowle but dyes,
Choakt wyth the pestlent sauours that aryse.
Hither we come, whence forth we still did pace,
In dreadfull feare amid the dreadfull place.

And first within the porch and iawes of Hell
Sate diepe Remorse of conscieuce, all be sprent
With teares: and to her selfe oft would she tell
Her wretchednes, and cursing neuer stent
To sob and sighe: but euer thus lament,
With thoughtfull care, as she that all in vayne
Would weare and wast continually in payne.

Her eyes vnstedfast rolling hereand there,
Whurld on ech place, as place that vengeaunce brought,
So was her mynde continually in feare,
Tossed and tormented with tedious thought
Of those detested crymes which she had wrought:
With dreadfull cheare and lookes throwen to the skie,
Wishing for death, and yet she could not dye.

Next saw we Dread all trembling how he shooke,
With foote vncertain profered here and there:
Benumbd of speach, and with a ghastly looke
Searcht euery place all pale and dead for feare,
His cap borne vp with staring of his heare,
Stoynd and amazdeat his owne shade for drede,
And fearing greater daungers than was nede.

                                                  And next

Maister Sackeuils induction.

And next within the entry of this lake
Sate fell Reuenge gnashing her teth for irc,
Deuising meanes how she may vengeaunce take,
Neuer in rest tyll she haue her desire:
But frets within so farforth with the fyer
Of wreaking flames, that now determines she,
To dy by death, or vengde by death to be.

When fell Reuenge with bloudy foule pretence
Had showd her selfe as next in order set,
With trembling lims we softly parted thence,
Tyll in our eyes another sight we met:
When fro my hart a sigh forthwith I fet,
Rewing alas vpon the woefull plight
Of Misery, that next appeard in sight.

His face was leane, and somedeale pyned away,
And eke his hands consumed to the bone,
But what his body was I cannot say,
For on his carkas raiment had he none
Saue clouts and patches pieced one by one.
With staffe in hand, and scrip on shoulder cast,
His chief defence against the winters blast.

His foode for most, was wylde fruites of the tree,
Vnlesse sometyme some crums fell to his share:
Which in his wallet long God wot kept he,
As on the which full daintely would fare
His drinke the running streame: his cup the bare
Of his palme closde, his bed the hard colde ground.
To this pore lyfe was Misery ybound.

P.ii. Whose

Maister Sackeuils induction.

Whose wretched state when we had well behelde
With tender ruth on him and on his feres,
In thoughtfull cares, forth then our pace we helde.
And by and by, another shape apperes
Of gredy care, still brushing vp the breres,
His knuckles knobde, his flesh depe dented in,
With tawed hands, and hard ytanned skin.

The morrowe gray no sooner hath begon
To spreade his light euen peping in our eyes,
When he is vp and to his worke yrun,
But let the nights blacke misty mantles rise,
And with foule darke neuer so much disguise
The fayre bright day, yet ceasseth he no while,
But hath his candels to prolong his toyle.

By him lay heauy slepe the cosin of death
Flat on the ground, and still as any stone,
A very corps, saue yelding forth a breth.
Small kepe tooke he whome Fortune frowned on
Or whome she lifted vp into the trone
Of high renowne, but as a liuing death,
So dead aliue, of life he drew the breath.

The bodies rest, the quyet of the hart,
The trauailes ease, the still nights feare was he.
And of our lyfe in earth the better part,
Reuer of sight, and yet in whome we see
Things oft that tyde, and oft that neuer bee.
Without respect esteming equally
King Cresus pompe, and Irus pouertie.

            And next

Maister Sackuils induction.

And next in order sad Olde age we founde
His beard all hoare, his eyes hollow and blynde,
With drouping chere still poring on the ground,
As on the place where nature him assynde
To rest, when that the sisters had but wounde
His vitall thred, and ended with their knyfe
The fleting course of fast declyning lyfe.

There hard we him with broken and hollow plaint
Rewe with him selfe his end approching fast,
And all for nought his wretched mynde torment,
With swete remembraunce of his pleasures past,
And fresh delytes of lusty youth forewaste.
Recounting which, how would he sob and shrike,
And to be yonge agayne of Ioue beseke.

But and the cruell fates so fixed be
That tyme forepast cannot retourne agayne,
This one request of Ioue yet prayed be:
That in such wichred plight, and wretched paine,
As elde (accompanied with his lothsome trayne.)
Had brought on him, all were it woe and griefe,
He might a while yet linger forth his lief,

And not so sone discend into the pit:
Where death, when he the mortall corps hath slaine,
With retchlesse hand in graue doth couer it,
Therafter neuer to enioye agayne
The gladsome light, but in the ground playne,
In depth of darknesse waste and weare to nought;
As he had neuer into the world bene brought.

P iii.   But who

Maister Sackeuills induction.

But who had seene him sobbing, how he stoode
Unto himselfe and how he would bemone
His youth forepast, as though it wrought him good
To talke of youth, all were his youth foregone,
He would haue mused, and meruayled much whereon
This wretched age should lyfe desire so fayne,
And knowes full well lyfe doth but length his payne.

Crookebackt he was, tooth shaken, and blere eyed,
Went on thre feet, and sometyme crept on fower,
With olde lame boanes, that ratled by his syde,
His scalpe all pilde, and he with eld forlore:
His withred fist still knocking at deaths dore,
Fumbling and driueling as he drawes his breath,
For briefe the shape and messenger of death.

And fast by him pale malady was plaste,
Sore sicke in bed, her coulour all foregone,
Bereft of stomacke sauour and of taste,
Ne could she brooke no meate but brothes alone,
Her breath corrupt, her kepers euery one
Abhorring her, her sickenes past recure,
Detesting phisicke, and all phisicks cure.

But oh the dolefull sight that than we see,
We tourned our looke and on the other side
A grieslye shape of famyne mought we see,
With gredy lookes, and gaping mouth that cryed,
And roarde for meate as she should there haue dyed,
Her body thin and bare as any bone,
Wherto was left nought but the case alone.

        And that

Maister Sackeuils induction.

And that alas was gnawen on euery where,
All full of holes, that I ne mought refrayne
From teares to se how shee her armes could teare
And with her teeth gnash on the bones in vayne:
When all for nought shee fayne would so sustayne
Her staruen corps, that rather seemd a shade,
Then any substaunce of a creature made.

Great was her force whome stonewall could not stay,
Her tearing nayles snatching at all she sawe:
With gaping iawes that by ne meanes ymay
Be satisfyed from hunger of her mawe,
But eates her selfe as she that hath no lawe:
Gnawing alas her carkas all in vayne,
Where you may count ech sinow, bone, and vayne.

On her while we thus firmly fixt our eyes,
That bled for ruth of such a drery sight,
Loe sodainly she shright in so huge wise,
As made hell gates to shiuer with the might.
Wherewith a dart we sawe how it did light,
Right on her brest, and therewithall pale death
Enthrilling it to reue her of her breath.

And by and by a dinn dead corps we sawe,
Heauy and colde, the shape of death aright,
That daunts all earthly creatures to his lawe:
Against whose force in vayne it is to fight
Ne Piers, ne Princes, nor no mortall wyght,
No townes, ne realmes, cittyes, ne strongest tower,
But all perforce must yelde vnto his power.

                       P iiii.   His dart

Maister Sackuils induction.

His dart anon out of the corps he tooke,
And in his hand (a dreadfull sight to see)
With great triumph eftsones the same he shoke,
That most of all my feares affrayed me:
His body dight with nought but bones perdye
The naked shape of man there saw I playne)
All saue the flesh, the sinowe, and the vayne.

Lastly stoode Warre in glittering armes yclad,
With visage grym, sterne lookes, and blackly hewed
In his right hand a naked sword he had,
That to the hilts was all with bloud embrued:
And in his left (that King and kingdomes rewed)
Famine and fyer he helde, and therewithall
He razed townes, and threw downe towers and all.

Cities he sakt, and realms that whilome flowred,
In honour, glory, and rule aboue the best,
He ouerwhelmde, and all their fame deuoured,
Consumde, destroyde, wasted, and neuer ceast,
Tyll he their wealth, their name, and all opprest.
His face forehewed with woundes, and by his side,
There hunge his targe with gashes depe and wyde.

In mids of which, depainted there we founde
Deadly debate, all full of snaky heare,
That with a bloudy fillet was ybound,
Outbrething nought but discord euery where.
And round about were portrayde here and there
The hugie hostes, Darius and his power,
His Kings, Princes, his Piers, and all his flower.

Whome

Maister Sackuils Induction.

Whom great Macedo vanquisht there in sight,
With deepe slaughter, despoyling all his pryde,
Pearst through his realms, and daunted all his might.
Duke Hanniball beheld I there besyde,
In Cannas field, victor how he did ryde,
And wofull Romaines that in vayne withstoode
And Consull Paulus couered all in blood.

Yet sawe I more the sight at Trasimene,
And Treberie fyeld, and eke when Hanniball
And worthy Scipio last in arms were seene
Before Carthago gate, to try for all
The worlds empyre, to whome it should befall.
There saw I Pompey, and Cæsar clad in arms,
Their hoasts allyed and all their ciuill harms.

With Conquerers hands forbathde in their owne bloud,
And Cæsar weping ouer Pompeis head:
Yet saw I Scilla and Marius where they stood,
Their great crueltie, and the diepe bludshed
Of frends: Cyrus I sawe and his hoast dead,
And how the Queene with greate despite hath flonge
His head in bloud of them she ouercome.

Xerxes the Percian King yet sawe I there
With his huge host that dranke the riuers drye,
Dismounted hills and made the vales vpreare,
His hoste and all yet saw I slayne perdye,
Thebes I sawe all razde how it did lye
In heapes of stones, and Tyrus put to spoyle,
With walls and towers flat euened with the soyle.

Bus

But Troy alas (me thought) aboue them all,
It made myne eyis in very teares consume:
When I behelde the wofull werd befall,
That by the wrathfull will of God was come:
And Ioues vnmoued sentence and foredoome
On Priam king, and on his towne so bent.
I could not lin, but I must there lament.

And that the more sith destenye was so shrewde,
As force perforce, there might no force auayle,
But she must fall: and by her fall we learne,
That cities, towers, wealth, world, and all shall quayle.
No manhood, might, nor nothing maught preuayle,
All were there prest full many a prince and piere
And many a knight that solde his death full dere.

Not worthy Hector worthyest of them all,
Her hope, her ioy, his force is now for naught:
O Troy, Troy, there is no boote but bale,
The hugie horse within thy walls is brought:
Thy turrets fall, thy knights that whilome fought
In armes, amid the field, are slayne in bed,
Thy Gods defylde, and all thy honour dead.

The flames vpprising, and cruelly they creepe
From wall to roofe, till all to cinders waste,
Some fyre the houses where the wretches sleepe,
Some rush in here, some run in there as fast,
In euery where or sword or fyre they taste:
The walls are torne, the towers whurld to the ground,
There is no mischiefe but may there be found.
                                    Cassandra

Maister Sackuills Induction. Folio. 112.

Cassandra yet there sawe I how they haled
From Pallas house, with sperclen tresse vndone,
Her wrists fast bound, and with Greeks rout empaled:
And Priam eke in vayne how he did runne
To armes, whome Pyrrhus with dispite hath done
To cruell death, and bathde him in the bayne
Of his sons bloud before the aultare slayne.

But how can I descryue the dolefull sight,
That in the shield so liuelye fayre did shyne?
Sith in this world I thinke was neuer wight
Could haue set forth the halfe, not halfe so fyne.
I can no more but tell how there is seene
Fayre Ilium fall in burning red gledes downe,
And from the soyle great Troy, Neptunus towne.

Herefrom when scarce I could mine eyes withdrawe
That fylde with teares as doeth the springing well,
We passed on so far forth tyll we sawe
Rude Acheron, a lothsome lake to tell
That boyles and bubs vp swelth as blacke as hell.
Where grisly Charon at their fixed tyde
Still ferries ghostes vnto the farther syde,

The aged God no sooner Sorow spied,
But hasting straite vnto the banke apace
With hollow call vnto the rowte he cryed,
To swarue apart, and geue the Goddesse place.
Strait it was done, when to the shoare we pace,
Where hand in hand as we than linked fast,
Within the boote we are together plaste.

And fourth

Maister Sackuils Induction.

And forth we launch full fraughted to the brinke,
Whan with the vnmoued waight, the rusty keele
Began to cracke as if the same should sinke.
We hoyse vp mast and saple, that in a while,
We set the shore, where scarcely we had while
For to argue, but that we hard anone
A three sound barke confounded all in one.

We had not long forth past, but that we sawe,
Blacke Cerberus the hydeous hound of hell,
With bristles reard, and with a three mouthed Iawe,
Foredinning the ayer with his horrible yell.
Out of the diepe darke caue where he did dwell,
The Goddesse straight he knew, and vp and vp
He peast and crouched, whils that we passed by.

Thence come we to the horrour and the hell,
The large greate kingdomes, and the dreadfull raygne
Of Pluto in his trone where he did dwell,
The wide wast places, and the hugie playne:
The waylings, shrikes, and sundry sortes of payne,
The sighes, the sobs, the diepe and deadly grones,
Earth, ayer, and all resounding playnt and moane.

Here pewed the babes, and here the maydes vnwed
With folded hands their sory chaunce bewayld,
Here wept the guiltlesse slayne, and louers dead,
That slew themselues when nothing els auayld:
A thousand sorts of sorrowes here that wayld
With sighs and teares, sobs, shrikes, and all yfere,
That (oh alas) it was a hell to heare.

           We stayed

Maister Sackeuils induction.

We staied vs strait, and with a rufull feare,
Behelde this heauy sight, while from myne eyes,
The vapored teares down stilled here and there,
And Sorrow eke in far more wofull wise.
Tooke on with plaint, vp heauing to the skies
Her wretched hands, that with her cry the rout
Gan all in heapes to swarme vs round about.

Loe here (quoth Sorowe) Princes of renowne,
That whilom sate on top of Fortunes whyele
Now layde full low, like wretches whurled downe,
Euen with one frowne, that stayed but with a smyle,
And now beholde the thing that thou erewhile,
Saw only in thought, and what thou now shalt heare
Recompt the same to Kesar, King, and Pier.

Then first came Henry Duke of Buckingham,
His cloake of blacke all pilde and quite forworne,
Wringing his hands, and Fortune oft doth blame,
Whiche of a Duke hath made him now her skorne.
With gastly lokes as one in maner lorne,
Oft sp;ed his armes, stretcht hands beioynes as fast,
With rufull cheare, and vapored eyes vpcast.

His cloake he reut, his manly breast he beat,
His heare all torne about the place it lay,
My hart so molte to see his griefe so great,
As felingly me thought it dropt awaye:
His eyes they whurlde about withouten staye,
With stormy sighes the place did so complaine,
As if his hart at erh had burst in twayne.

Henry Stafforde

Thrise he began to tell his dolefull tale,
And thrise the sighes did swalow vp his voice,
At ech of which he shriked so withall
As though the heauens riued with the noyse:
Tyll at the last recouering his voice,
Supping the teares that all his brest berainde.
On cruell Fortune weping thus he plainde.

FINIS.

The complaint of Henry Duke of Buckingham.

Who trusts to much to honours highest throne
And warely watch not slye dame Fortunes snare:
Or who in court wil beare the swinge alone,
And wisely weygh not how to wield the care,
Beholde he me, and by my death beware:
Whome flattering Fortune falsely so begylde,
That loe she slewe, where erst ful smoth she smylde.

And Sackuille sith in purpose now thou hast
The wofull fall of princes to descrpue,
Whome Fortune both vplift and eke downe cast,
To shewe thereby the vnsuertye in this lyfe,
Harke well my fall, which I shall shew belyue,
And paynt it forth that all estates may knowe:
Haue they the warning, and be myne the woe,

For noble

Duke of Buckingham.

For noble bloud made me both prince and pier
Yea pierles too, had reason purchast place,
And God with gifts endowed me largely beare.
But what auailes his giftes where failes his grace?
My mothers sire sprönge of a kingly race
And cald was Edmund Duke of Somerset,
Bereft of lyfe ere tyme by nature set.

Whose faythfull hart to Henry sixt so wrought
That neuer he him in weale or woe forsooke,
Till lastly he at Tewkesbury fyeld was cought
Where with an axe his violent death he tooke:
He neuer could King Edwards party brooke,
Tyll by his death he voucht that quarrell good,
In which his sire and graundsire spilt their bloud.

And such was erst my fathers cruell chaunce,
Of Stafford Earle by name that humfrey hight,
Who euer prest did Henries part auaunce,
And neuer ceast tyll at Saynt Albones fight
He lost his life as than did many a knight:
Where eke my graundsire Duke of Buckingham
Was wounded sore and hardly scapt vntane.

But what may boot to stay the sisters three?
When Atropos perforce will cut the threde:
The dolefull day was come when you might see
Northampton field with armed men orespred,
Where fate would algates haue my graundsire dead:
So rushing forth amids the fiercest fight,
He lyued and dyed there in his maisters right.

             In place

Henry Stafforde

In place of whome as it befell my lot,
Like on a stage, so stept I in straite way,
Enioying there but wofully God wot,
As he that had a slender part to play:
To teach therby, in earth no state may stay,
But as our partes abridge or length our age
So passe we all while others fyll the stage.

For of my selfe the dreery fate to plaine,
I was sometyme a prince withouten peere,
When Edward fift began his rufull raigne,
Ay me, than I began that hatefull peare,
To compasse that which I haue bought so deare:
I bare the swinge, I and that wretched wight,
The Duke of Glocester that Richard hight.

For when the fates had reft that royall prince
Edward the fourth, chief mpyrour of that name,
The Duke and I fast ioyned euer since,
In faithfull loue, our secret driftes to frame:
What he thought best, to me so seemde the same,
My selfe not bent so much for to aspyre,
As to fulfill that greedy Dukes desyre.

Whose restlesse mynde sore thirsting after rule,
When that he saw his nephewes both to bene
Through tender yeares as yet vnfit to rule,
And rather ruled by their mothers kin,
There sought he first his mischief to begin,
To plucke from them their mothers frends assynde,
For well he wist they would withstand his mynde.

                                                                                                 Ta folowe.

Duke of Buckingham.

To follow which he ran so headlong swyft,
With eigre thirst of his desired draught,
To seke their deaths that sought to dash his drift,
Of whome the chief the Quenes allies he thought,
That bent therto with mounts of mischief fraught,
He knew their liues would be so sore his let,
That in their deaths his onzly help he set.

And I most cursed caityfe that I was,
Seeing the state vnstedfast how it stoode,
His chiefe complice to bring the same to passe,
Unhappy wretch consented to their blood:
Yea Kings and Piers that swim in worldly good,
In seeking bloud the end aduert you playne,
And see if bloud eye aske not bloud agayne.

Consider Cyrus in your cruell thought,
A makelesse prince in riches and in might,
And weigh in mynde the bloudy dedes he wrought,
In sheading which he set his whole delight:
But see the guerdon lotted to this wight,
He whose huge power no man might ouerthrowe,
Tomyris Quene with great dispite hath slowe.

His head dismembred from his mangled corps,
Her selfe she cast into a vessell fraught
With clottered bloud of them that felt her force:
And with these words a iust rewarde she taught:
Drinke now thy fill of thy despsed draught.
Lee marke the fyne that did this prince befall:
Marke not this one, but marke the ende of all.

Q.i.   Beholde

Henry Stafforde

Beholde Cambises and his fatall daye,
Where murders mischief impyrour lyke is left:
While he his brother Mergus cast to slay,
A dreadful thing his wits were him bereft.
A sword he caught werwith he pearced eft
His body gored, which he of lyfe benooms:
So iust is God in all his dreadfull dooms.

O bloudy Brutus rightly didst thou rewe,
And thou Cassius iustly came thy fall,
That with the sword wherewith thou Cæsar slewe
Murdrest thy selfe, and reft thy lyfe withall.
A mirrour let him be vnto you all
That murderers be, of murder to pour meede:
For murder cryeth out vengeaunce on your seede

Loe Bessius he that armde with murderers knife,
And traytours hart against his royall king,
With bloudy hands bereft his maisters life,
Aduert the fine his foule offence did bring:
And loathing murder as most lothly thing
Beholde in him the iust deserued fall,
That euer hath, and shal betyde them all.

What booted him his false vsurped raygne,
Wherto by murder he did so ascend:
When lyke a wretch led in an yron chayne
He was presented by his chiefest frend
Vnto the foes of him whome he had slayne:
That euen they should venge so fowle a gilt,
That rather sought to haue his bloud yspilt

Duke of Buckingham.

Take hede ye princes and ye prelates all
Of this outrage, whice though it slepe a while
And not disclosde, as it doth seeld befall,
Yet God that suffreth silence to beguyle
Such gilts, wherewith both earth and ayre ye file,
At last discryes them to your fowle deface,
You see th'examples set before your face.

And dieply graue within your stony harts,
The drery dewle that mighty Macedo,
With tears vnfolded wrapt in deadly smarts,
When he the death of Clitus sorrowed so,
Whome erst he murdred with the deadly blowe
Raught in his rage vpon his frend so deare,
For which beholde loe how his pangs appeare.

The launced speare he wrythes out of the wound,
From which the purple blud spins in his face:
His heynous gilt when he returned found,
He throwes himselfe vpon the corps alas.
And in his armes how oft doth he imbrace
His murdred frend: and kissing him in vayne,
Forth flowe the fluds of salt repentant rayne.

His frends amazde at such a murder done,
In fearefull flocks begin to shrinke away.
And he therat with heapes of grief fordone,
Hateth him selfe, wishing his later daye,
Now he likewise perceiued in lyke staye,
As is the wylde beast in the desert bred,
Both dreading others and him selfe adred.

Q.ii. He calles

Henry Stafforde

He calles for death, and loathing lenger lyfe,
Bent to his bane, refuseth kindely foode:
And plounged in depth of death and dolours strife,
Had queld him selfe, had not his frends withstoode.
Loe he that thus hath shed the guiltles bloud,
Though he were King and Kesar ouer all
Yet chose he death to guerdon death withall.

This prince whose pier was neuer vnder sonne
Whose glistening fame the earth did ouerglyde,
Which with his power welny the world had wonne,
His bloudy hands himselfe could not abyde,
But fully bent with famine to haue dyed:
The worthy prince deemed in his regarde,
That death for death could be but iust rewarde:

Yet we that were so drowned in the depth
Of diepe desyre to driuke the guiltlesse bloud,
Lyke to the wolfe, with griedy lookes that lepth
Into the snare, to feede on deadly foode,
So we delighted in the state we stoode,
Blinded so far in all our blinded trayne
That blinde we sawe not our destruction playne.

We spared none whose lyfe coulde ought forlet
Our wicked purpose to his passe to come.
Fower worthy knights we headed at Pomfret
Gyltlesse (God wote) withouten lawe or dome.
My hart euen bledes to tel you all and some,
And how Lord Hastings when he feared least,
Dispiteously was murdred and opprest.

These

Duke of Buckingham.

These rocks vpraught, that threatned most our wrecke
We seemde to sayle much surer in the streame:
And Fortune faring as she were at becke
Layde in our lap the rule of all the realme.
The Nephewes strait deposde were by the same,
And we aduaunst to that we bought full deare,
He crowned king, and I his chiefest Peer.

Thus hauing wonne our long despyed pray,
To make him king that he might make me chief,
Downthrowe we strait his his self Nephewes tway,
From princes pompe, to wofull prisoners lyfe:
In hope that now stint was all furder strife.
Sith he was King and I chief stroke did beare
Who ioyed but we, yet who more cause to feare?

The giltlesse bloud which we vniustly shed,
The royall babes deuested from their trone,
And we like traitours raigning in their sted,
These heauy burdens passed vs vpon,
Tormenting vs so by our selues alone,
Much like the felon that pursued by night,
Starts at ech bush as his foe were in sight.

Now doubting state, now dreading losse of lyfe,
In feare of wracke at euery blast of wynde,
Now start in dreames through dread of murdrers knyfe,
As though euen then reuengement were assynde.
With restlesse thought so is the guilty mynde
Turmoyld, and neuer feeleth ease or stay,
But liues in feare of that which followes aye.

Q.iii.   Well

Henry Stafforde

Well gaue that Judge his dome vpon the death
Of Titus Clelius that in bed was slayne:
When euerye wight the cruell murder leyeth
To his two sonnes that in his chamber layen,
That Judge, that by the proofe perceiueth plaine,
That they were found fast slepyng in their bed,
Hath deemde them giltlesse of this bloud yshed.

He thought it could not be, that they which brake
The lawes of God and man in such outrage
Could so foorthwith them selues to slepe betake:
He rather thought the horrour and the rage
Of such an haynous gilt, could neuer swage.
Nor neuer suffer them to slepe or rest,
Or dreadles breath one breath out of their brest.

So gnawes the grief of conscience euermore
And in the hart it is so diepe ygraue,
That they may neither slepe nor rest therfore,
Ne thinke one thought but on the dread they haue.
Still to the death foretossed with the waue
Of restlesse woe, in terrour and dispeire.
They lead a lyfe continually in feare.

Lyke to the deare that striken with the dart,
Withdrawes himselfe into some secrete place,
And feeling greue the wound about his hart,
Startlesse with pangs tyll he fall on the grasse,
And in greate feare lies gasping there a space,
Foorth braying sighes as though ech pang had brought
The present death whiche he doth dread so oft:

                            So we

Duke of Buckingham.

So we diepe wounded with the bloudy thought,
And gnawing worme that grieued our conscience so,
Neuer tooke ease, but as our hart outbrought
The stayned sighes in witnesse of our woe,
Such restles cares our falte did well beknowe:
Wherewith of our deserued fall the feares
In euery place rang death within our eares.

And as yll grayne is neuer well ykept,
So fared it by vs within a while:
That which so long with such vnrest we reapt,
In dreade and daunger by all wit and wyle,
Loe see the fyne, when once it felt the whele
Of slypper Fortune, stay it mought no stowne,
The wheele whurls vp, but strait it whurleth downe.

For hauing rule and riches in our hand,
Who durst gainsay the thing that we auerde?
Wyll was wysedome, our lust for law did stand,
In sort so straunge that who was not afeard
When he the sounde but of king Richard heard?
So hatefull wart the hearing of his name,
That you may deeme the residue of the same.

But what auailde the terrour and the feare,
Wherewith he kept his lieges vnder awe?
It rather wan him hatred euery where,
And fayned faces forst by feare of lawe:
That but while Fortune doth with fauour blaw,
Flatter through feare: for in their hart lurkes aye
A secrete hate that hopeth for a daye.

Henry Stafforde

Recordeth Dionisius the Kinge,
That with his rigour so his realme oppzest,
As that he thought by cruell feare to bring
His subiects vnder, as him lyked best:
But loe the dread wherewith himselfe was strest,
 And you shall see the fyne of forced feare,
Most myrrour lyke in this proud prince appeare.

All were his head with crowne of golde yspzad,
And in his hand the royall scepter set:
And he with princely purple richly clad,
Yet was his hart with wretched cares ozefret:
And inwardly with deadly feare beset,
Of those whome he by rygour kept in awe,
And sore oppzest with might of tyrants law.

Against whose feare, no heapes of golde and glee,
No strength of gard, nor all his hyred power,
Ne proude high towers that preaced to the skie,
His cruell hart of saftie could assure:
But dreading them whome he should deme most sure,
Him selfe his beard with burning brand would ceare,
Of death deserude so depd him the feare.

This might suffise to represent the fyne
Of tyrants force, their feares, and their vnrest,
But heare this one, although my hart repine
To let the sound once sincke within my brest:
Of fell *Phereus*, that aboue the rest,
Such lothsome cruelty on his people wrought,
As (oh alas) I tremble with the thought.

Some

Some be encased in the coates of Bears,
Among wilde beasts deuoured so to be:
And some for pray vnto the hunters speares,
Lyke sauage beasts withouten ruth to dye.
Sometyme to encrease his horrible cruelty,
The quicke with face to face engraued hee,
Ech others death that ech mought liuing see.

Loe what more cruell horrour mought be found,
To purchase feare, if feare could stay his raigne?
It booted not, it rather strake the wounde
Of feare in him to feare the lyke agayne.
And so he did full oft and not in vayne:
And in his life his cares could witnesse well
But most of all his wretched end doth tell.

His owne deare wife whome as his lyfe he loued,
He durst not trust, nor proch vnto her bed,
But causing first his slaue with naked swordе
To go before, him selfe with trembling dread
Strait foloweth fast, and whurling in his head
His rolling eyin, he searcheth heare and there
The diepe daunger that he so sore did feare.

For not in vayne it ran still in his breast,
Some wretched hap should hale him to his end.
And therfore alway by his pillow prest
Had he a sword, and with that sword be wende,
In vayne (God wote) all perils to defende.
For loe his wife foreyrked of his raygne,
Sleping in bed this cruell wretch hath slaine.

What

What should I more now seke to saye in this
Or one iote farder linger foorth my tale?
With cruell Neros or with Phalaris,
Caligula Domitians and all
The cruell route: or of their wretched fall?
I can no more, but in my name aduert
All earthly powers beware of tyrants hart.

And as our state endured but a throwe,
So best in vs the stay of such a state
May best appeare to hang on ouer throwe,
And better teach tyrants deserued hate,
Than any tyrants death tofore or late.
So cruell seemde this Richad third to me,
That loe my selfe now loathde his crueltee.

For when alas, I saw the Tyrant King
Content not onely from his Nephues twayne
To ryue worlds blisse, but also all worlds being,
Sauns earthly gilt ycausing both be slaine,
My hart agriefde that such a wretch shoulde raygne,
Whose bloudy brest so saluaged out of kinde,
That Phalaris had neuer so bloudy a mynde.

Ne coulde I brooke him once within my brest,
But with the thought my teeth would gnash withall:
For though I earst were his by sworne behest,
Yet when I sawe mischief on mischiefe fall,
So diepe in bloud, to murder prince and all.
Ay then thought I, alas, and wealaway,
And to my selfe thus mourning would I say.

Of neither

Duke of Buckingham.

If neither loue, kinred, ne knot of bloud,
His owne alleageaunce to his prince of due,
Nor yet the state of trust wherein he stoode,
The worlds defame, nor nought could forme him true
Those giltlesse babes, could they not make him rue?
Nor could their youth, nor innocence withall
Moue him from reuing them their lyfe and all?

Alas it coulde not moue him any iote,
Ne make him once to rue or wete his eye,
Stird him no more than that that stirreth not:
But as the rocke or stone that will not plye,
So was his hart made hard with crueltie,
To murder them, alas I weepe in thought,
To thinke on that whiche this fell wretche hath wrought.

That now when he had done the thing he sought,
And as he woulde, complisht and compast all,
And sawe and knewe the treason he had wrought
To God and man, to slay his prince and all,
Then seemde he first to doubt and dread vs all,
And me in chief, whose death all meanes he might,
He sought to worke by mallice and by might.

Such heapes of harms vpharbard in his brest
With enuious hart my honour to deface,
And knoweing he that I which wated best
His wretched dryfts, and all his wretched case,
If euer sprang within me sparke of grace,
Must nedes abhorre him and his hatefull race:
Now more and more can cast me out of grace.

Which

Henry Stafforde.

Which sodayne chaunge when I by secret chaunce
Had well perceiued by proofe of enuious frowne,
And saw the lot that did me to aduaunce
Him to a King that sought to cast me downe,
To late it was to linger any stowne:
Syth present choise lay cast before myne iye,
To worke his death or I my selfe to dye.

And as the knight in field among his foes,
Beset with swords, must slay or there be slayne:
So I alas lapt in a thousand woes,
Beholding death on euery syde so playne,
I rather chose by some sly secret trayne
To worke his death, and I to liue thereby,
Than he to lyue, and I of force to dye.

With heauy choise so hastened me to chose,
That I in parte agrieued at his disdayne,
In parte to wreake the dolefull death of those
Two tender babes, his selfe Nephewes twayne,
By him alas commaunded to be slaine,
With painted chere humbly before his face,
Straight tooke my leaue and roade to Breeknocke place.

And there as close and couert as I might,
My purposed practise to his passe to bring,
In secret drifts I lingered day and night:
All how I might depose this cruell King,
That seemd to all so much desperd a thing,
As therto trusting I emprisde the same:
But to much trusting brought me to my bane.

f.ij.

Duke of Buckingham,

For while I now had Fortune at my becke
Mistrusting I no earthly thing at all,
Unwares alas, least looking for a checke,
She matcht me in tourning of a ball:
When least I feard, then nerest was my fall,
And when whole hoasts were prest to stop my fane,
She chaungde her cheare and left me post alone.

I had vprayſde a mighty band of men,
And marched forth in order of array,
Leading my power amid the forest Dene,
Agaynſt the tyrant banner to display:
But loe my souldiers cowardly shranke away.
For such is Fortune when she lift to frowne,
Who semes most sure, him soneſt whurls she downe.

O let no prince put truſt in commontie,
Nor hope in faith of giddy peoples mynde,
But let all noble men take heede by me,
That by the proofe to well the payne do fynde:
Loe, where is truth or truſt: or what could bynde
The vayne people, but they will swerue and swaye,
As chaunce brings chaunge, to vpyue and draw that way:

Rome thou that once aduaunced vp ſo hye,
Thy ſtay, patron, and flower of excellence,
Haſt now throwne him to depth of miſerie,
Exiled him that was thy whole defence,
Ne compteſt it not an horrible offence:
To reueu him of honour and of fame,
That wan it thee when thou hadſt loſt the ſame.

Beholde

Henry Stafforde.

Beholde Camillus, he that erst reuiued
The state of Rome, that dyeng he did fynde,
Of his owne state is now alas depriued,
Bannisht by them whom he did thus vet bynde:
That cruell folke, vnthankefull and vnkynde,
Declared well their false inconstancy,
And Fortune eke her mutabilytie.

And thou Scipio, a mirrour maist thou be
To all nobles, that they learne not to late,
How they once trust the bustable commontie.
Thou that recuredst the torne dismembred state,
Euen when the conquerer was at the gate,
Art now exilde, as though thou not deserued
To rest in her, whome thou hadst so preserued.

Ingratefull Rome hast shewed thy crueltie,
On him, by whome thou liuest yet in fame,
But nor thy dede, nor his desert shall dye,
But his owne wordes shall witnes ay the same:
For loe his graue doth the most iustly blame,
And with disdayne in Marble sayes to thee:
Unkinde countrey thy bones shalt thou not see.

What more vnworthy than this his exile?
More iust than this the wofull plaint he wrote?
Or who could shewe a playner proofe the whyle,
Of moste false faithe, than they thus forgot
His great deserts? that so deserued not?
His cindres yet loe, doth he them deny,
That him denyed amongst them for to dye.

                                                   Miltiades

Duke of Buckingham.

Milciades, O happy hadst thou be,
And wel rewarded of thy country men,
If in the field when thou hadst forst to flye
By thy prowes, three hundred thousand men,
Content they had bene to exile thee then:
And not to cast thee in depth of prison so,
Laden with gyues to end thy lyfe in woe.

Alas how hard and steely harts had they
That not contented there to haue the dye,
With fettred gyues in prison where thou lay,
Increast so far in hatefull crueltye,
That buriall to thy corps, they eke denye:
Ne will they graunt the same tyll thy sonne haue
Put on thy gyues to purchase thee a graue.

Loe Hanniball as long as fixed fate,
And brittle Fortune had ordayned so,
Who euermore aduaunst his countrey state
Then thou that liuedst for her and for no moe:
But when the stormy waues began to growe,
Without respect of thy deserts erwhile,
Art by thy countrey throwen into exile.

Unfrendly Fortune shall I the now blame?
Or shall I fault the fates that so ordayne?
Or art thou Ioue the causer of the same?
Or crueltie her selfe doth she constrayne?
Or on whome els alas shall I complayne?
O trustlesse world I can accusen none,
But fickle faith of commontie alone.

The Poli-

Henry Stafforde

The Polipus nor the Chameleon straunge,
That tourne themselues to euery hewe they see
Are not so full of vayne and fickle chaunge
As is this false vnstedfast commontye.
Loe I alas with myne aduersitye
Haue tryed it true, for they are fled and gone,
And of an oast there is not left me one.

That I alas in this calamitie
Alone was left, and to my selfe mought playne
This treason, and this wretches cowardye,
And eke with tears beweepen and complayne
My hatefull hap, still loking to be slayne.
Wandring in woe and to the Gods on hye
Cleaping for vengeaunce of this treachery.

And as the turtle that hath lost her make,
Whome griping sorowe doth so sore attaint,
With dolefull voice and sound that she doth make
Mourning her losse fills all the groue with plaint,
So I alas forsaken, and forsayut,
With restlesse foote the wood came vp and downe,
Which of my dole all shiurring doth resowne.

And being thus alone and all forsake,
Amyd the thicke, forewandred in despayer,
As one dismayed ne wist what way to take,
Untill at last gan to my minde repayer
A man of myne called Humfrey Banastaier:
Wherwith me feeling much recomforted,
In hope of succour to his house I fled.

Who be-

Who being one whome erst I had vp brought
Euen from his youth, and loued and lyked best,
To gentry state auauncing him from nought,
And had in secret trust aboue the rest,
Of speciall trust now being thus distrest
Full secretly to him I me conueyed
Not doubting there but I should fynde some ayde.

But out alas on cruell trecherie,
When that this captife once an inkling hard,
How that King Richard had proclaimde, that he
Which me descryed should haue for his rewarde
A thousand pounds, and farther be prefarde,
His truth so turnde to treason, all distainde
That faith quite fled, and I by trust was trainde.

For by this wretch I being strait betrayed,
To one Ihon Mitton, shiriffe of Shropshire then,
All sodenly was taken, and conuayed
To Salisburie, with rout of harnest men,
Vnto King Richard there encamped then:
Fast by the cittie with a mightye hoast
Withouten dome where head and lyfe I lost.

And with these words as if the are euen there
Disinembred had his head and corps aparte,
Dead fell he downe: and we in wofull feare
Stoode mazed when he would to lyfe reuert:
But deadly griefs still grewe about his hart,
That still he lay, sometyme reuyued with payne,
And with a sigh becomming dead againe.

Henry Stafforde

Midnight was come, when euery vitall thing
With swete sound slepe their weary lyms did rest,
The beasts n ere still, the litle byrds that syng,
Now sweetly slept besydes their mothers brest:
The olde and all were shrowded in their nest.
The waters calme, the cruell Seas did ceas,
The woods, the fylds, and all things held their peace.

The golden stars were whyrld amyd their race,
And on the earth did laugh with twinkling light,
When ech thing nestled in his resting place,
Forgat dayes payne with plesure of the night:
The Hare had not the gredy hounds in sight,
The fearefull Deare of death stoode not in doubt,
The Partridge drept not of the Falcons foote.

The ougly Beare now mynded not the stake,
Nor how the cruell mastiues do him teare,
The stag lay still vnroused from the brake,
The fomy Boare feard not the hunters speare:
All thing was still in desert, bush and brear.
With quyet hart now from their trauayles rest,
Soundly they slept in midst of all their rest.

When Buckingham amid his plaint opprest,
With surging sorrowes, and with pinching paines
In sort thus sowned, and with a sigh he ceast.
To tellen forth the trechery and the traynes,
Of Banastar, which him so sore distraines.
That from a sigh he falls into a sounde,
And from a sound lyeth raging on the ground,

                                                            So twy-

Duke of Buckingham.

So twiching were the pangs that he assayed,
And he so sore with rufull rage distraught.
To thinke vpon the wretch that him betrayed,
Whome erst he made a gentilman of naught
That more and more agreued with this thought,
He stormes out sighes, and with redoubled sore,
Stroke with the furies, rageth more and more.

Who so hath seene the Bull chased with darts,
And with diepe wounds foregalde and gorde so,
Tyll he oppressed with the deadly smarts,
Fall in a rage and run vpon his foe,
Let him I say, beholde the raging woe
Of Buckingham, that in these gripes of griefe
Rageth gainst him that hath betrayed his lyfe.

With bloud red iyen he stareth here and there,
Frothing at mouth, with face as pale as cloute:
When loe my lyms were trembling all for feare,
And I amazde stoode still in dread and doubt,
While I mought see him throwe his armes about:
And gainst the ground him selfe plounge with such force
As if the lyfe forthwith should leaue the corps.

With smoke of sighs somtyme I might beholde
The place all dimde, lyke to the morning mist:
And strait again the teares how they downrolde.
Alongst his cheekes, as if the riuers hist:
Whose flowing streames ne were no soner whist,
But to the stars such dreadfull shoutes he sent,
As if the trone of mighty Ioue should rent,

R ii.   And I

Henry Stafforde

And I the while with sprites welny bereft,
Beheld the plight and panges that did him strayne.
And how the bloud his deadly coulour left,
And strait returnde with flaming red agayne:
When sodaynly amyd his raging payne,
He gaue a sigh and with that sigh he sayed,
Oh Banaſtar, and strait agayne he sayed,

Dead lay his corps as dead as any stone,
Evll swelling sighes stormning within his brest
Vpstayed his head, that downeward fell anone,
With lookes vpcast, and sighes that neuer ceaſt:
Forth streamde the teares records of his vnreſt,
When he with shrikes thus groueling on the ground,
Ybrayed these words with shrill and dolefull sounde.

Heauen and earth and ye eternall lamps
That in the heauens wrapt, wyll vs to reſt,
Thou bright Phœbe, that cleareſt the nights damps
Witneſſe the plaints that in these pangs oppreſt
I wofull wretch vnlade out of my breſt.
And let me peelde my laſt words ere I parte,
You, you, I call to record of my ſmart.

And thou Alecto feede me with thy foode
Let fall thy serpents from thy snaky heare,
For such reliefe well ſits me in this moode;
To feede my plaint with horrour and with feare,
While rage afreſh thy venomde worme areare.
And thou Sibilla when thou ſeeſt me faynte,
Addreſſe thy selfe the gyde of my complaint.

                                  And thou

Duke of Buckingham.

And thou O Ioue, that with thy deepe fordoome
Dost rule the earth, and raygne aboue the skies,
That wreakest wrongs, and geuest the dreadfull doine
Against the wretch that doth thy name despise,
Receiue these words and wreake them in such wyse,
As heauen and earth may witnesse and beholde,
Thy heapes of wrath vpon this wretch vnfolde.

Thou Bannaster gainst the I clepe and call
Unto the Gods, that they iust vengeaunce take
On thee, thy bloud, thy stayned stocke and all:
O Ioue to the aboue the rest I make
My humble plaint, guyde me that what I speake,
May be thy will vpon this wretch to fall,
On the Banastar, wretch of wretches all.

O would to God the cruell dismall day,
That gaue me light fyrst to beholde thy face,
With foule eclipse had reft my sight away:
The vnhappy hower, the tyme, and eke the day:
The Sonne and Moone, the sters, and all that was
In their aspetts helping in ought to thee,
The earth and ayre, and all accursed bee.

And thou captyfe, that lyke a monster swarued,
From kinde and kindenes, hast thy master lorne,
Whome neither truth, nor trust wherin thou serued,
Ne his deserts, coulde moue, nor thy faith sworne,
How shall I curse, but with that thou vnborne
Had bene, or that the earth had rent in twayne,
And swallowed the in cradell as thou laye.

R.iii. To this

Henry Stafforde

To this did I euen from thy tender youth
Witſaue to bring thee vp: dyd I therefore
Beleue the oath of thy vndoubted troth:
Aduaunce thee vp, and truſt thee euermore:
By truſting thee that I ſhould dye therfore:
O wretch, and worſe than wretch, what ſhall I ſay:
But cleape and curſe gainſt thee and thyne for aye

Hated be thou diſdaynd, of euery wight,
And pointed at where euer that thou go.
A trayterous wretch, vnworthy of the light,
Be thou eſteemed: and to encreaſe thy woe.
The ſounde be hatefull of thy name alſo:
And in this ſort with ſhame and ſharpe reproch
Leade thou thy lyfe tyll greater grief approch.

Dole and diſpayre, let thoſe be thy delight,
Wrapped in woes, that can not be vnfolde,
To wayle the day, and wepe the weary night,
With raynye eyin and ſighes cannot be tolde,
And let no wight thy woe ſeeke to witholde:
But count thee worthy (wretch) of ſorrowes ſtore,
That ſuffring much, oughteſt ſtill to ſuffer more.

Deſerue thou death, yea be thou demed to dye
A ſhamefull death. To end thy ſhamefull life:
A ſight longed for, ioyfull to euery eye,
When thou ſhalt be arraygned as a thief,
Standing at bar, and pleading for thy lyfe,
With trembling tongue in dread and dolours rage,
Lade with white locks, and fowerſcore yeares of age.

          Yet ſhall

Duke of Buckingham.

Yet shall not death deliuer the so soone
Out of thy woes, so happy shalt thou not be:
But to the eternall Ioue this is my boone,
That thou maist liue thine eldest son to se,
Reft of his wits, and in a foule bores stye
To end his dayes in rage and death distrest,
A worthy tombe where one of thyne shoulde rest.

Yet after this yet pray I more thou may
Thy seconde sonne see drowned in a dyke,
And in such sort to close his later day,
As heard or sene erst hath not bene the lyke:
Strangled in a puddle not halfe so depe
As halfe a foote that such hard losse of lyfe,
So cruelly chaunst, may be the greater grief.

And not yet shall thy huge sorowes cease,
Ioue shall not so witholde his wrath fro thee,
But that thy plagues may more and more encrease,
Thou shalt still liue that thou thy selfe maist se
Thy deare daughter stroken with leprosye:
That she that earst was all thy whole delight,
Thou now maist loath to haue her come in sight.

And after that, let shame and sorowes grief
Feede forth thy yeares continually in woe,
That thou maist liue in death, and dye in lyfe,
And in this sort, forwayde and weried so,
At length thy ghost to parte thy body fro:
This pray I Ioue, and with this later breath
Vengeaunce I aske vpon my cruell death.

R iiii. This

Henry Stafforde

This sayde, he flong his retchlesse arms abroade,
And groueling flat vpon the grounde he laye,
Which with his teeth he all to gnasht and gnawde:
Depe groanes he fet, as he that would awaye.
But loe in vayne hee did the death assay:
Although I thinke was neuer man that knewe,
Such deadly payns where death did not ensue.

So stroue he thus a whyle as with the death,
Now pale as leade and colde as any stone.
Now still as calme, now storming forth a breath.
Of smoaky sighes, as breath and all were gone:
But euery thing hath end: so he anone
Came to himselfe when with a sigh outbrayed.
With wofull cheare these wofull words he sayde.

Ah where am I, what thing, or whence is this?
Who reft my wits? or how do I thus lye?
My lyms do quake, my thought agasted is,
Why sigh I so? or wherunto do I
Thus graule on the grounde? and by and by
Vpraysde he stood, and with a sigh hath sayde,
When to himselfe retourned thus he sayde.

Suffiseth now this plaint and this regrete,
Wherof my hart his bottome hath vnfraught:
And of my death let piers and princes mete
The worlds vntrust, that they therby be taught.
And in her wealth, sith that such change is wrought,
Hope not to much, but in the mids of all
Thinke on my death, and what may them befall.

Duke of Buckingham.

So long as fortune woulde permit the same,
I liued in rule and riches with the best:
And past my tyme in honour and in fame,
That of mishap no feare was in my brest:
But false Fortune when I suspected least,
Did tourne the wheele, and with a dolefull fall
Hath me berefte of honour lyfe and all.

Loe what auayles in riches floud̃s that flowes:
Though he so smylde as al the world were his:
Euen Kings and Kesars byden Fortunes throwes,
And simple sort must beare it as it is.
Take heede by mee that blithde in balefull blisse:
My rule, my riches, royall bloud and all,
When Fortune frounde the feller made my fall.

For hard mishaps that happens vnto such,
Whose wretched state erst neuer fell no chaunge,
Agreue them not in any parte so much,
As their distresse to whome it is so straunge,
That all their liues nay passed pleasures raunge:
Their sodain woe that ay wielde welth at will,
Algates their harts more pearcingly must thrill.

For of my byrth, my bloud was of the best,
First borne an Earle, then Duke by due discent:
To swinge the sway in court among the rest,
Dame Fortune me her rule most largely lent:
And kynde courage so my corps had blent,
That loe on whome but me did she most smyle:
And whome but me lo, did she most begyle?

Not

Now hast thou harde the whole of my vnhap
My chaunce, my chaunge, the cause of all my care:
In wealth and woe, how Fortune did me wrap,
With worlde at will to win me to her snare.
Bid Kings, bid Kesars, by all states beware,
And tell them this from me, that tryed it true.
Who reckelesse rules, right sone may hap to rue.

FINIS. T. S.

How like you this my maysters (quoth I)
very well said one: the tragedy excelleth: the
inuention also of the inductiion, & the descriptions are notable. But where as hee
fayneth to talke with the princes in hell, that I am
sure will be mislyked, because it is most certaine, that
some of their soules be in heauen. And although he
herein do follow allowed Poets, in their descriptiō
of hell, yet it sauoreth so much of Purgatorie, whiche the Papists haue digged therout, that the ignorant may therby be deceiued. Not a whit I warrant you (saide I) for he meaneth not by his Hell
the place eyther of damned soules, or of suche as lye
for their fees, but rather the graue, wherin the deade
bodies of all sorts of people do rest tyll tyme of the resurrection. And in this sence is hell taken often in the
scriptures, and in the wrytings of learned christians.
And so (as he himselfe hath tolde me) he meaneth, &
so wold haue it taken. Tush (quoth another) what
stand we here vppon? it is a poesy and no deuinity,
and

Collingbourne.

and it is lawfull for Poets to fayne what they lyst, so it be appertinent to the matter: And therfore let it passe euen in such sort as you haue read it. With a good will (quoth I) But whereas you say a poet may fayne what he list: In dede my thinke it shuld be so, and ought to be well taken of ye hearers: but it hath not at all tymes beene so allowed. Ye saye troth quoth the reader: For here followeth in the story, that after the death of this Duke, one called Collingbourn was cruelly put to death for making of a ryme. I haue his tragedy here (said I) For the better perceiuing wherof, you muste ymagin ye you see him a maruailous well fauoured man, holding in his hand, his owne hart, newly ripped out of his breast and smoaking forth the lyuely spiryt: & with his hand, beckeninge to and fro, as it were to warne vs to auoyde: and with his faint tong and voyce, saying as couragiously as hee may, these wordes that followe.

How Collingbourne was cruelly executed for makinge a foolishe ryme.

Beware, take hede, take hede, beware, beware
You Poets you, that purpose to rehearce
By any arte what tyrants doings are,
Erinnis rage is growen so fell and fearce
That vicious acts may not be toucht in verse:
The Muses fredome, graunted them of elde,
Is harde, sly reasons treasons bye are helde.

Be rough

Collingbourne.

Be rough in ryme, and then they say you rayle,
As Iuuenal was, but that makes no matter:
With Ieremye you shall be had to iayle,
Or forst with Martial, Cæsars faults to flatter,
Clarkes must be taught to clawe and not to clatter:
Free Hellicon and franke Pernassus hylls,
Are belly haunts, and ranke pernicious ylls.

Touch couertly in terms, and then you taunt
Though praysed Poets, alway did the lyke,
Controll vs not, els traytour vyle auaunt,
What passe we what the learned do mislike?
Our syns we see, wherin to swarme we seeke,
We passe not what the people say or thinke.
Their shittle hate maketh none but cowards shrinke.

We knowe (say they) the course of Fortunes wheele,
How constantly it whyrleth still about,
Arrearing now, while elder headlong reele.
How all the riders alway hang in doubt.
But what for that? we count him but a loute
That sticks to mount, and basely lyke a beast
Lyues temperately for feare of blockam feast.

In deede we woulde of all be deemed Gods
What euer we do; and therfore partely hate
Rude preachers that dare threaten vs plagues and rods,
And blase the blots wherby we stayne our state:
But nought we passe what any such do prate.
Of course and office they must say theyr pleasure,
And we of course must heare and mend at leasure.

But when

Collingbourne.

But when these pelting poets in their rymes,
Shall taunt, or ieast, or paint our wicked workes,
And cause the people knowe and curse our crymes,
This ougly fault, no tyrant lyues but yrkes.
Wherfore we loth such taunters worse than Turks,
Whose meaning is to make vs knowe our misse,
And so to mend, but they but doate in this.

We knowe our faults as well as any other,
We also doubt the daungers for them due:
Yet still we trust so right to guyde the rother,
That scape wee shall the sourges that ensue.
We thinke we knowe moe shifts than other knewe,
In vayne therfore for vs are counsailes writ:
We knowe our faults and wil not mend a whit.

These are the feats of the vnhappy sort,
That preace for honours, wealth, and pleasure bayne.
Ceasse therfore Baldwin, ceasse I thee exhort,
Withdraw thy pen, for nothing shalt thou gayne
Saue hate, with losse of paper, ynke and payne.
Fewe hate their faults, all hate of them to heare
And fautiest, from fault would seme most cleare.

Thy entent I knowe is honest, playne, and good,
To warne the wyse, to fray the fond fro yll:
But wicked worldlings are so witles wood,
That to the worst they all things construe still.
With rygour oft they recompence good will:
They racke the wordes tyll tyme their sinowes burst,
In doubtfull sences, strayning still the worst.

A paynfull

Collingbourne.

A painfull proofe taught me the truth of this,
Through tyrants rage, and Fortunes cruell tourne:
They murdred me, for metring things amisse.
For wotst thou what? I am that Collingbourne
Which made the ryme, wherof I may well mourne.
The Cat, the Rat, and Louell our Dog,
Do rule all England vnder a Hog.

Wherof the meaning was so plaine and true,
That every foole perceyued it at furst:
Most lyked it, for moste that most things knewe,
In hugger mugger, muttred what they durst.
The tyrant prince, of most was held accurst,
Both for his owne, and for his counsails faults,
Of whom was three the naughtiest of all naughts.

Catesby was one whome I called a Cat,
A crafty lawer catching all he coulde.
The second Ratcliffe, whome I named a Rat,
A cruell beast to gnaw on whome he should.
Lord Louell barkt and bit whome Richard would,
Whom I therfore did rightly terme our Dog,
Wherwith to ryme I calde the King a Hog.

Tyll he the crowne had caught, he gaue the Bore,
In which estate would God he had deceased,
Than had the realme not ruined so sore.
His Nephewes raigne should not so sone haue ceassed,
The noble bloud had not bene so decreased.
His Rat, his Cat, and Bloudhound had not noyed
Such liegemen true, as after they destroyed.

Their

Collingbourne.

Their lawlesse acts, good subiects did lament,
And so dyd I, and therfore made the rymes
To showe my wit how well I could inuent,
To warne withall the carelesse of their crymes,
I thought the fredome of the auncient tymes
Stoode still in force. Ridentem dicere verum
Quis vetat? Nay nay, Veritas est pessima rerum

Belyke no tyrants were in Horace dayes,
And therfore Poets freely blamed vyce.
Witnesse their Satyrs sharpe, and tragicke playes,
With chiefest princes chiefly had in price.
They name no man, they mixe their gall with spice,
No more do I, I name no man outright,
But riddle wise, I meane them as I might,

When bruite had brough this to their gilty eares,
Whose right surnames were notes in the ryme,
They all conspyred lyke most gredy bears.
To charge me straight with this most greuous cryme:
And damned me the gallowe tre to clyme,
And then strangled, in quarters to be cut,
Which should on high ouer London gates be put,

This iudgement geuen so behement and sore
Made me exclame against their tyranny.
Wherwith encenst, to make my pain the more,
They practised a shamefull vilany:
They cut me downe alyue and cruelly,
Ript vp my paunch and bulke to make me smart,
And lingered long ere they toake out my hart.

Pier

Collingbourne.

Here tyrant Richard played the eager Hog,
His gnashing tuskes my tender gristles shore:
His bloudhound Louell played the rauening Dog,
His wuluish teeth, my giltlesse carkasse tore:
His Rat, and Cat, did what they might, and more,
Cat Catesby clawed my guts to make me smart,
The Rat Ratcliffe gnawed me to the hart.

If Iewes had kilde the iustest King alyue,
If Turkes had burnt vp churches, Gods, and all,
What greater payne coulde cruell harts contryue,
Than that I suffred, for this trespas small?
I was no prince nor pier, but yet my fall
Is worthy to be thought vpon for this,
To see how canckard tyrants mallice is.

To teach also all subiects to take heede
They medle not with magistrates affayres,
But pray to God to mend them if it nede:
To warne also all Poets that be strayers,
To kepe them close in compasse of their chayers,
And when they touch, that they would wish amended
To sause them so, that fewe nede be offended.

And so to mixe their sharpe rebukes with mirth,
That they may pearce, not causing any payne,
Saue such as followeth euery kindely byrth,
Requited strait, with gladnesse of the gayne.
A Poet must be pleasaunt, not to playne,
Faults to controwl, ne yet to flatter vice
But sound and sweete, in all things ware and wise

The Gro

Collingbourne.

The Grekes do paynt a Poets office whole
In Pegasus, their fayned horse with wings,
Whome shaped so Medusaes bloud did foale,
Who with his feete strake out the Muses springs
Fro flintie rockes to Hellicon that clings.
And then flewe vp into the starry skye,
And there abydes among the gods on hye.

For he that shall a perfect Poet be,
Must first be bred out of Medusaes bloud:
He must be chast and vertuous as was she,
Who to her power the Ocean God withstoode.
To th'ende also his dome be iust and good,
He must (as she) looke rightly with one eye
Truth to regarde and write nothing a wrye.

In courage eke he must be lyke a horse,
He may not feare to register the right,
What though some frowne, thereof he may not force,
No bit nor reyne his tender iawes may twight.
He must be armed with strength of wit and spite.
To dash the rocks, darke causes and obscure,
Tyll he attayne the springs of truth most pure.

His hooues also must plyant be and strong,
To riue the rockes of lust and errors blynde,
In braynlesse heades, that alway wander wrong:
These must he brise with reasons playne and kynde,
Tyll springs of grace do gush out of the mynde,
For till affections from the fond be dryuen,
In vayne is truth tolde, or good counsayle geuen.

S i.   Lyke

Collingbourne.

Like Pegasus a Poet must haue winges,
To fly to heauen or where him liketh best:
He must haue knowledge of eternall things,
Almighty Ioue must harber in his brest,
With worldly cares he may not be opprest,
 The wingz of wit and skill must heaue him hyer,
 With greate delight to satisfye desyer.

He must also be lusty, fre, and swift
To trauayle far to viewe the trades of men,
Greate knowledge oft is goten by the shift:
Things that impart he must be quicke to pen,
Reprouing vices sharpely now and then.
He must be swift when touched tyrants chafe,
 To gallop thence to kepe his carkas safe.

If I had well these quallities considered,
Especially that which I touched last,
With spedy flyght my feete should haue deliuered
My feble body from a most boistous blast,
They should haue caught me, ere I had be cast,
But to much trust vnto a tyrants grace,
I neuer shronke, nor chaunged port or place.

I thought the Poets auncient liberties
For pleas had bene allowed at the bar.
I had forgot how new founde tyrannies
With truth and fredome were at open warre,
That lust was lawe that might did make and marre
That among tyrants this is and euer was
Sic volo, sic iubeo, stet pro ratione voluntas.

 Where

Collingbourne.

Where lust is law it boteth not to pleade,
No priuelege nor liberties auayle.
But with the learnde whome law and wisdome leade
Although through rashenes Poets hap to rayle,
A plea of dotage may all quarells quayle:
Their olde licence their writings to expounde,
Doth quit them clere from faults by Momus founde.

This fredome olde ought not to be debard
From any wight that speaketh ought, or writeth.
The authors meaning should of right be herd,
He knoweth best to what end he enditeth:
Words somtyme beare more then the hart behiteth.
Admit therfore the authors exposition.
If playne for truth: if forst, for his submission.

In case of sclaunder the lawes requyre no more
Saue to amend that seemed not well sayde:
Or to vnsay the slaunders sayd afore,
And aske forgeuenes for the hasty brayde:
To Heretikes no greater payne is layde
Then to recant their errours or retract:
And worse than these can be no writers acte.

Yes (quoth the Cat) thy rayling words be treason:
And treason is far worse then heresye.
Then must it follow by this awkwarde reason,
That Kings be more than God in maiestie,
And soules be lesse then bodies in degree.
For heretikes both soules and God offend,
Traytours but seeke to bring mans lyfe to end.

S.ii.   I speake

Collingbourne.

I speake not this to abase the haynous fault,
Of trayterous acts abhorde by God and man,
But to make playne their iudgement to be naught
That heresye for lesser sin do ban,
I curse them both as depe as any can,
And alway did: yet through my foolish ryme,
They stayned me with that most hatefull cryme.

I neuer ment the King or counsayle harme,
Vnles to wish them safety were offence:
Agaynst their power I neuer lifted arme,
Neyther pen nor tougue for any ill pretence.
The ryme I made, though rude, was found in sence,
For thei therin whome I so fondly named,
So ruled all that they were foule defamed.

This was no treason but the very troth,
They ruled all, none could deny the same:
What was the cause then why they were so wroth?
What, is it treason in a ryming frame
To clip, to stretch, to adde, or chaunge a name?
And this reserued, there is no ryme nor reason,
That any craft can clout to seeme a treason.

For where I meant the King by name of Hog,
I onely alluded to his badge the Bore:
To Louels name I added more our Dog,
Because most dogs haue borne that name of yore:
These metaphors I vse with other more,
As Cat, and Rat, the halfe names of the rest,
To hyde the sence which they so wrongly wrest.

I pray

Collingbourne.

I pray you now what treason fynde you heare
Enough: you rubbed the gilty on the gaule,
Both sence and names do note them very neare,
I graunt that was the chiefe cause of my faule,
Yet can you fynde therein no treason at all:
There is no word against the prince or state,
No harme to them whome all tha realme did hate.

But sith the gilty alwayes are suspicious,
And dread the ruine that must sewe by reason,
They cannot chose but count their counsayle vicious,
That note their faults, and therfore call it treason:
All grace and goodnes with the lewde is geason.
This is the cause why they good things do wrest
Wher as the good take yll things to the best.

And therfore Baldwin boldly to the good
Rebuke their falt, so shalt thou purchase thankes
As for the bad, thou shalt but moue their moode,
Though pleasauntly thou touch their naughty prankes:
Warne Poets all, no wyse to passe the banks
Of Hellicon, but kepe within the bound:
So shall their fredome vnto no harme redound.
           S iii.   Gods

FINIS.

Collingbourne.

GOds blessing on his hart that made this (sayd one) specially for reuiuing our auncient liberties. And I pray God it maye take such place with the Magistrates, ý they may ratifye our olde fredome, Amen saide another: for that shalbe a meane both to stay and vpholde themselues from fallyng: and also to preserue many kynde, true, zealous, & wel meaning myndes from slaughter and infamy. If kinge Richard and hys counsaylours had allowed, or at the leaste but wynked at some such wits, what great commodities might they haue taken thereby.

First, they should haue knowen what ý people mislyked and grudged at, (whiche no one of their flatterers either wolde or durst haue tolde them) and so mought haue found meane, eyther by amendment (which is best) or by some other pollicy to haue staied the peoples grudge: the forerunner commenly of rulers destructions. *Vox populi, vox dei.* in this case is not so famous a prouerb, as true: The experiēce of all tymes do approue it. They should also haue bene warned of theyr owne sinnes, whiche call continually for Gods vengeaunce, which neuer fayleth to fall on their necks sodainly and horribly, vnles it be stayed with harty repentaunce.

These weighty commodities moughte they haue taken by Collingbourns vayne ryme. But as all thinges worke to the best in them that be good, so best things heape vp mischief in the wicked, and all to hastē their vtter destruction. For after this pore
wretches

K. Richarde the iii.

wretches lamentable persecution, (the common rewarde of best endeuours) straite folowed the fatall destruction both of this tyrant, and of his tormentours. Whiche I wishe mighte be so set foorthe, that they might be a warning for euer, to all in authoritie to beware howe they vsurpe or abuse theyr offices. I haue here (quoth I) kinge Richards tragedy. Reade it we praye you (quoth they) wyth a good wil quoth I) For the better vnderstanding wherof, ymagine that you see him tormented with Diues in the diepe pit of hel and thence howling this whiche folloeth.

How Richard Plantagenet Duke of Glocester, murdred his brothers children ysurping the crowne, and in the third yeare of his raigne was most worthely depriued of lyfe and kingdome in Bosworth plaine, by Henry Earle of Richmond after called kinge Henry the vii. the 22. of August. 1485.

What hart so harde, but doth abhorre to heare
The rufull raygne of me the third Richard:
King vnkindely cald though I ye crowne did weare,
Who entred by rigour, but right did not regard,
By tyranny proceding in killing king Edward,
Fift of that name, right heir vnto the crowne,
With Richard his brother, Princes of renowne.

R iiii.   Of trust

K. Richarde the iii.

Of trust they were committed vnto my gouernaunce,
But trust turned to treason to truly it was tryed,
Both against nature dueti and allegiaunce,
For through my procurement most shamefully they dyed
Desyre of a Kingdome forgetteth all kinred,
As after by discourse it shalbe shewed here,
How cruelly these innocents in prison murdered were.

The Lords and Commons all with one assent,
Protectour made me both of land and King,
But I therewith alas was not content:
For mynding mischiefe I ment another thing,
Which to confusion in short tyme did me bring,
For I desyrous to rule and raygne alone,
Sought crowne and kingdome, yet title had I none.

To all piers and princes a president I may be,
The lyke to beware how they do enterprise,
And learne their wretched falles by my fact to forsee,
Which rufull stand bewayling my chaunce before their eyes,
As one cleane bereft of all felicities:
For right through might I cruelly defaced,
But might helped right, and me agayne displaced.

Alas that euer prince shoulde thus his honour staine
With the bloud of innocents most shamefull to be tolde
For these two noble imps I caused to be slaine,
Of yeares not full rype as yet to rule and raygne.
For which I was abhorred both of yong and olde,
But as the dede was odious in sight of God and man,
So shame and destruction in the end I wan.

Both

K. Richarde the iii.

Both God, nature, dutye, allegiaunce all forgot,
This vile and haynous acte unnaturally conspyred:
Which horrible dede done, alas, alas, God wot
Such terrours me tormented, and so my sprites fired
As unto such a murder and shamefull dede required,
Such broyle dayly felt I breding in my brest,
Wherby more and more, increased myne unrest.

My brothers children were right heires unto the crowne
Whome nature rather bound to defend than distroy,
But I not regarding their right nor my renowne
My whole care and study to this end did imploye,
The crowne to obtayne, and them both to put downe:
Wherein I God offended, prouoking iust his ire,
For this my attempt and most wicked despre.

To cursed Cayn compare my carefull case,
Which did vniustly slay his brother iust Abel,
And did not I in rage make run that rufull race
My brother Duke of Clarence, whose death I shame to tell
For that so straunge it was, as it was horrible:
For sure he drenched was and yet no water neare,
Which straunge is to be tolde to all that shall it heare.

The but he was not whereat I did shoote,
But yet he stoode betwene the marke and me,
For had he liued, for me it was no boote
To tempt the thing that by no meanes could be,
For I third was then of my brethren three:
But yet I thought the elder being gone,
Then needes must I beare the stroke alone.

De$3

K. Richarde the iii.

Desyre of rule made me alas to rewe,
My fatall fall I could it not forsee,
Puft vp in pryde, so hawtye then I grewe,
That none my peare I thought now could be,
Disdayning such as were of high degree:
Thus dayly rising and pulling other downe,
At last I shot how to win the crowne.

And dayly deuising which was the best way
And meane how I might my Nephewes both deuour
I secretly then sent without further delay
To Brackynburie then lieutenant of the tower,
Requesting him by letters to helpe vnto his power,
For to accomplish this my desyre and will,
And that he would secretly my brothers children kill.

He aunswered plainely with a flat nay,
Saying that to dy he would not do that dede:
But fynding then a proffer to my pray,
Well worth a frend (quoth I) yet in tyne of nede.
James Tyrrill hight his name, whome with all spede,
I sent agayne to Brackinbury, as you heard before,
Commaunding him deliuer the keyes of euery dore.

The keyes he rendered but partaker would not be
Of that flagitious fact. O happy man I say,
As you haue heard before, he rather chose to dye
Then on those sely lambes his violent hands to laye.
His conscience him pricked, his prince to betray:
O constant mynde that would not condiscend,
Thee may I prayse, and my selfe discommend.

What

K. Richarde the iii.

What though he refuses, yet be sure you may,
That other were as ready to take in hand that thing,
Which watched and wayted as duly for their pray,
As euer did the Cat for the Mouse taking,
And how they might their purpose best to passe bring:
Where Tyrrell he thought good to haue no bloud shed,
Becaſt them to kill by ſmothering in their bed.

The wolues at hand were ready to deuour
The ſely lambes in bed wheras they laye
Abiding death and loking for the hower,
For well they wiſt, they could not ſcape away.
Ah woe is me, that did them thus betray,
In aſſigning this vile dede to be done,
By Myles Forreſt and wicked Jhon Dighton.

Who priuely into their chamber ſtale,
In ſecret wiſe ſomewhat before midnyght,
And gan the bed together tug and hale,
Bewrapping them alas in wofull plight,
Keping them downe, by force, by power, and might,
With haling, tugging, turmoyling, turnde and toſt,
Tyll they of force were forced yeld the ghoſt.

Which when I heard, my hart I felt was eaſed
Of grudge, of griefe, and inward deadly payne,
But with this dede the Nobles were diſpleaſed,
And ſayde: O God, ſhall ſuch a tyrant raygne,
That hath ſo cruelly his brothers children ſlayne?
Which bruite once blowen in the peoples eares,
Their dolour was ſuch, that they braſt out in tears.

But

K. Richarde the iii.

But what thing may suffyse vnto the gredy man,
The more he bathes in bloud, the bloudier he is alwayes:
By proofe I do this speake, which best declare it can,
Which onely was the cause of this princes decaye.
The wolfe was neuer greuier than I was of my pray,
But who so vseth murder full well affirme I dare,
With murder shall be quit, ere he therof beware.

And marke the sequell of this begon mischief,
Which shortly after was cause of my decay,
For high and low conceiued such a grief
And hate against me, which sought day by day,
All wayes and meanes that possible they may,
On me to be reuenged for this sinne,
For cruell murdering vnnaturally my kyn.

Not onely kin, but King the truth to saye
Whome vnkindely of kingdome I bereft,
His lyfe from him I also raught away,
With his brothers, which to my charge was left.
Of ambition beholde the worke and weft,
Prouoking me to do this haynous treason,
And murder them against all right and reason.

After whose death thus wrought by violence,
The Lords not lyking this vnnaturall deede,
Began on me to haue greate diffidence,
Such brinning hate gan in their harts to breede,
Which made me doubt and sore my daunger dredde:
Which doubt and drede proued not in vayne,
By that ensued alas vnto my paryne.

K. Richarde the iii.

For I supposing all things were as I wished,
When I had brought these sely babes to bane,
But yet in that my purpose far I missed:
For as the moone doth chaunge after the wane,
So chaunged the harts of such as I had tane
To be moste true, to troubles did me tourne,
Such rage and rancour in boyling breasts do burne.

And sodainly a bruite abroade was blowen,
That Buckingham the Duke both sterne and stout,
In field was ready, with divers to me knowen,
To gyue me battaile if I durst come out:
Which daunted me and put me in great doubt,
For that I had no army then prepared,
But after that I litle for it cared.

But yet remembring, that oft a litle sparke
Suffered doth growe vnto a greate flame,
I thought yt wisdome wisely for to warke,
Mustered then men in every place I came,
And marching forward dayly with the same,
Drectly towards the towne of Salisburie,
Where I gat knowledge of the Dukes army.

And as I passed ouer Salisburie downe,
The rumour ran the Duke was fled and gone,
His host dispersed besydes Shrewesburie towne,
And he dismayed was left there post alone,
Bewayling his chaunce and making great moane:
Towards whome I hasted withall expedition,
Making due serch and diligent inquisition.

But as

But at the fyrst I coulde not of him heare,
For he was scaped by secrete bywayes,
Unto the house of Humfrey Banastar,
Whome he had much preferred in his dayes,
And was good lorde to him in all assayes:
Which he full euell requited in the end,
When he was driuen to seeke a trusty frend.

For it so happened to his mischap, alas,
When I no knowledge of the Duke could heare
A proclamation by my commaundement was
Published and cryed throughout euery shyre,
That who so coulde tell where the Duke were,
A thousand marke should haue for his payne,
What thing so hard but money can obtayne.

But were it for mony, mede, or drede,
That Banastar thus betrayed his ghest,
Diuers haue diuersly deuined of this dede,
Some deme the worst, and some iudge the best,
The doubt not dissolued nor plainly exprest,
But of the Dukes death he doubtles was cause,
Which dyed without iudgement or order of lawes.

Lo this noble Duke I brought thus vnto bane,
Whose doings I doubted and had in greate dred,
At Banastars house I made him to be tane,
And without iudgement be shortened by the head,
By the shriue of Shropshyre to Salisbury led.
In the market place vpon the scaffolde newe
Where all the beholders did much his death rewe.

And after

And after this done I brake vp my hoste,
Greatly applauded with this heauy hap,
And forthwith I sent to euery sea coste
To foresee all mischieues and stop euery gap,
Before they should chaunce or light in my lap,
Geuing them in charge to haue good regarde
The sea coast to kepe with good watch and warde.

Directing my lettres vnto euery shriue,
With strait commaundement vnder our name,
To suffer no man in their partes to aryue
Nor to passe forth out of the same,
As they tendered our fauour, and voyde would our blame,
Doing therein their payne and industry,
With diligent care and vigilant eye.

And thus setting things in order as you heare:
To preuent mischieues that might then betyde,
I thought my selfe sure, and out of all feare,
And for other thiugs began to prouide:
To Notingham castle strait did I ryde,
Where I was not very long space,
Straunge tydings came which did me sore amaze.

Reported it was, and that for certainty,
Th'erle of Richemond landed was in Wales
At Milford hauen, with an huge army,
Dismissing his nauy which were many sayles:
Which at the first I thought flying tales,
But in the end did otherwise proue,
Which not a litle did me vexe and moue.

                                                    Thus

K. Richarde the iii.

Thus fawning Fortune gan on me to frowne,
And cast on me her scornefull lowring looke:
Then gan I feare the fall of my renoune,
My hart it fainted, my sinowes sore they shooke,
This heauy hap a scourge for sin I tooke,
Yet did I not then vtterly dispayre,
Hopinge storms past the weather shoulde be fayre.

And then with all spede possible I might,
I caused them muster throughout euery shyre,
Determining with the earle spedely to fyght,
Before that his power much encreased were,
By such as to him greate fauour did beare:
Which were no small number by true report made,
Dayly repayring him for to ayde.

Directing my letters to diuers noble men,
With earnest request their power to prepare,
To Notingham castle whereas I lay then.
To ayde and assist me in this waighty affayre:
Where strait to my presence did then repayre,
Iohn Duke of Northfolke, his eldest son also,
With Th'erle of Northumberland and many other mo.

And thus being furnisht with men and munition,
Forwarde we marched in order of battayle ray,
Making by scouts euery way inquisition,
In what place the Earle with his campe lay:
Towards whome directly we tooke then our way,
Euermore mynding to seeke our most auayle,
In place conuenient to geue to him battaile.

Sol.

K. Richarde the iii.

So long we laboured, at last our armies met
On Bosworth playne besydes Lecester towne,
Where sure I thought the garland for to get,
And purchase peace, or els to lose my crowne.
But fickle Fortune alas on me dyd frowne,
For when I was encamped in the fielde,
Where most I trusted I soonest was begylde.

The brand of mallice thus kindling in my brest
Of deadly hate which I to him dyd beare,
Pricked me forward, and bad me not desist,
But boldly fight and take at all no feare,
To win the field, and the earle to conquere:
Thus hoping glory great to gayne and get,
Myne army then in order did I set.

Betyde me lyfe or death I desperately ran,
And ioyned me in battayle with this Earle so stoute,
But Fortune so him fauoured that he the battayle wan
With force and greate power I was beset about,
Which when I did beholde, in mids of the whole route
With dent of sword I cast me on him to be reuenged,
Wherein the midst of them my wretched lyfe I ended.

My body was hurried and tugged lyke a dog,
On horsebacke all naked and bare as I was borne.
My head, hands, and feete, downe hanging lyke a hog,
With dirt and bloud besprent, my corps all to torne,
Cursing the day that euer I was borne.
With greuous wounds bemangled moste horrible to se
So sore they did abhorre this my vile cruelty e.

Ti. Loe here

K. Richarde the iij.

Loe heare you may beholde the due and iust rewarde
Of tyranny and treason which God doth most detest,
For if vnto my duety I had taken regarde,
I might haue liued still in honour with the best,
And had I not attempt the thing that I ought leste.
But desyre to rule alas did me so blynde,
Which caused me to do against nature and kynde.

Ah cursed captife why did I clymbe so hye,
Which was the cause of this my balefull thrall.
For still I thirsted for the regall dignitie,
But hasty rising threatneth the sodayne fall,
Content your selues with your estates all,
And seeke not right by wrong to suppresse,
For God hath promist ech wrong to redresse.

See here the fyne and fatall fall of me,
And guerdon due for this my wretched deede,
Which to all princes a myrrour now may be
That shall this tragicall story after reede,
Wishing them all by me to take heede,
And suffer right to rule as it is reason,
For, tyme tryeth out both truth and also treason.

FINIS. F. Seg.

K. Richarde the iii.

When I had read this, we had much talke about it. For it was thoughte not vehement enough for so violent a mā as king Richarde had beene. The matter was well ynoughe lyked of some, but the meetre was mislyked almoste of all.

And when diuers therfore woulde not allowe it, what (quoth one). You knowe not whereuppon you stycke: elles you woulde not so muche mislyke this because of the vncertaine Meetre. The cumlynes called by the Rhetoricians Decorum, is specially to be obserued in all things. Seyng than that king Richard neuer kept measure in any of his doinges, seyng also he speaketh in hell, whereas is no order: it were againste ye Decorum of hys personage to vse eyther good meeter or order.

And therfore if his oration were far woorse, in my opinion it were more fyt for him. Mars and the Muses dyd neuer agree. Neither is to be suffered that theyr mylde sacred arte should seeme to procede frō so cruell and prophane a mouth as his: seeinge they them selues do vtterly abhorre it.

And although we reade of Nero, that hee was excellent both in musycke, and in versifyinge, yet do not I remember that euer I sawe any songe or verse of his makinge: Minerua iustly prouiding that no monument shoulde remayne of any such vniuste vsurpation. And therfore let this passe euen as it is whiche the writer I knowe both could and would amend in many places, saue for keping the Decorū,

T.ii. which

The blacke Smith.

whych he purposely hath obserued herein.
In deede (quoth I) as you saye : It is not meete
that so dysorderlye and vnnaturall a man as kynge
Richarde was, shoulde obserue any metricall order
in his talke: which not withstanding in many places of his oration is verye well kepte : it shall passe
therefore euen as it is, though to good for so euell a
person.   Then they wylled me to reade the
black Smith. With a good will (quoth
I) but fyrst you must ymagin that
you see hym standing on a ladder ouer shrined with the
Tybourne, a meete
stage for all such rebelles and traytoures: and there stoutlye
saying as followeth.

The blacke Smith.

The wllfull fall of blacke Smith, and the foolishe ende of the Lorde Awdeley in Iune anno. 1496.

Who is more bould than is the blynde Beard?
Where is more craft than in the clowted shone?
Who catch more harme than such as nothing feard?
Where is more guile then where mistrust is none?
No plaisters helpe before the grief beknowen,
So seemes by me who could no wisdome lere,
Untill such tyme I bought my wit to deare.

Who being boistous stout, and brapnlesse bolde,
Puft vp with pryde, with fyer and furies fret,
Incenst with tales so rude and plainely tolde,
Wherin deceit with double knot was knyt,
I trapped was as sely fyshe in net,
Who swift in swimming, not doubtfull of disceit,
Is caught in gyn wherin is layde no bayt.

Such force and vertue hath this dolefull plaint,
Set forth with sighes and teares of Crocodile,
Who semes in sight as simple as a saynt,
Hath layde a bayte the wareles to begyle,
And as they weepe they worke disceit the whyle,
Whose rufull cheare the rulers so relent,
To worke in hast that they at last repent.

Michaell Ioseph.

Take hede therfore ye rulers of the land,
Be blynde in sight and stop your other eare,
In sentence slow tyll skill the truth hath scande,
In all your doomes both loue and hate forbeare,
So shall your iudgement iust and right appeare:
It was a southfast sentence long agoe,
That hasty men shall neuer lacke much woe.

Is it not truth? Baldwin what sayest thou?
Say on thy mynde, I pray the muse no more,
Me thinke thou starest and lokest I wote not howe,
As though thou neuer sawest a man before:
By lyke thou musest why I teach this lore,
Els what I am that here so boldly dare,
Among the prease of princes to compare.

Though I be bolde, I pray the blame not me,
Lyke as men sowe, such corne nedes must they reape,
And nature hath so planted in ech degree,
That Crabs like Crabs will kindely crall and crepe:
The suttle Foxe vnlyke the sely shepe:
It is according to myne education,
Forward to prease in rout and congregation.

Beholde my cote burnt with the sparkes of fyer,
My lether apron fylde with the horse shoe nayles,
Beholde my hammer and my pincers here,
Beholde my lockes a marke that seldome fayles:
My chekes declare I was not fed with quailes,
My face, my clothes, my tooles with all my fashion,
Declare full well a prince of rude creation.

          A prynce

The blacke Smith.

A prince I sayde, a prince I say agayne,
Though not by byrth, by crafty vsurpation,
Who doubts but some men princehoode do obtayne,
By open force and wrongfull domination,
Yet while they rule are had in reputation:
Eu'nso by me, the whyle I wrought my feate,
I was a prince at least in my conceyte.

I dare the bolder take on me the name,
Because of him whome here I leaue in hand,
Tychet Lord Awdley a Lorde of byrth and fame,
Which with his strength and power serude in my band,
I was a prince while that I was so mande:
His Butterfly still vnderneath my shielde,
Displayed was from Wells to blackeheath fielde.

But now beholde he doth bewayle the same:
Thus after wits their rashnes do depraue,
Beholde dismayde he dare not speake for shame,
He lookes lyke one that late came from the graue,
Or one that came forth of Trophonius caue,
For that in wit he had so litle pith,
As he a Lord to serue a traitour Smith.

Such is the courage of the noble hart,
Which doth despyse the vyle and baser sort,
He may not touch that sauers of the cart,
Hym listeth not with ech Iacke lout to sport,
He lets him passe for payzing of his porte,
The iolly Egles catch not litle flees,
The courtly silkes match seeld with homely frees.

C.iiii.   But

Michaell Joseph.

But surely Baldwyn if I were allowde
To say the trouth, I could somewhat declare:
But clarkes will say, this Smyth doth waxe to proude,
Thus in preceptes of wisdome to compare,
But Smiths must speake that clarkes for feare ne dare.
It is a thing that all men may lament,
When clarkes kepe close the truth least they be shent.

The Hostler, Barber, Myller and the Smith,
Heare of the sawes of such as wisdom ken,
And learne some wit although they want the pith,
That clarkes pretend: and yet both now and then,
The greatest clarkes proue not the wisest men:
It is not right that men forbid should be,
To speake the truth all were he bond or free.

And for because I haue vsed to fret and fome,
Not passing greatly whome I should displease,
I dare be bolde a while to play the mome,
Out of my sacke some others faultes to lease,
And let myne owne behynde my backe to pepse.
For he that hath his owne before his eye,
Shall not so quicke anothers fault espye.

I say was neuer no such wofull case,
As is when honour doth it selfe abuse:
The noble man that vertue doth imbrace,
Represseth pride, and humblenes doth vse,
By wisdome workes, and rashnes doth refuse
His wanton will and lust that brydell can,
In dede is gentill both to God and man.

But

The blacke Smith.

But where the nobles want both wit and grace,
Regarde no rede, care not but for their lust,
Oppresse the poore, set will in reasons place,
And in their wordes and doines be found vniust,
Wealth goeth to wracke, tyll all lye in the dust:
There Fortune frownes, and spite beginneth to growe,
Till high, and lowe, and all be ouerthrowe.

Then sith that vertue hath so good rewarde,
And after vice so duly waiteth shame,
How hapth that princes haue no more regarde,
Their tender youth with vertue to enflame?
For lacke whereof their wit and will is lame,
Infect with folly, prone to lust and pryde,
Not knowing how themselues or theirs to guyde.

Wherby it hapneth to the wanton wight,
As to a shyppe vpon the stormy seas,
Which lacking sterne to guide it selfe aright,
From shore to shore the wynde and tyde do teese,
Fynding no place to rest or take his ease,
Tyll at the last it sinke vpon the sande:
So fare they all that haue not vertue cand

The plowman first his land doth dresse and tourne,
And makes it apt or ere the seede be sowe,
Wherby he is full like to reape good corne,
Where otherwise no seede but weede would growe:
By which ensample men may easely knowe,
When youth haue welth before they can well vse it
It is no wonder though they do abuse it.

How

Michaell Ioseph

How can he rule well in a common wealth,
Which knoweth not himselfe in rule to frame?
How should he rule himselfe in ghostly health,
Which never learnd one lesson for the same:
If such catch harme their parents are to blame:
For nedes must they be blynde, and blyndly led,
Where no good lesson can be taught or read.

Some thinke their youth discret and wysely taught,
That brag, and boast, and weare their fether braue,
Can roist, and rout, both lowre, and looke aloft,
Can swere and stare, and call their felowes knaue,
Can pyll and poll, and catch before they craue,
Can carde and dyce, both cog and foyst at fare,
Play on vnthrifty, tyll their purse be bare.

Some teach their youth to pype, to syng, and daunce,
To hauke, to hunt, to choose and kill their game,
To wynde their horne, and with their horse to praunce,
To play at tenis, set the lute in frame,
Run at the ring and vse such other game:
Which feates although they be not all vnfyt,
Yet cannot they the marke of vertue hit.

For noble youth, there is nothing so meete
As learning is, to knowe the good from yll:
To knowe the toungs and perfectly endyte,
And of the lawes to haue a perfect skill,
Things to reforme as right and iustice will:
For honour is ordeyned for no cause,
But see right mainteined by the lawes,

The blacke Smith.

It spytes my hart to heare when noble men
Cannot disclose their secrets to their frend,
In sauegarde sure with paper, inke, and pen,
But fir stthey must a secretary fynde,
To whome they showe the bottome of their myndes
And be he false or true, a blab or close.
To him they must their counsayle nedes disclose.

And where they rule that haue of lawe no skill,
There is no boote, they nedes must seeke for ayde:
Then ruled are they, and rule as others will:
As he that on a stage his parte hath playd:
But he was taught nought hath he done or sayde.
Such youth therfore seeke science of the sage,
As thinke to rule when that ye come to age.

Where youth is brought vp in feare and obedience,
Kept from yll company, brydeled of their lust,
Do serue God duely and know their allegiaunce,
Learne godly wisdome which tyme nor age can rust:
There prince, people, and piers nedes prosper must:
For happy are the people and blessed is that land,
Where truth and vertue haue got the ouer hand.

I speake this Baldwyn of this rufull Lord,
Whome I perforce do here present to thee,
He faynts so sore he may not speake a worde:
I pleade his cause without rewarde or fee,
And am inforst to speake for him and mee:
If in his youth he had bene wysely tought,
He should not now his wit so dere haue bought.

Michaell Ioseph

For what is he that hath but halfe a wit,
But may well know that rebelles cannot spede:
Marke well my tale, and take good hede to it,
Recount it well and take it for good rede,
If it proue vntrue I will not trust my crede.
Was neuer rebell before the world, nor since,
That could or shall preuaile against his prince,

For ere the subiect beginneth to rebell,
Within himselfe let him consider well,
Forsee the daunger, and beat well in his brayne,
How hard it is his purpose to obtayne,
For if he once be entered to the brears,
He hath a raging wolfe fast by the ears.

And when he is once entred to rule the beastly rout
Although he would he can no way get out:
He may be sure none will to him resorte,
But such as are the vile and rascall sorte:
All honest men, as well the most as lest,
To tast of treason will vtterly detest.

Then let him way how long he can be sure,
Where faith nor frendship may no while endure:
He whome he trusteth most, to gayne a grote
Will fall him from and assay to cut his throte,
Among the knaues and slaues where vice is rooted,
There is no other frendship to be loked.

With flashers, slaues, and snuffers so falshod is in price
The simple faith is deadly sinne, and vertue counted vice.
And where the quarrell is so vyle and bad,   What

The blacke Smith.

What hope of ayde then is there to be had?
Thinks he that men will run at this or that,
To do a thing they knowe not how or what?

Nor yet what daunger may thereof betyde,
Where wisdome would they should at home abyde,
Rather then seeke and knowe not what to fynde.
Wise men will first debate this in their mynde:
Full sure they are if that they go to wrecke,
Without all grace they loose both head and necke.

They lose their lands and goods, their childe and wife
With sorrow and shame shall leade a wofull lyfe,
If he be slayne in field he dyeth accurst,
Which of all wrecks we should accompt the worst:
And he that dyeth defending his liege Lord,
Is blist and blist agayne by Gods owne worde.

And where the souldiers wages is unpayde,
There is the Captaine slenderly obayde,
And where the souldier is out of feare and drede,
He will be lacke when that there is most nede,
And priuately he seekes his ease and leasure,
And wil be ruled but at his will and pleasure.

And where some drawe foorth, and other do drawe backe,
There in the end must nedes be woe and wracke:
To hope for ayde of Lords it is but vayne,
Whose foretaught wit of treason knoweth the payne,
They knowe what power a prince hath in his land,
And what it is with rebells for to stand.

They

Michaell Ioseph.

They knowe by treason honour is defaced,
Their offspringe and their progeny disgraced,
They knowe to honour is not so worthy a thing,
As to be true and faithfull to their king,
Aboue cognisaunce or armes, or pedigrewe a far,
An vnspotted cote is lyke a blasing star:

Therfore the rebell is accurst and mad,
That hopeth for that which rebell neuer had:
Who trusting still to tales doth hang in hope,
Till at the last he hang fast by the rope,
For though that tales be tolde that hope might feede,
Such foolish hope hath still vnhappy speede.

It is a custome that neuer will be broken,
In broyles the bag of lyes is euer open,
Such lying newes men dayly will inuent,
As can the hearers fancy best content,
And as the newes do run and neuer cease,
So more and more they dayly do encrease.

And as they encrease they multiply as fast,
That ten is ten hundred, ten thousand at the last,
And though the rebell had once got the fielde,
Thinkes he therby to make his prince to yelde?
A princes power within his owne region,
Is not so sone brought vnto confusion.

For Kings by God are strong and stoutly harted,
That they of subiects will not be subuerted:
If Kings would yeld, yet God would them restrayn,   Of.

The blacke Smith.

Of whome the prince hath grace and power to raygne:
Who straitly chargeth vs aboue all thing,
That no man shoulde resist against his king.

Who that resisteth his dreade soueraigne Lorde,
Doth dampne his soule by Gods owne very worde.
A christen subiect shoold with honour due,
Obey his soueraigne though he were a Iewe:
Wherby assured when subiects do rebell,
Gods wrath is kindled and threatneth fyre and hell.

It is soone knowen when Gods wrath is kyndled,
How they shall spede with whome he is offended:
If God geue victory to whome he lyketh best,
Why looke they for it whome God doth most detest:
For treason is hatefull and abhord in Gods sight,
Example of Iudas that most wicked wight:

Which is the chiefe cause no treason preuayles,
For yll must he spede whome Gods wrath assayles:
Let traitours and rebels looke to speede then,
When Gods mighty power is subiect to men.
Much might be sayde that goeth more nere the pith,
But this suffiseth for a rurall Smith.

Baldwin when thou hearest my reason in this case,
Belyke thou thinkest I was not very wyse,
And that I was accurst, or els lacked grace,
Which knowing the end of my fond enterprise,
Would thus presume against my prince to ryse:
But as there is a cause that moueth euery woe,
Somewhat there was wherof this sore did growe.

And

Michaell Ioseph

And to be playne and simple in this case,
The cause why I such matter tooke in hand,
Was nothing els but pride and lacke of grace,
Vayne hope of helpe, and tales both false and fond:
By meane wherof I did my prince withstand,
Denyed the taxe assest by conuocation
To maintaine war against the scottish nation.

Whereat the Cornishe men did much repyne,
For they of Golde and Siluer were full bare,
And liued hardly digging in the Myne,
They sayde they had no money for to spare:
Began first to grudge and then to sweare and stare,
Forgot their due obeysaunce and rashly fell to rauing,
And sayde they would not beare such polling and such shauing.

They first accusde the King as authour of their griefe,
And then the Bishop Moreton, and sir Reinold Bray
For they then were about the King most chief,
Because they thought the hole fault in them lay:
They did protest to rid them out of the way.
Such thanke haue they that rule about a prince,
They beare the blame of other mens offence.

When I perceiued the commons in a roare,
Then I and Flamoke consulted both together,
To whome the people resorted more and more,
Lamenting and crying, helpe vs now or neuer,
Breake this yoake of bondage then are we free for euer:
Wherat we inflamed in hope to haue a fame,
To be their capitaines tooke on vs the name.

Then

The blacke Smith.

Then might you heare the people make a shoute,
And crye, God saue the Captaines, and send vs all good spede
Then he that fainted was counted but a lout,
The ruffians ran abroade to sowe seditious seede:
To call for companie then there was no nede
For euery man laboured another to entyce,
To be partaker of his wicked vice.

Then all such newes as made for our auayle,
Was brought to me, but such as sounded ill,
Was none so bolde to speake or yet bewayle:
Euerich was so wedded vnto his will,
That foorth they cryed with bowes, sword, and byll.
And what the rufler speake the loute tooke for a verdite,
For there the best was worst, the worst was best regarded.

For when men go a madding, there still the viler parte
Conspyre together and will haue all the swaye,
And be it well or yll they must haue all the porte,
As they will do, the rest must needs obay,
They prattle and prate as doth the Popingaye:
They crye and commaund the rest to kepe th'array,
While s they may range and rob for spoyle and pray.

And when we had prepared euery thing,
We went to Tawnton with all our prouision,
And there we slewe the prouost of Penryn,
For that on the subsedy he sate in commission:
He was not wyse, nor yet of greate discretion,
That durst approche his enemies in their rage,
When wit nor reason coulde their yre asswage.

U.i. From

Michaell Joseph

From thence we went to Wels, where we were receiued
Of this Lorde Awdeley as of our chief captaine,
And so had the name, but yet he was deceiued,
For I in dede did rule the clubbish trayne,
My cartly knights true honour did disdaine:
For like doth loue his like, it will be none other,
A chorle will loue a chorle before he will his brother.

Then from Wels to Winchester, and so to Blackheath feild,
And there we encamped looking for more ayde,
But when none came, we thought our selues begilde,
Such Cornyshmen as knew they were betrayde,
From their fellowes by nyght away they strayde:
There myght we learne how vayne it is to trust,
Our fayned frends in quarrels so vniust.

But we the sturdy captaines y[t] thought our power was strōg,
Were bent to try our Fortune what euer should betyde
We were the bolder, for that the King so long
Deferred battaile: which so increast our pryde,
That sure we thought the King himselfe did hyde
Within the citty, therfore with courage hault,
We did determyne the citty to assault.

But he working contrary to our expectation,
Was fully mynded to let vs run our race,
Tyll we were from our domesticall habitation,
Where that of ayde or succour was no place,
And then to be plaged as it should please his grace,
But all doubtfull plaints, how euer they did sound,
To our best vayle we alway did expound.

When

The blacke Smith.

When that the King sawe tyme, with courage bolde
He sent a power to circumuent vs all:
Where we enclosed as simple shepe in folde,
Were slaine and murdred as beasts in butchers stall,
The King himselfe, what euer chaunce might fall,
Was strongly encamped within saynt Georges field,
And there aboue tyll that he hard vs yelde.

Then downe we kneled, and cryed to saue our lyfe,
It was to late our folly to bewayle,
There were we spoiled of armour, cote, and knyfe:
And we which thought with pryde the citye to assaile,
Were led in prisoners naked as my naile,
But of vs two thousand they had slaine before,
And we of them three hundred and no more.

This my Lord and we the captaines of the West,
Tooke our Inne at Newgate, fast in fetters tyde,
Where after tryall we had but litle rest,
My Lord throw London was drawen on a slyde,
To Tower hill where with an axe he dyed,
Clad in his cote armour painted all in paper,
Torne and reuersed in spite of his behauer.

And I with Thomas Flamoke, and other of our bent,
As traytours at Tyborne our iudgement did obay:
The people looked I should my fault lament,
To whome I boldly spake that for my fond assaye,
I was sure of fame that neuer should decaye:
Wherby ye may perceiue vayne glory doth enflame
As well the meaner sort as men of greater name.

But

But as the sickle patient, sometyme hath desyre
To tast the things that phisicke hath denied,
And hath both paine and sorowe for his hyre,
The same to me right well may be applied,
Which while I caught for fame on shame did slyde,
And seeking fame, brought forth my bitter bane,
As he that fyred the temple of Diane.

I tell the Baldwin, I muse right oft, to see
How euery man for wealth and honour gapeth,
How euery man would climbe aboue the skye,
How euery man th'assured meane so hateth,
How froward Fortune oft their purpose mateth:
And if they hap their purpose to obtaine,
Theyr wealth is woe, their honour care and paine.

We see the seruaunt more happy than his Lord,
We see him lyue when that his Lord is dead,
He slepeth sound, is mery at his boorde,
No sorow in his hart doth vexe his head:
Happy then is he that pouerty can wed,
What gaine the mighty conquerours when they be dead
By all the spoile and blowes that they haue shed?

The terrible tower where honour hath his seate,
Is hye on rockes more slipper than the yse,
Where still the whorling wynde doth roare and beate,
Where sodain qualmes and peryls still aryse,
And is beset with many sundry vice,
So straunge to men when first they come thereat,
They be amased, and do they wote not what,

He

The blacke Smith.

He that preuailes and to the tower can clyme,
With trouble and care must nedes abridge his dayes,
And he that slydes may curse the hower and tyme,
He did attempt to geue so fond assaies,
And al his lyfe to sorrowe and shame obayes.
Thus slyde he downe or to the top ascend,
Sure himselfe repentaunce is the end.

Wherfore good Baldwyne do thou record my name,
To be ensample to such as credit lyes,
Or thirst to sucke the sugred cup of fame,
Or do attempt against their prince to ryse,
And charge them all to kepe within their syse:
Who doth assay to wrest beyond his strength,
Let him be sure he shall repent at length.

And at my request admonish thou all men,
To spend well the talent which God to them hath lent,
And he that hath but one, let him not toile for ten,
For one is to much, vnlesse it be well spent:
I haue had the proofe, therfore I now repent,
And happy are those men, and blist and blist is he,
As can be well content to serue in his degree.

FINIS. Maister Cauyll.
V. iii.

Shores wyfe.

It is pity (quoth one) that the meeter is no better seing ye matter is so good: you maye do very well to helpe it, and a lytle fylinge would make it formall. The authour him selfe (quoth I) coulde haue done that, but he woulde not, and hath desyred me that it maye passe in suche rude sorte as you haue hearde it: for hee obserueth therein a dowble Decorum both of the Smith, and of hymselfe: for he thynketh it not meete for the Smyth to speake, nor for himselfe to wryte in any exact kynde of meter. Well sayde another: the matter is notable to teach al people as wel officers as subiects to consider their estates and to lyue in loue and obedyence to the hyeste powers, what so euer they be, whom God eyther by byrth, lawe, succession, or vniuersall election, doth or shall aucthorise in his own roume to execute his lawes and iustice, among any people or nacion: for by all these meanes God placeth his deputies. And in my iudgement there is no meane so good either for the common quiet of the people, or for gods fre choise, as the naturall order of enheritaunce by lineall dyscent: for so it is left in Godes handes, to create in the wombe what prince he thinketh metest for his purposes: The people also knowe their princes, and therfore the more gladly and willyngly receiue and obay them. And although some realmes more carefull than wyse, haue entailed their crown to th'eir male thinking it not mete for the feminine sexe to beare the royall office: yet if they consider all
circum-

circumstaunces, and the chiefest vses of a prince in a realme, they shall see how they are deceiued. For princes are Gods lieutenauntes or deputyes, to see Gods lawes executed among their subiectes, not to rule accordyng to their own lustes or deuises, but by the prescript of Gods lawes: so ẏ the chiefest poynt of a Princes offyce consistethe in obedience to God and to his ordinaunces, and what shoulde let but ẏ a woman may be as obedient vnto god as a man? The second point of a princes office is to prouide for the impotent, nedy, and helples, as widowes, orphanes, lame, and decrepite persōs: and seing women are by nature tender harted, mylde, and pittyfull, who may better then they discharge this duty? Yea but a woman lacketh courage, boldnesse, and stomacke, to withstand the aduersarye, and so are her subiects an open spoile to their enemies. Debora, Iaell, Iudith, Thomiris, and other do proue ẏ contrary. But graunt it were so: what harme were that seing victory consisteth not in witte or force, but in Gods pleasure. I am sure that whatsoeuer prince doth his duty in obaying God, and causinge iustice to be ministred accordyng to Gods lawes, shall not onely lacke warre (be he man woman or childe) but also be a terrour to all other princes. And if god suffer any at any tyme to be assailed, it is for ẏ destruction of the assailer, whether he be rebell or forreyne foe, & to the honour & profite of ẏ vertuous prince, in whose behalfe rather then he shall miscary God him selfe will fight with enfections & earthquakes.

U. iiii. from

Shores wyfe.

from the lande and waters, and with stormes and lyghtenings from the ayre and skies. Moe warres haue bene fought through the wilfull & hautye courages of kinges, and greater destructions happened to realmes therby, than by any other meanes. And as for wisdome and pollicy, seing it consisteth in folowing the counsaile of many godly, learned, & long experienced heades, it were better to haue a woman, who consyderinge her owne weakenes and inabilyty, should be ruled therby, thā a man which presuming vpon his owne fond brayne, will heare no aduise saue his owne. You muse peraduenture wherfore I saye this. The frantike heades whyche disable our Quene, because she is a woman, & oure kinge because he is a straunger, to be our princes & chief gouernours, hath caused me to say thus much For what so euer man, woman, or chylde, is by the consent of the whole realme established in the royall seate, so it haue not bene iniuriously procured by rygour of sworde and open force, but quietly by tytle, eyther of enheritaunce, succession, lawful bequeste, common consent, or election, is vndoubtedly chosē by God to be his deputye: and whosoeuer resisteth any suche, resisteth againste God him selfe, and is a ranke traitour and rebell, and shalbe sure to prosper as well as the Blacke Smith and other suche haue done. All resist that wilfully breake any lawe, not being against Gods law, made by common consēt for the wealthe of the realme, and commaunded to be kept by the authority of the prince: or ῷ denie to

paye

Shores wife Folio. 161

paye such duties, as by consent of the high court of parliament, are appointed to the Prince for the defence and preseruation of the realme. You haue saide very truely herein,(quoth I)and I trust this terrible example of the blacke Smithe, will put all men in mynde of their duties and teach them to bee obediente to all good lawes, and lawfull contributions. The scriptures do forbid vs to rebell,or forcibly to withstand Princes, though they commaūd vniust things: yet in any case we may not do them but receiue quietly at the princes hand whatsoeuer punishement God shall suffer to be layd vpon vs for our refusall, God will suffer none of his to be tempted aboue their strēgth.But because these two persons last before rehersed were thoughte not onelye obscure in y̑ matter but also crabbed in the meeter,(I haue here redy to supply that which
lacked in the) Shores wyfe, an eloquēt
wench, which shall fynish out both
in meter & matter, that which
could not comlily be said
in their persons.
Marke I praye you what shee
sayth and tell me how
you lyke it.

Shores wyfe.

Howe Shores wyfe, Kinge Edwarde the fowerths Concubine, was by Kinge Richarde despoyled of all her goods, and forced to doo a pen penaunce.

Among the rest by Fortune overthrowen,
I am not least, that most may wayle her fate:
My fame and bruite abroade the world is blowen,
Who can forget a thing thus done so late?
My greate mischaunce, my fall, and heauy state,
Is such a marke wherat ech tounge doth shote,
That my good name is pluct vp by the roote.

This wandring world bewitched me with wyles,
And won my wits with wanton sugred ioyes,
In Fortunes frekes who trustes her when she smiles,
Shall fynde her false, and full of fickle toyes,
Her triumphes all but fil our eares with noyse,
Her flattring gifts are pleasures mixt with payne,
Yea all her woords are thunders threatning rayne.

The fond desyre that we in glory set,
Doth thirle our harts to hope in slipper hap,
A blast of pompe is all the fruite we get,
And vnder that lies hid a sodaine clap:
In seeking rest vnwares we fall in trap,
In groping flowers with nettles stong we are,
In labouring long, we reape the crop of care.

Shores wyfe

Oh darke disceite with painted face for showe,
Oh poysoned bayte that makes vs eger still,
Oh fayned frend deceiuing people so,
Oh world of the we cannot speake to yll,
Yet foeles we are that ben so to thy skill,
The plague and scourge that thousands dayly feele,
Should warne the wise to shun thy whirling whele.

But who can stop the streame that runnes full swift?
Or quench the fyer that is crept in the strawe?
The thirsty drinkes, there is no other shift,
Perforce is such, that nede obeyes no lawe,
Thus bound we are in worldly yokes to drawe,
And can not stay, nor turne againe in tyme,
Nor learne of those that sought to high to clyme.

My selfe for proofe, loe here I now appeare,
In womans weede with weping watred eyes,
That bought her youth and her delights full deare,
Whose lowde reproch doth sound vnto the skies
And bids my corse out of the graue to ryse,
As one that may no longer hyde her face,
But nedes must come and show her piteous case.

The shete of shame wherein I shrowded was
Did moue me oft to playne before this daye,
And in myne eares did ring the trumpe of brasse,
Which is defame that doth ech vice bewraye.
Yea though full dead and lowe in earth I laye,
I heard the voice of me what people sayde,
But then to speake alas I was afrayde.

Shores wyfe.

And now a tyme for me I see preparde,
I beare the liues and falles of many wights:
My tale therfore the better may be heard,
For at the torch the litle candell lights.
Where pageants be, small things fill out the sights,
Wherefore geue care, good Baldwin do thy best,
My tragedy to place among the rest.

Because the truth shall witnes wel with thee,
I will rehearce in order as it fell,
My lyfe, my death, my dolefull destenie,
My wealth, my woe, my doing euery deale,
My bitter blisse, wherein I long did dwell:
A whole discourse by me Shores wyfe by name,
Now shalt thou heare as thou hadst seene the same.

Of noble bloud I cannot boast my byrth,
For I was made out of the meanest molde,
Myne heritage but seuen foote of the earth,
Fortune ne gaue to me the gifts of golde:
But I could brag of nature if I would,
Who filde my face with fauour fresh and fayre,
Whose beauty shone lyke Phœbus in the ayre.

My shape some sayde was seemly to ech sight,
My countinaunce did showe a sober grace,
Myne eyes in lookes were neuer proued light,
My tongue in words were chast in euery case,
Myne eares were deafe, and would no louers place,
Saue that (alas) a prince did blot my browe,
Loe, there the strong did make the weake to bowe.

Shores wyfe.

The maiesty that Kings to people beare,
The stately port, the awfull cheare they showe,
Doth make the meane to shrinke and couch for feare,
Lyke as the hound, that doth his maister knowe:
What then, since I was made vnto the bowe:
There is no cloake, can serue to hyde my fault,
For I agreed the fort he should assault.

The Eagles force subdues ech bird that flies,
What mettall may resist the flaming fyre?
Doth not the sonne, dasill the clearest eyes,
And melt the yse, and make the frost retyre?
Who can withstand a puissaunt Kings desyre?
The stiffest stones are perced through with tooles,
The wisest are with princes made but fooles.

Yf kynde had wrought my forme in common frames,
And set me foorth in coulours blacke and browne,
Or beauty had bene perched in Phœbus flames,
Or shamefast wayes had pluct my fethers downe,
Then had I kept my fame and good renowne:
For natures gifts was cause of all my griefe,
A pleasaunt pray entyseth many a thiefe.

Thus woe to the that wrought my peacocks pryde
By clothing me with natures tapistrye,
Wo worth the hewe wherin my face was dyed,
Which made me thinke I pleased euery eye:
Lyke as the sterres make men beholde the skye,
So beauties showe doth make the wyse full fond,
And brings free harts full oft to endlesse bond.

But

Shores wyfe.

But cleare from blame my frends cannot be founde,
Before my tyme my youth they did abuse:
In mariage, a prentise was I bounde,
Then that meere loue I knewe not how to vse.
But welaway, that cannot me excuse,
The harme is myne though they deuised my care,
And I must smart and sit in slaundrous snare.

Yet geue me leaue to pleade my cause at large,
Yf that the horse do runne beyond his race,
Or any thing that kepers haue in charge
Do breake their course, where rulers may take place,
Or meate be set before the hungries face,
Who is in fault? the offender yea or no,
Or they that are the cause of all this woe?

Note well what stryfe this forced mariage makes,
What lothed lyues do come where loue doth lacke,
What scratching breers do growe vpon such brakes,
What common weales by it are brought to wracke,
What heauy loade is put on pacients backe,
What straunge delights this braunch of vice doth brede,
And marke what graine springs out of such a seede.

Compell the hauke to sit that is vnmande,
Or make the hound vntaught to drawe the dere,
Or bring the free against his will in band,
Or moue the sad a pleasaunt tale to heare,
Your tyme is lost and you are neuer the neare:
So loue ne learnes of force the knot to knit,
She serues but those that feele sweete fancies fit.

The

Shores wyfe.

The lesse defame redounds to my dispraise,
I was entyste by trapnes, and trapt by trust:
Though in my power remayned yeas and nayes,
Unto my frendes yet nedes consent I must,
In euery thing, yee lawfull or vniust.
They brake the bowes and shakte the tree by sleight,
And bent the wand that mought haue growen full streight.

What helpe is this, the pale thus broken downe,
The deere must nedes in daunger run astray:
At me therfore why should the world so frowne,
My weakenes made my youth a princes pray.
Though wisdome should the course of nature stay,
Yet try my case wholist, and they shall proue,
The ripest wits are soonest thralles to loue.

What nede I more to clere my selfe to much?
A King me wan, and had me at his call:
His royall state his princely grace was such,
The hope of will (that women seeke for all,)
The ease and wealth, the gifts which were not small,
Besieged me so strongly round about,
My power was weake I could not holde him out.

Duke Hanniball in all his conquest greate,
Or Cæsar yet, whose triumphes did excede,
Of all their spoiles which made them toyle and sweate,
Were not so glad to haue so rich a meede.
As was this prince when I to him agreed.
And yelded me a prisoner willinglye,
As one that knewe no way away to flye.

The

Shores wyfe.

The Nightingale for all his mery voice
Nor yet the Larke that still delights to sing,
Did neuer make the hearers so reioyce,
As I with words haue made this worthy King:
I neuer iarde in tune was euery string,
I tempered so my tong to please his eare,
That what I sayde was currant euery where.

I ioynde my talke, my iestures, and my grace
In witty frames that long might last and stand,
So that I brought the King in such a case,
That to his death I was his chiefest hand.
I gouerned him that ruled all this land:
I bare the sword though he did weare the crowne,
I strake the stroke that threwe the mighty downe.

If iustice sayde that iudgement was but death,
With my sweete words I could the King perswade,
And make him pause and take therin a breath,
Tyll I with suite the fautors peace had made:
I knewe what way to vse him in his trade,
I had the arte to make the Lyon meeke,
There was no point wherein I was to seeke.

If I did frowne, who then did looke awrye?
If I did smyle, who would not laugh outright?
If I but spake, who durst my words denye?
If I pursued, who woulde forsake the flight?
I meane my power was knowen to euery wight.
On such a height good hap hat built my bower,
As though my sweete should neuer haue turnde to sower.

Shores wife

My husband then as one that knewe his good,
Refused to kepe a princes Concubine,
Forseing the end and mischiefe as it stoode,
Against the King did neuer much repine,
He sawe the grape whereof he dranke the wyne,
Though inward thought his hart did still torment,
Yet outwardly he semde he was content.

To purchase praise and win the peoples zeale,
Yea rather bent of kynde to do some good,
I euer did vpholde the common weale,
I had delight to saue the giltlesse bloud:
Ech suters cause when that I vnderstoode,
I did prefer as it had bene myne owne,
And helpe them vp that might haue bene orethrowne.

My power was prest to right the poore mans wrong,
My hands were free to geue where nede required,
To watch for grace I neuer thought it long,
To do men good I nede not be desyred.
Nor yet with gyfts my hart was neuer hyred.
But when the ball was at my foote to guyde,
I playde to those that Fortune did abyde.

My want was wealth, my woe was ease at will,
My robes were rich and brauer than the sonne:
My Fortune then was far aboue my skill,
My state was great, my glasse did euer runne,
My fatall threede, so happely was sponne,
That then I sate in earthly pleasures clad,
And for the tyme a Goddesse place I had,

X.i.   But

Shores wyfe.

But I had not so sone this lyfe possest,
But my good hap began to slyp asyde.
And Fortune then did me so sore molest,
That vnto plaints was tourned all my pryde.
It booted not to rowe against the tyde:
Myne oares were weake my hart and strength did faile,
The wynde was rough I durst not beare a saile.

What steps of stryfe belong to high estate?
The climing vp is doubtfull to endure,
The seate it selfe doth purchase pryuy hate,
And honours fame is fickle and vnsure,
And all she bryngs, is flowers that be vnpure:
Which fall as fast as they do sprout and spring,
And cannot last they are so vayne a thing.

We count no care to catch that we do wishe,
But what we win is long to vs vnknowen,
Tyll present paine be serued in our dish,
We scarce perceiue wheron our grief hath growen:
What graine proues well that is so rashly sowen?
Yf that a meane did measure all our deedes,
In stede of corne we should not gather weedes.

The setled mynde is free from Fortunes power,
They nede not feare who looke not vp aloft,
But they that clymbe are carefull euery hower,
For when they fall they light not very softe:
Examples hath the wisest warned oft,
That where the trees the smallest braunches bere,
The stormes do blowe and haue most rygoure there.

Where

Shores wife

Where is it strong but nere the ground and roote?
Where is it weake but on the highest sprayes?
Where may a man so surely set his foote,
But on those bowes that groweth lowe alwayes?
The little twygs are but vnstedfast stayes,
If they breake not they bend with every blast,
Who trusts to them shall neuer stand full fast.

The wynde is greate vpon the highest hylles,
The quiet lyfe is in the dale belowe,
Who treades on yse shall slyde against their wills,
They want not cares that curious artes would know.
Who lyues at ease and can content him so,
Is perfect wise, and sets vs all to schole,
Who hates this lore may well be called a foole.

What greater grief may come to any lyfe,
Than after sweete to tast the bitter sower?
Or after peace to fall at war and strife,
Or after myrth to haue a cause to lower?
Under such props false Fortune buildes her bower,
On sodaine chaunge her flittring frames be set,
Where is no way for to escape her net.

The hasty smart that Fortune sends in spite
Is hard to brooke where gladnes we imbrace,
She threatens not, but sodainly doth smyte,
Where ioy is most there doth she sorrow place.
But sure I thinke, this is to straunge a case,
For vs to feele such griefe amyd our game,
And knowe not why vntill we tast the same.

L.ii.   As

Shores wyfe.

As earst I sayde, my blisse was turnde to bale,
I had good cause to wepe and wring my hands,
And showe sad cheare with countinaunce full pale,
For I was brought in sorrow wofull bands:
A pirry came and set my shyp on sands,
What should I hyde, or coulour care and noy,
King Edward dyed in whome was all my ioye.

And when the earth receiued had his corse,
And that in tombe, this worthy prince was layde,
The worlde on me began to showe his force,
Of troubles then my part I long assayed:
For they, of whome I neuer was afrayde,
Auoid me most, and wrought me such dispyte,
That they bereft me from my pleasure quite.

As long as lyfe remaynde in Edwards brest,
Who was but I: who had such frends at call:
His body was no soner put in chest,
But well was he that could procure my fall:
His brother was myne enemy most of all,
Protectour then, whose vice did still abound,
From yll to worse tyll death did him confound.

He falsely fayned, that I of counsaile was
To poyson him which thing I neuer ment,
But he could set theron a face of brasse,
To bring to passe his lewde and false entent,
To such mischiefe this Tyrants hart was bent.
To God, ne man, he neuer stoode in awe,
For in his wrath he made his will a lawe.

Lorde

Shores wyfe.

Lord Hastings bloud for vengeaunce on him cryes,
And many moe, that were to long to name:
But most of all: and in most wofull wyse
I had good cause this wretched man to blame.
Before the worlde I suffered open shame,
Where people were as thicke as is the sand,
I penaunce tooke with taper in my hand.

Ech eye did stare, and looke me in the face,
As I past by the rumours on me ran,
But patience then had lent me such a grace,
My quiet lookes were praysed of euery man:
The shamefast bloud brought me such coulour than,
That thousands saide, which sawe my sobre chere,
It is great ruth to see this woman here.

But what preuailde the peoples pitie there?
This raging wolfe would spare no giltles bloud.
Oh wicked wombe that such ill fruite did beare,
Oh cursed earth that yeldeth forth such mud,
The hell consume all thinges that did the good,
The heauens shut their gates against thy spzite,
The world tread downe thy glory vnder feete,

I aske of god a vengeaunce on thy bones,
Thy stinking corps corrupts the ayre I knowe:
Thy shamefull death no earthly wight bemones,
For in thy lyfe thy workes were hated so,
That euery man did wish thy ouerthrowe:
Wherfore I may, though perciall now I am,
Curse euery cause whereof thy body came.

Wo worth the man that fathered such a chylde:
Wo worth the hower wherin thou wast begate,
Wo worth the brests that haue the worlde begylde,
To norrish thee that all the world did hate,
Wo worth the Gods that gaue thee such a fate,
To lyue so long, that death deserued so oft.
Wo worth the chaunce that set thee vp aloft.

Ye princes all, and rulers euerychone,
In punishment beware of hatreds yre.
Before ye scourge, take heed, looke well thereon:
In wrothes ill wyll if mallice kindle fyre,
Your harts wyll burne in suche a hote desyre,
That in those flames the smoake shall dym your sight,
Ye shall forget to ioyne your iustice right.

You should not iudge till things be well discerned,
Your charge is still to maintain vpright lawes,
In conscience rules ye should be throughly learned,
Where clemency bids wrath and rashnes pause,
And further saith strike not without a cause,
And when ye smyte do it for iustice sake,
Then in good parte ech man your scourge will take.

Yf that such zeale had moued this tyrants mynde,
To make my plague a warrant for the rest,
I had small cause such fault in him to fynde,
Such punishment is vsed for the best:
But by yll will and power I was opprest,
He spoyled my goodes and left me bare and pore,
And caused me to beg from dore to dore.

What

Shores wyfe.

What fall was this, to come from princes fare,
To watch for crums among the blynde and lame:
When almes were delt I had an hungry share,
Because I knew not how to aske for shame,
Tyll force and nede hand brought me in such frame,
That starue I must, or learne to beg an almes,
With booke in hand to say S. Dauids Psalmes.

Where I was wont the golden chaynes to weare,
A paire of beades about my necke was wound,
A lynnen cloth was lapt about my heare,
A ragged goune that trayled on the ground,
A dish that clapt and gaue a heauy sound,
A staying staffe and wallet therewithall,
I beare about as witnesse of my fall.

I had no house wherein to hyde my head,
The open strete my lodging was perforce,
Full oft I went all hungry to my bed,
My flesh consumed, I loked lyke a corse,
Yet in that plight who had on me remorse?
O God thou knowest my frends forsooke me than,
Not one holpe me that succred many a man.

They frownd on me that fawnd on me before,
And fled from me that followed me full fast,
They hated me, by whome I set much store,
They knew full well my fortune did not last,
In euery place I was condemnd and cast:
To pleade my cause at bar it was no boote,
For euery man did treade me vnder foote.

X iiii.   Thus

Shores wyfe.

Thus long I liued all weary of my lyfe,
Tyll death approcht and rid me from that woe:
Example take by me both maide and wyfe,
Beware, take hede, fall not to folly so,
A mirrour make by my greate ouerthrowe:
Despe this world, and all his wanton wayes,
Beware by me that spent so yll her dayes.

FINIS.

Tho. Churcheyarde.

IMPRINTED AT LON
don by Thomas Marsh, *dwelling*
in Fleetstrete, neare vnto Sainte
Dunstanes Churche.
1571.

www.ingramcontent.com/pod-product-compliance
Lightning Source LLC
Chambersburg PA
CBHW030734230426
43667CB00007B/707